# RURAL-URBAN DIVIDE
## Changing Spatial Pattern of Social Variables

**About the Authors**

**Dr. (Mrs.) Sneh Sangwan** obtained her M.Phil as well as Ph.D. from Maharshi Dayanand University, Rohtak. She was a University Research Scholar during her Ph.D. research work. She is a perceptive researcher and has contributed a number of research papers to various professional journals. Dr. (Mrs.) Sangwan is a life member of several professional and academic bodies and participated in various conferences/ seminars. Currently, Dr. (Mrs.) Sangwan is Sr. Lecturer, Department of Geography, B.P.S.M. Girls College, Khanpur Kalan (Sonipat). She also taught at Govt. College for Women, Rohtak and A.I. Jat H.M. College, Rohtak.

**Dr. Randhir Singh Sangwan,** M.Sc., M.Phil, Ph.D., LL.B., B.Ed., is a Lecturer (Selection Grade) in the Department of Geography, University College, Maharshi Dayanand University, Rohtak.

Dr. Sangwan has authored a Book entitled *Dynamics of Urban Land-use: Ecology of Residential Mobility (2000)*. He has contributed a number of research papers to various professional journals and books. His research interests are focused on Urban Geography, Population Geography and Environmental Hazards.

Besides being a Life Member of several professional and academic bodies, Dr. Sangwan was on the Executive Committee of National Association of Geographers, India (NAGI), New Delhi (1997-2000), and Governing Council of Indian Institute of Geographers (IIG), Pune (1998-2001).

Currently, Dr. Sangwan is Vice-President (North-West Region) of National Association of Geographers, India (NAGI).

# RURAL-URBAN DIVIDE
## CHANGING SPATIAL PATTERN OF SOCIAL VARIABLES

SNEH SANGWAN

RANDHIR SINGH SANGWAN

CONCEPT PUBLISHING COMPANY PVT. LTD.
NEW DELHI-110059

**ISBN: 978-81-8069-016-7**

First Published 2022

*Published and Printed by*

Concept
Since 1974

**Concept Publishing Company Pvt. Ltd.**
A/15-16, Commercial Block, Mohan Garden,
New Delhi-110059 (India)
*T* : 91-11-41101460
*E* : publishing@conceptpub.com, *W*: www.conceptpub.com

# FOREWORD

*Rural-Urban Divide: Changing Spatial Pattern of Social Variables,* jointly written by wife-husband duo Dr. (Mrs.) Sneh Sangwan and Dr. Randhir Singh Sangwan is a well-researched publication designed to highlight the emerging levels of disparities in social situation in India as exhibited by sex ratio, literacy, vital rates, and size of households.

Rural-urban divide has been a research theme of great interest in India for the last several decades. The roots of rural poverty and backwardness have often been traced in urban bias in development policy from the pre-colonial days. Easy access to time series data churned out by the decadal censuses for each village and town of the country is another reason for continuing engagement of researchers in the study of rural-urban differentials.

The present study aims at 'describing and interpreting the trends in, and regional aspects of, rural-urban differentials' in respect of select demographic features: sex ratio, literacy, vital rates, and size of households. The analysis is primarily based on the last five census returns (1951-1991) and covers 25 states, 7 union territories and 466 districts as in 1991. Modified Sopher's Index was used to derive the differentials. However, to make the study more relevant and valuable, the data for the demographic aspects like growth of population, density of population, sex ratio and literacy rates have appreciably been updated on the basis of Paper-1 and Paper-1 (Supplement) of 2001 published so far by Registrar General and Census Commissioner, India, New Delhi.

Sex ratio in India has remained adverse right from the beginning of the census operations. In 2001, it declined to 933 from 972 females per thousand males in 1901. It is a sign of low status of women in the society. Wide regional differences in sex ratio and the rates at which they are widening or narrowing, have been highlighted by the authors. The rural-urban differentials are declining but at different paces. The areas of low differentials constitute a broad dry belt running through Rajasthan, Gujarat, Madhya Pradesh, Maharashtra, Karnataka, Andhra Pradesh and Tamil Nadu.

As regards literacy, the rural-urban differentials are really large and matter of great concern. Literacy rate of urban India in 1991 was 73.08 per cent, as compared to 44.69 per cent for rural areas. Over dependence of rural population on traditional agriculture and related activities, is the major cause of low literacy. Traditional agriculture does not require skilled manpower. Children learn to cultivate land as helps for their parents. And hence, there is reluctance to go to school and those who go to school leave it prematurely to remain illiterate. Literacy rates are improving fast particularly in rural areas. This has salutary influence on rural-urban differentials. Southern states show lower differentials, while the states of the Ganga valley barring West Bengal show up high differentials.

In matters of vital rates, rural-urban differentials are predictably acute. Low urban fertility was caused by such factors like unbalanced sex ratio, high cost of living in cities forcing the poor to leave their families back home in the village, economic insecurity and unemployment, social capillarity, higher rate of female literacy, and adoption of family planning measures in cities. But with spread of the message of family planning in rural parts of the country, the differentials are tending to decline.

Fertility rates have declined all over the country and across all regions; but the general notion that the rates decline, as the level of development improves, does not always hold good. Punjab and Haryana are the two states which are marked with high per capita income and high rates of fertility. Poverty is not also an antidote for fertility as indicated by the states of Bihar and Orissa. The authors suggest that success of a sufficiently large number of enterprising persons triggers of a change in the mentality of the people more than slow doses of overall improvement in the economy. Liberalization of the economy giving greater opportunities for private initiatives, in their view, may prove beneficial in the long run in so far as the reduction in the rates of fertility in rural areas is concerned.

The mortality rates also differ widely across the states and districts. Kerala has the lowest, while Uttar Pradesh has the highest rate of mortality. Much depends on the overall socio-economic development and effectiveness of the health services. Rural-urban differentials in this respect are higher in the eastern states and lower in the relatively developed states like Kerala, Haryana, and Gujarat.

Analysis of the size of households indicated that the rural-urban differentials in this respect, contrary to widespread belief, were marginal suggesting a rural-urban continuum in traditional joint family structure. There are regional differences though. For example, the differentials are larger in developed states and districts. More than 40 per cent of the districts of the southern states show up larger size of urban households probably because of local endogamy.

The research conducted by Sangwans points to a multiplicity of factors responsible for rural-urban differentials in social change. While there is definite link between development, no matter how we measure it, and social change, differing geographic, social and economic base of each state and district of the country, has its own implications and impacts thus making simple correlation misleading. There are wide differences among the rural districts of not only different states but also the same states. The same is true for urban districts also.

Analysis of the type Sangwans have attempted is important from the point of view of social and economic planning. Development policies formulated at the national level are often oblivious of the regional peculiarities of Indian society. Treating the national space as uniform and giving equal treatment to all regions and areas irrespective of the intensity of the problem to be solved often proves wasteful. It negates the concept of equity. Many schemes have failed because some areas marked with high intensity of the problem, did not get adequate attention while others with low intensity received over attention. In the latter case, the resources were wasted, while in the case of the former resources available did not reach the critical minimum to make any impact.

Studies of the type Sangwans have done form an important input in planning and policy making for social development and change. They deserve congratulations. The book will certainly add to the growing literature on social change in India.

Allahabad
January 1, 2002

**Bhoogol Ratna Prof. R.P. Misra**
Mahatma Gandhi National Fellow

# PREFACE

Population refers to a reference element of geographic study. The group of people that signifies population, has created the ecumene world—the world of culture. The cultural landscape is inseparable part of geo-economic and socio-cultural milieu. The population element has, however, been found changing and evolving both in number and kind. In other words, the quantitative and qualitative faces of population element have been constantly changing and evolving through time and space. The number and the behaviour of population have contributed towards creating different faces of the world.

There is the Ecumene world. There are world segments of major population agglomerations. There are regions of moderate to high population and there are areas of still scarce population. Different world segments, regions and areas of the Ecumene have been growing and developing in response more to human character and actions than to any other elements.

The population is the sum total of growing human number which, in itself, depends on varied demographic attributes including birth and death, age and sex, skill and mobility and the likes. The nature and the extent, which world population phenomenon observes in the rural-urban component, are apparently manifested in these select demographic elements.

The rural-urban differentials, in terms of different select demographic attributes of population, are most apparently viewed in spatio-temporal dimensions. The contemporary perspectives of population phenomenon has, however, brought a situation in which the intensity and the extent of rural-urban divide has progressed to fade and wane. People have been expressing the ideas of "rural-urban dichotomy", "rural culture", "urban culture", "rural-urban differentials", "continuous gradation from rural to urban", "differences between rural and urban ways of life" and "rural-urban continuum".

All such expressions suggest that the issues of rural-urban differentials with respect to demographic attributes assume enhanced implications of socio-economic relevance. The science of geography and other social sciences have accordingly, accorded adequate interests in matters of analyzing dynamics of rural-urban differentials with reference to select demographic traits of population. The science of Geography has, however, been persistently pursuing such analyses in spatio-temporal dimensions. The present book is an attempt to provide a spatial view of rural-urban differentials in some select aspects of demography in India. The contents of the book and approach to the population analysis will provide new insights for population policy makers and planners as also for students and researchers pursuing study in the disciplines of Geography, Sociology, Economics and other social sciences and agricultural science as well.

We are deeply indebted to Bhoogol Ratna Prof. R.P. Misra, Mahatma Gandhi National Fellow, Allahabad; Prof. Nandeshwar Sharma, Head, Department of Geography, L.N. Mithila University, Darbhanga; Dr. (Mrs.) Swaranjit Mehta, Professor, Department of Geography, Panjab University, Chandigarh; Prof. S.P. Sinha, former Chairman, Department of Geography, Kurukshetra University, Kurukshetra; Dr. (Mrs.) Nina Singh, Reader, Department of Geography, M.D. University, Rohtak; Shri S.C. Gupta, Lecturer (Retd.) from Department of Geography, Govt. P.G. College, Jhajjar, for their valuable suggestions, encouragement and unstinted moral support in completing the work.

We would like to place on record our deep sense of gratitude to all those officials with whom we have been associated in this task. We express our gratitude especially to Shri S.K. Sinha, Deputy Registrar General; A.K. Saxena, Assistant Director of Census Operations, Vital Statistics Division and Shri Krishan Lal, Assistant Director, Office of the Registrar General of India for the help and co-operation they extended whenever we visited the office. We are also grateful to the staff members of the libraries of Maharshi Dayanand University, Rohtak; Jawahar Lal Nehru University, New Delhi; University of Delhi (Ratan Tata Library), Delhi; National Institute of Urban Affairs, New Delhi; Teen Murti Bhawan, New Delhi and Panjab University, Chandigarh.

We take the opportunity to express our thanks to Shri Arun Srivastva, System Analyst, New Delhi and Harish Malik, Computer Operator, PGIMS, Rohtak who were very helpful in getting the data processed.

We are also greatly beholden to our parents and in-laws whose blessings helped us in completing this work. For our children, Mahima and Himanshu we have nothing but admiration for the sporting manner in which they took the difficulties faced by them due to our pre-occupation with this work. We also thank our nephew Balwan Singh, Lecturer in

Geography, Government College for Women, Sampla, who extended a helping hand to us at every stage. All our near and dear ones who helped us in any manner also deserve our thanks.

It would be highly gratifying for us if our humble effort proves to be thought provoking and opens up new vistas.

Our special thanks are also due to Shri Ashok Mittal, Concept Publishing Company, New Delhi for readily agreeing to publish this book and bringing it out expeditiously and efficiently.

For a few errors that may have crept into the book, we crave the indulgence of readers and own sole responsibility.

February 4, 2002

SNEH SANGWAN
RANDHIR SINGH SANGWAN

# CONTENTS

# LIST OF FIGURES

# LIST OF TABLES


2.15: India: Literacy Rates by Sex, 1951-2001 82

# 1

# INTRODUCTION

Diversities and inequalities are discernible in almost all types of physical and cultural phenomena at various spatial scales ranging from global to local. They also distinguish themselves as urban and rural.

There is an ancient world-wide tradition of differentiating rural and urban people. Every country displays a specific history of the so-called rural-urban dichotomy. Rural-urban differences get revealed in occupation, environment, size of community, density of population, heterogeneity, social differentiation, mobility and system of social interaction. The rural areas are generally at the receiving end of these inequalities. The differences between rural and urban populations represent contrasts between the old and the new. Whereas, the urban sector contains most of the articulateness, organization and power, the rural areas with ever increasing population pressure on land and natural resources, the rise of rural cities and aggravation of landlessness, the worsening of the welfare of the rural poor and in many instances absolute decline in income of the lower 40 per cent of the population, the environmental degradation and the breakdown of rural society present an alarming perspective.

Notwithstanding the fact that rural and urban areas constitute a functional system of settlements in a given region, the rural-urban divide is a part of the prevalent political ethos in India. The urban is said to symbolize *India* (exploitator or ruler) and the rural *Bharat* (exploited or ruled). Rural is portrayed as indigenous and the urban something exogenous meant to subjugate and exploit the former. It is essentially a thing passed to us by our predecessors. Most of the development during the British rule was urban biased. Urban areas were primarily the centres of administration and power, collection centres of export-oriented raw materials and distribution centres of imported manufactured goods. In urban areas, the facilities of good education, health, water-supply, sanitation, electricity and other civic amenities were easily available, which, in turn, raised the standard of living of people in these areas.

Most of the industries were also established in urban areas. So, the urban population differed strongly from rural population in distribution, density, way of life, structure and growth. Because of this favouritism for urban areas, the gap between rural and urban areas increased and became so noticeable that cannot be ignored. Cities came to be seen as the exploiter of the countryside (rural areas) (Krishan, 1991).

After Independence, the main aim was to fill-up this gap between rural and urban areas. So, various programmes were launched to develop the rural areas, to mention a few—Community Development Programme, Multi-Purpose Irrigation and Power Projects, Integrated Rural Development Programme, Rural Electrification, Establishment of Small Scale and Cottage Industries, Agricultural Development Programmes, Minimum Needs Programme, Special Areas Programme, National Rural Employment Programme, Training Scheme for Rural Youth for Self-Employment, Scheme for Providing Self-Employment to Educated Unemployed Youth, Poverty Eradication Programmes, Rural Landless Employment Guarantee Programme and Nehru Rojgar Yojna, etc. All these schemes were started to boost up the rural areas, to come at the level of urban areas.

Inspite of the fact that there has been a significant shift in focus from urban based strategies to rural development priorities in regional development planning by Government of India, the problem of rural-urban disparity still remains. This gets best reflected in the demographic attributes.

## Basic Objectives of Study

The aim of the present work is to describe and interpret the regional aspects of rural-urban differentials of social variables of the Indian population, on the basis of statistical analysis and mapping of the 1991 census data for all the 452 districts (excluding the state of Jammu & Kashmir) in the country. In 1991, there were 25 states, 7 union territories and 466 districts in the country.

The main objectives of study are:

1. To study the trend of rural-urban differentials in India (state-wise) for the social variables like size of household, vital rates, sex-ratio and literacy.
2. To study the spatial patterns of rural-urban differentials (district-wise) for the social variables like size of household, vital rates, sex ratio and literacy.

It is primarily an empirical investigation of the rural lag in literacy, urban lag in sex ratio, size of household, etc, in relation to the economy, society, urbanization, industrialization, modernization and educational history of different parts of India. Rural-urban differences are essentially a function of the differential rates of change occurring in towns and villages. The degree of urban influence and the intensity of rural-urban interaction are evidently the two major factors involved in the reduction of disparities between urban and rural sex ratio, literacy rates and in other demographic attributes. Keeping in consonance with the purpose, only those aspects for which the data was available, could be chosen for study. These were size of household, sex ratio, vital rates, and literacy.

**Review of Literature**

There are some schools of thought that question the existence of a rural-urban dichotomy. Belonging to this stream are scholars who explain that there is no such rural-urban dichotomy, but these are two extremes of the continuum, *i.e.* the distribution is not really two-fold one in which one part of the population is wholly rural and the other wholly urban, but a graduated distribution along a continuum from the least urban to the most urban or from the most rural to the least rural. Consequently, the line that is drawn between rural and urban for statistical or census purposes is necessarily arbitrary (United Nations, 1950).

In a regional seminar on rural-urban differential in South Asian countries held in Delhi in December 1962, under the direction of Professor (Ms.) Ruth Glass, Director Research Centre for Urban Studies, University College, London, the main emphasis was given to the review of criteria of urban-rural differential in which Ruth Glass (1962) felt that in most areas of the world, rural-urban differences are becoming inconsistent and rather faint. Besides, in industrialised world, the main current of development is not the urban growth in physical and occupational terms, but the urban diffusion in cultural terms.

Dewey (1960) said that there is no such thing as urban culture or rural culture but only various cultural contents somewhere on the rural-urban continuum. He said that there can be and most assuredly are, small rural communities which are secular, civilized, dynamic and highly literate as well as large, religious, essentially primitive, illiterate and relatively static urban communities.

While making a study of United States, Queen and Carpenter (1953) observed that there is a continuous gradation from rural to urban rather than a simple rural-urban dichotomy and as human communities are arrayed along this rural-urban continuum, consistent variations occur in patterns of behaviour.

Oscar Lewis, an anthropologist, also doubts that there are any criteria for universally distinguishing rural from urban environments. Louis Wirth (1938) explains that the city and the country may be regarded as two poles in reference to one or the other of which all human settlements tend to arrange themselves. Similarly, Sorokin and Zimmerman (1929) said that there is no absolute boundary line which would show a clear-cut distinction between the rural and the urban community.

Inspite of the fact that certain schools of thought question the existence of a rural-urban dichotomy (Pocock, 1960), the rural and urban, as opposing concepts exist since the dawn of history. There were only a few rural-urban differences in times of nomadic life but they started increasing as the cities were founded. The rural-urban differences are a function of the process of development, origin normally being the urban place. The nature of change varies from society to society and from one historical epoch to the next. The amount of difference between the two is in part a function of changes in the rural sector which originated in cities. As the diffusion of development takes place, in time perspective, these rural-urban differences tend to minimize. So, it can be emphasized that the magnitude of rural-urban differential depends upon the differential rates of development (Gibbs, 1961).

The comparative analysis of these differences has always revealed societies in transition. Societies tend to be dominated by either rural or urban social structures. Therefore, when rural-urban differences are most pronounced, the societies are experiencing the greatest dynamics of social change. There have always been rural-urban differences, but they were less important in colonial period and nineteenth century and became prominent with passage of time. In contrast to developed world where rural-urban differences have rapidly diminished in the face of advanced urbanized social organisation, these differences in Third World countries are at their peak in the present century. India falls in line with the latter. The major cause of increasing rural-urban differentials in India is that with factory development came job proliferation due to which migration increased and streams of migration were primarily rural to urban. These developments contributed to marked differences between urban and rural ways of life. (Taylor and Jones, 1964)

Unequal allocation of resources among rural and urban areas also resulted into wider disparities between the two. But if the resources are allocated equally without urban bias, the results will be more encouraging in rural than in urban areas. Even after the existence of urbanized social organization in developed world, some differences continue to exist but they are more of degree than of kind. They present a distortion of development process (Lipton, 1986).

Similarly, Stewart (1958) describes that the distinction between rural and urban population is entrenched in most census reports and in many and varied demographic series. Vital statistics, economic and sociological data in great profusion have been compiled, which distinguish between rural and urban components. The rural-urban dichotomy is often used as a crude yardstick for international comparisons and as a rough measure of the socio-economic evolution of each country. All these series assume that the distinction between rural and urban population is relevant and significant for the social sciences. So, the scholars of this school of thought adhere to the view that there exists rural-urban dichotomy at one or the other level.

## Geography and Rural-Urban Differential Studies

The available literature on rural-urban differentials reveals that the issue has received slight attention from geographers.

Baker (1986) in his study of northern Ethiopia explained that distinction between rural and urban areas is firmly established in census reports and social and economic statistics.

D'Souza (1982) examined the inter-state differences in the rural-urban literacy rates for the year 1981.

Lipton (1977) believes that among different kinds of class conflicts, the one between rural and urban is most critical. A strong urban bias in allocation of resources in developing countries is underlined by him. The suggestion is for treating the urban and the rural as separate entities and for giving a priority to the rural areas in development investment.

Smith and Zopf (1970) have examined the inequalities in education in U.S.A. in terms of sex, residence, colour or race and state.

Zachariah (1962) said that migration is a vital factor in rural-urban differential. This type of migration blurs the rural-urban differentials generally, though may increase the differences also. For example, migration of literates from rural areas to urban areas might affect the educational standards of both areas.

Kingsley Davis (1951) observed the differences between city and country (rural areas). In case of India, in his view, the rural-urban differences were expected to increase immediately after Independence, especially in literacy. Davis felt that while cities of new world represented a diffusion of western civilization, the cities of India represented a partial diffusion.

All these studies mainly stress on the trends in rural-urban differentials, factors or determinants of rural-urban differentials and urban bias in allocation of resources.

A few geographers have studied the rural-urban differential for various demographic parameters at macro and micro scales.

Krishan (1991) recognized wide rural-urban gaps in some select demographic and social indicators while critically examining the rural-urban relations in India. These aspects were birth rate, death rate, infant mortality rate, sex ratio, literacy, size of household, and percentage of households with tap water supply and electricity. He observed that there exists a wide gap between rural and urban areas in respect of physical quality of life.

Jolly (1991), while describing strategies to attain Universal literacy in India by 2001, identified the rural-urban differentials in literacy.

Premi (1991) studied the literacy scenario in India and found that as a result of National Policy on Education and other new policy thrusts, the literacy rates have improved gradually despite tremendous increase in population, but the rural-urban literacy differentials continue to be high even in 1991.

Nain (1988) examined inter-state change of rural-urban differentials in literacy, vital rates, sex ratio and size of household in India during 1971-81.

Gill and Singh (1985) viewed the rural-urban differentials in sex ratio in Rajasthan. Mamoria (1981) also studied the state-wise rural-urban differentials in literacy. Misra (1980) in his book *An Introduction to the Study of Population* covered almost all demographic aspects of population. He considered rural-urban differences in sex ratio, population composition, age at marriage and marital composition, rural-urban distribution of non-workers and differences in literacy rates among scheduled castes and scheduled tribes residing in rural and urban areas.

Sinha (1979) observed the rural-urban differentials in fertility and mortality rates.

Gosal (1979) made a study of literacy in spatial perspective and found that as in several other characteristics of population, so in literacy and education, the villages and towns in India stand in marked contrast to each other. Krishan and Chandna (1974) explained that rural-urban differential in literacy had an adverse correlation with general literacy. Desai (1969) calculated rural-urban differentials in sex ratio for India as a whole. Gosal (1964) studied the rural-urban differentials in literacy in India and said that the rural and urban areas stand in marked contrast to each other in the field of literacy.

Clarke (1960) made an attempt to find out the differentials in rural-urban sex ratios in England and Wales.

Burnight *et al.* (1956) examined the rural-urban differential in fertility in Mexico and concluded that Mexican fertility is subject to the differential effect of urbanization in much the same way as has been fertility in the industrialized countries of the West and urban dominance significantly reduced the fertility ratio.

Among state level studies, Chandna (1972) examined literacy differentials in Haryana. Gurumurthy (1976) calculated fertility differentials for Andhra Pradesh. Ram (1981), Usha Rao (1981), Mathur (1982), Sharma (1985) and Ahmad and Nuna (1986) analysed literacy differentials in Punjab, Karnataka, Uttar Pradesh, Assam and Maharashtra respectively. Goel (1994) made an attempt to examine the rural-urban differentials in literacy and size of household in Uttar Pradesh by taking the 1971-81 census data. Ali (1995) had studied the rural-urban differentials in Andhra Pradesh in terms of some demographic and economic variables and concluded that rural-urban disparities are widening.

Finally, there are those studies which evolved some new methodology to study rural-urban differentials. Ogburn (1936) observed that the rural-urban differences within regions are frequently of greater magnitude than inter-regional differences, when the latter are measured by a gross ratio or average pertaining to the region as a whole.

Gosal (1964) had used the simple technique of scanning the two sets of data (male literates and female literates), visually comparing the two mapped patterns and getting the ratio between the two groups.

Sopher (1974) made a notable contribution in computing differentials by using his own formula, *i.e.*

$$D_s = log\,(X_2 / X_1) + log\,(100 - X_1) / (100 - X_2)$$

where $X_2 \geq X_1$, $X_1$ and $X_2$ are demographic indicators of *alphas* and *non-alphas* respectively.

Krishan and Shyam (1978) described the regional aspects of the rural-urban differential in literacy in India on the basis of 1971 census data by using the formula, *i.e.*

$$ID = Urban - Rural/Total$$

Krishan and Rana (1980) studied rural-urban differentials in size of the household in India by using crude method of rural-urban differential, *i.e.*

$$ID = Rural - Urban$$

Naik (1971), Chitnis (1972, 1974), Sen (1973), Banerjee (1975), Shastri (1985), Gosal (1988) and Nain (1988) calculated rural-urban differentials in literacy with the help of this method. Nain (1988) used this method also for calculating rural-urban differential in sex ratio, vital rates and size of the household in India. Goel (1994) also calculated rural-urban differentials in size of the household in Uttar Pradesh by this method.

Victor S. D'Souza (1980) evolved a new formula for the measurement of educational inequalities among scheduled castes of Punjab, *i.e.*

$$\text{Coefficient of Equality} = \frac{A/B}{C/D} \times 100$$

where

$A$ = Scheduled Castes Literate Population
$B$ = Scheduled Castes Total Population
$C$ = Non-Scheduled Castes Literate Population
$D$ = Non-Scheduled Castes Total Population

Kundu and Rao (1982) made a comparative study on the nature and patterns of inequalities in literacy rates between 1961 and 1971. They modified Sopher's formula of differential index and incorporated a new one, *i.e.*

$$D_s = \log (X_2 / X_1) + \log (Q - X_1) / (Q - X_2)$$

where $Q \geq 200$
$X_2 \geq X_1$ and $X_1$ and $X_2$ are demographic indicators of *alphas* and *non-alphas* respectively.
So, $D_s = \log (Rural/Urban) + \log (200 - Urban) / (200 - Rural)$

Raza and Aggarwal (1986) looked into the regional dimension of inequality in the level of literacy in India. They also proposed an alternative formulation of Sopher's disparity index and the new index has been defined as:

$$W = log\,(L_2/L_1) + log\,[(100+I_1)\,/\,(100 + I_2)]\; L_2\; 3/8\; L_1 > 0$$

where $L_1$ and $L_2$ are the literacy rates and $I_1$, and $I_2$ are the corresponding illiteracy rates for the two elements between which disparity index is to be calculated.

Sagar (1990), in his study of rural-urban differentials in literacy, has modified D'Souza's formula and gave his own to calculate differentials, *i.e.*

$$DI = 100\;\; [1 - (Y_i\,/\,X_i)]$$

where,

$DI$ stands for the differential index.

$X_i$ stands for the ratio of the property of one item in the *i-th* areal units.

$Y_i$ stands for the ratio of the property of the other item in the *i-th* areal unit.

In order to measure the differentials or inequality of various demographic aspects among two relevant population groups, these statistical techniques have been adopted by different scholars. As we can see from the above methodological studies, most of these have been conducted to calculate literacy differentials mainly.

## Data Sources and Limitations

The study is mainly based on the secondary sources of data. Data, though provisional, obtained from two papers published so far [Paper-I and Paper-I (Supplement) of 2001] have been used along with the data from census of India (1991). The data, therefore, have mainly been obtained from the Office of the Registrar General & Census Commissioner, India, New Delhi. However, the data for vital rates have been obtained from the "Vital Statistics Division", Office of the Registrar General, India, New Delhi. Some relevant data meant for the purpose have also been obtained from previous year's publications of the Census of India. Various occasional papers published by Census of India, Office of the Registrar General & Census Commissioner, India, New Delhi, were also consulted.

Since the data for 2001 by rural-urban residence are not available yet, the rural-urban differential indices of social variables, such as sex ratio, literacy, vital rates and size of the household, for all the districts, states and union territories have been computed on the basis of 1991 data. As most of the data required for the study is at district level, but due to non-availability of district level data on vital rates, they have been examined for state level.

**Methodology**

Disparity or differentials can be absolute or relative. In an absolute sense, it may be calculated by simply subtracting the lesser values from the higher values. For instance, if literacy rate for urban population in a region is 60 per cent, for rural population it is 40 per cent, then absolute disparity will be equal to 20 per cent (*i.e.* 60 – 40 = 20). The relative disparity may be derived by working out the ratio between the literacy rates of both the regions *i.e.* $U : R = 60 : 40 = 3 : 2$. Though these are two different views of disparity from different angles, but both suffer from a common vagary of grouping dissimilar areas into the same type. An area with urban literacy rate of 80 per cent and rural literacy rate of 60 per cent would have the same absolute disparity as an area with 50 per cent of urban literacy and 30 per cent of rural literacy rates.

Likewise, the relative disparity in an area with 80 per cent male and 40 per cent female literacy rates would be the same as in an area having 60 per cent urban literacy and 30 per cent rural literacy rates.

Thus, both absolute and relative measures have been used to measure disparities between various binomial elements. However, the major difficulty with both of these measures is that the disparity between *alphas* and *non-alphas* is not the same as between *non-alphas* and *alphas*. Hence, a more sophisticated technique for the measurement of disparity is required to overcome this difficulty. David E. Sopher (1974) has proposed an alternative measure known as *Sopher's Disparity Index*, that gives the same value in the two cases mentioned above. Sopher's disparity index was originally stated as follows:

$$D_s = log\,(X_2 / X_1) + log\,(100 - X_1) / (100 - X_2)$$

where $X_2 \geq X_1$ and $X_1$ and $X_2$ are demographic indicators (such as literacy rates, sex-ratio, vital rates and size of household) of *alphas* and *non-alphas* respectively.

But this disparity index has also some limitations such as (i) for a given set of data, the disparity between *alphas* and *non-alphas* would be numerically the same but directionally opposite to that between *non-alphas* and *alphas*. This seriously restricts the analytic application of the index; (ii) It fails to distinguish between situations, each defined by two observations, when one of the two observations is zero or 100.

Therefore, in measuring the rural-urban differentials in size of household, vital rates, sex ratio and literacy rates, an index that satisfies all the four axioms of additive and multiplicative monotonicity, redistribution and repetitive transfers has been employed. This is the Sopher's index which was further modified by Kundu and Rao (1982), *i.e.*

$$D_s = log\,(X_2 / X_1) + log\,(200 - X_1) / (200 - X_2)$$

where $X_2 \geq X_1$ and $X_1$ and $X_2$ are various demographic aspects of *alphas* and *non-alphas* respectively.

It was found that most of the other techniques suffer from a limitation that the areas of high as well as low literacy may display similar differential index value if the two segments being differentiated are at the same level of literacy although they are simple and easy to comprehend.

Keeping in view the above mentioned disparity index, the first and foremost step in the analysis was the selection of binomial elements, in terms of which disparity was to be measured. The choice or selection of these aspects was highly constrained by the availability of data. For example, data on vital rates for 1991 were available only on state level. The differential index for various demographic attributes for the different districts of India was computed on the basis of disparity index given by Kundu and Rao (1982). Therefore, since spatial concept occupies a central position in every geographic inquiry, map is an important tool. On calculating differential index for various demographic indicators, the districts of India were classified into various categories and represented cartographically so as to present a regional perspective, showing spatial patterns of rural-urban differentials in size of the household, vital rates, sex ratio and literacy. The Census Maps of India for 1991 and 2001 showing district boundaries have been adopted as the base maps (Maps 1.1 and 1.2).

Wherever necessary, correlations have been calculated to determine the relationship between the dependent as well as the independent demographic and socio-economic variables. The coefficients of variability have also been computed to seek the spatial disparity of sex ratio and vital rates.

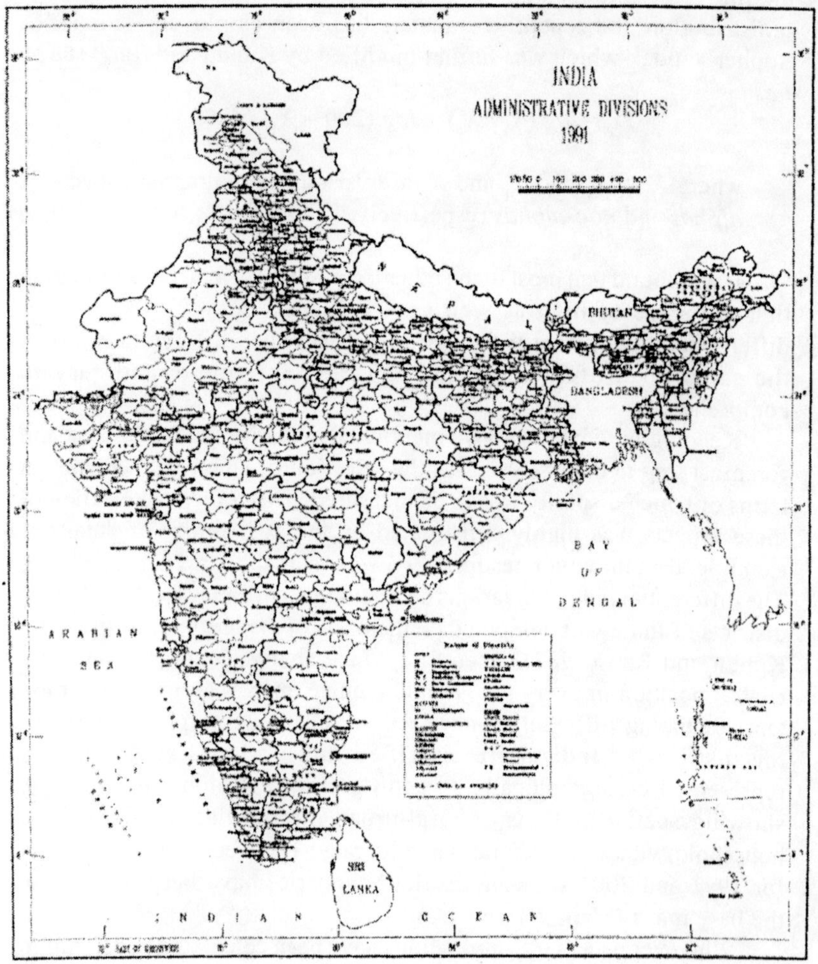


**Map 1.1**: India: Administrative Divisions, 1991

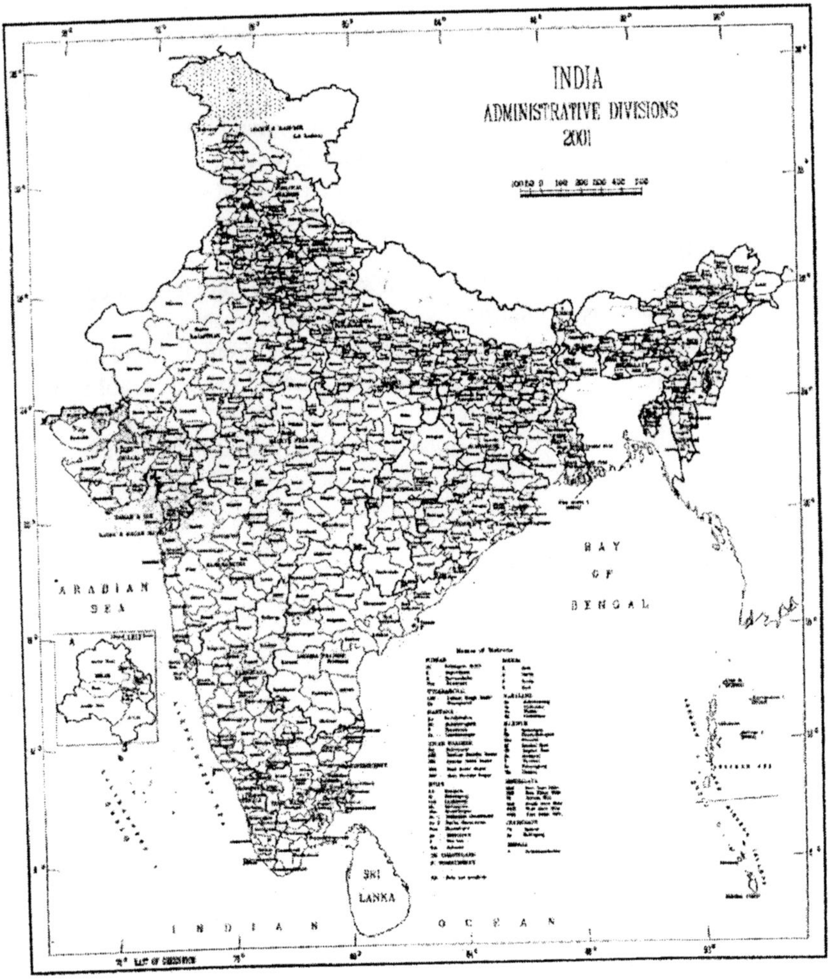


**Map 1.2:** India: Administrative Divisions, 2001

## Organisation of the Study

The present study has been organised into six main chapters followed by a summary of conclusions.

The first chapter is introductory in nature and deals with the problem under study, review of literature, methodology and data sources.

The second chapter presents a comprehensive view of the population profile of India.

The third chapter deals with the trends and spatial patterns of rural-urban differentials in sex ratio both at state and district level.

The fourth chapter presents a view of the trends and spatial patterns at state and district level for the rural-urban differentials in literacy.

In the fifth chapter the trends and spatial patterns of rural-urban differentials in vital rates have been discussed only on state level because of the non-availability of district level data on vital rates.

The sixth chapter explains the rural-urban differential trends and the spatial patterns of these differentials in size of the household in India at state as well as district level.

Lastly, a summary of conclusions has been given. It is followed by Bibliography.

# 2

# POPULATION PROFILE

India is a vast country, a nation of 1027 million people as per 2001 census. It is the second largest populous country next to China. India has thus about 16.7 per cent of the population of the world living on only 2.4 per cent of the total land area of the world. During 1981-91, the increase in population was more than 163 million persons from 683 million in 1981 to 846 million in 1991. In this way, India added in a decade, the size of population greater than *either* the population of Japan *or* that of Brazil (World Development Report, 1992). Not only this, but the 1991 population was three and a half times the population of the country at the beginning of twentieth century and two and a half times the population at the time of Independence. It was almost twice the population of Latin America and one and a quarter times the population of the whole of Africa. The increase in population during the 1980s was just a little less than the total population of the Western Europe comprising Austria, Belgium, France, Germany, Luxemburg, Netherlands, and Switzerland. In terms of annual increase, we add almost the total population of Australia or of Sri Lanka every year (Premi, 1997). However, during the decade 1991-2001, the population of India has increased by a whopping 180.6 million. This absolute addition to the population during the decade 1991-2001 is more than the estimated population of Brazil, the fifth most populous country in the world (Census of India, 2001).

The first comprehensive census of India conducted in 1881 recorded the country's population as 210.9 million. However, at the turn of the twentieth century, the population of India was recorded around 238.4 million which increased by more than four times in a period of hundred years to reach 1027 million at the dawn of the twenty-first century. Interestingly, the population of India grew by one and half times in the first-half of the twentieth century, while in the later half it recorded almost a phenomenal three-fold increase. Since the annual rate of population growth happens to be 1.9 per cent during 1991-2001, India became only the second country in the world after China to officially cross the one billion mark. At the current rate, India will attain the first rank in terms of the size of population by overtaking China as the most populous nation in the world some time between 2050-2075AD.

It is indeed alarming that more than 600 million people have been added to India's population in just about 90 years since 1901. It may lead to serious repercussions in the socio-economic and political set-up of the country. The dynamics of the past, present and anticipated growth of population is so complex and related to diversified socio-economic, environmental and demographic structure of the country that a simple generalization of this problem at the national level will not suffice the cause. Studies on population growth and its components, such as fertility and mortality, indicate significant regional variations. This is expressed in corresponding statistical analysis usually by the amount of variance that is not explained and that is quite considerable in some case. Therefore, with regard to the regional diversities of India, a geographical characterization of population growth by time will help as a first step in arriving at a reasonable understanding of the process of population growth.

## POPULATION GROWTH (1901-2001)

"The growth of population is often used to connote the change in the number of people living in a particular area during a specific period of time, irrespective of the fact whether the change is negative or positive". The growth of population is positive if there is increase in population and negative if there is decrease in population between two given points of time. The net change between two points of time is expressed in percentage and is described as the *growth rate* of population.

The growth of population is a function of fertility, mortality and migration. The prevalence of high birth and death rates during the early years of the demographic history of India restricted the growth rate and the size of population. This phenomenon was at its peak in 1921 when the country registered a negative growth rate. It gets momentum very abruptly and maintains an upward swing continuously with certain ups and downs (Table 2.1, Fig. 2.1).

### Population Growth: A Temporal Analysis

India has had a very chequered demographic history, more so during

**Table 2.1**: India: Growth of Population and Decadal Variations, 1901-2001

| *Census Year* | *Population (millions)* | *Decadal Growth* | | *Average Annual Exponential Growth Rate (per cent)* |
|---|---|---|---|---|
| | | *Absolute* | *Per cent* | |
| 1901 | 238.4 | — | — | — |
| 1911 | 252.1 | 13.7 | 5.75 | 0.56 |
| 1921 | 251.3 | –0.8 | –0.31 | –0.03 |
| 1931 | 279.0 | 27.7 | 11.00 | 1.04 |
| 1941 | 318.7 | 39.7 | 14.22 | 1.33 |
| 1951 | 361.1 | 42.4 | 13.31 | 1.25 |
| 1961 | 439.2 | 78.1 | 21.64 | 1.96 |
| 1971 | 548.2 | 109.0 | 24.80 | 2.20 |
| 1981 | 683.3 | 135.1 | 24.66 | 2.22 |
| 1991 | 846.3 | 163.1 | 23.86 | 2.14 |
| 2001 | 1027.0 | 180.6 | 21.34 | 1.93 |

*Source*: Census of India (2001), *Provisional Population Totals*, Paper-1 of 2001, Series-1, India, Statement 2, p. 34.

*Notes*: (i) The population of India includes the estimated population of entire Kachchh district, Morvi, Maliya-Miyana and Wankaner talukas of Rajkot district, Jodiya taluka of Jamnagar district of Gujarat state and entire Kinnaur district of Himachal Pradesh where population enumeration of Census of India, 2001, could not be conducted due to natural calamities.

(ii) The 1981 census could not be held owing to disturbed conditions prevailing in Assam. Hence the population figures for 1981 of Assam have been worked out by 'interpolation'.

(iii) The 1991 census could not be held owing to disturbed conditions prevailing in Jammu & Kashmir. Hence the population figures for 1991 of Jammu & Kashmir have been worked out by 'interpolation'.

the twentieth century. A perusal of population data for this period (Table 2.1) reveals that there have been significant demographic divides like the census years of 1921, 1951, and 1981. Thus, the demographic history of India can be divided into four distinct phases of population growth from 1901 to 2001.

| | | | |
|---|---|---|---|
| (i) | Phase I: | 1901-1921 | Very slow growth |
| (ii) | Phase II: | 1921-1951 | Steady growth |
| (iii) | Phase III: | 1951-1981 | Rapid high growth |
| (iv) | Phase IV: | 1981-2001 | High growth with definite signs of slowing down |

*Phase I: 1901-1921*

The first phase of 20 years (1901-1921) has often been recognized as

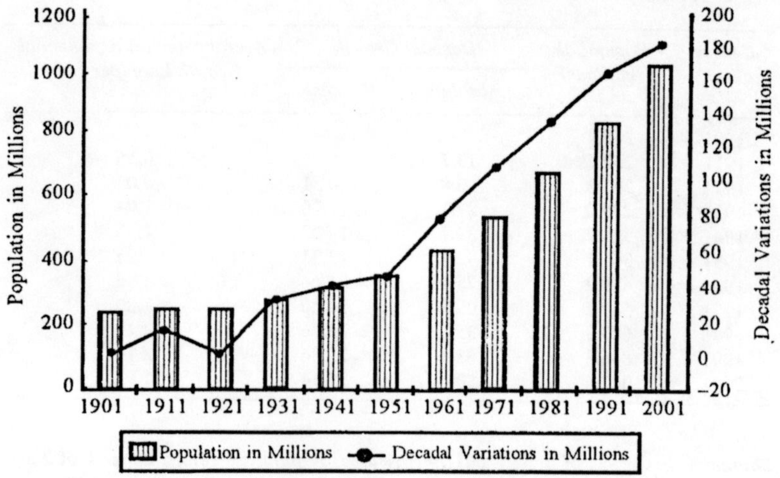


**Fig. 2.1:** India : Growth of Population and Decadal Variations, 1901-2001

the period of *very slow growth* of population. During this period, India's population increased from 238.4 million in 1901 to 251.3 million in 1921 *i.e.* just by 12.9 million. The growth of population was held in check by the prevalence of high death rate against a high birth rate, both being above 40 per 1000. Such a high mortality rate during this period was the product of large-scale abnormal deaths due to epidemics like plague (1907, 1915), malaria (1908, 1917), small pox (1912) and influenza (1918), and famines like droughts, food-shortages, etc. Influenza alone caused an estimated 7 per cent of the total population to die in 1918 (Mitra, 1978). This resulted in a net decrease of 0.3 per cent during the decade 1911-21 for the century as a whole. Thus, the year 1921 turned out to be a significant demographic divide as in the post-1921 period the population started showing signs of steady increase. India was in the first stage of demographic transition during 1901-1921.

*Phase II: 1921-1951*

The second phase started after 1921 and continued till 1951. During this period, the annual population growth rate increased by three times. Thus, the year 1921 can also be termed as a great divide in the demographic history of the country (Fig. 2.2). During this period the population increased from 251.3 million in 1921 to 361.1 million in 1951. The net gain of 109.8 million people was more than eight times than that of 1901-21. The fall in the death rate after 1921 is generally accepted as the plausible reason for this increase (Table 2.1, Fig. 2.2). The crude death rate (CDR) reduced by 19.8 points to 27.4 per 1000, whereas the crude birth rate (CBR) decreased only by 8.1 points to 40 per 1000. However, the trend of sharp decline in death rates was relatively slower during 1931-51 and, therefore, the overall growth rate of population remained under control particularly during 1941-51. The decline in death rate was the result of a gradual and significant reduction in the incidence of epidemics and famines.

Thus, the second phase of 30 years (1921-1951) emerged as a period of steady population growth. India had started its entry into the second phase of demographic transition during this period.

*Phase III: 1951-2001*

The year 1951 can be considered as another great divide because on the one hand, accelerated decline in the CDR was witnessed and on the other, CBR remained stubbornly high in the post-1951 period upto 1981. In 1951, the country had a CBR of 40 per 1000 and a CDR of 27 per

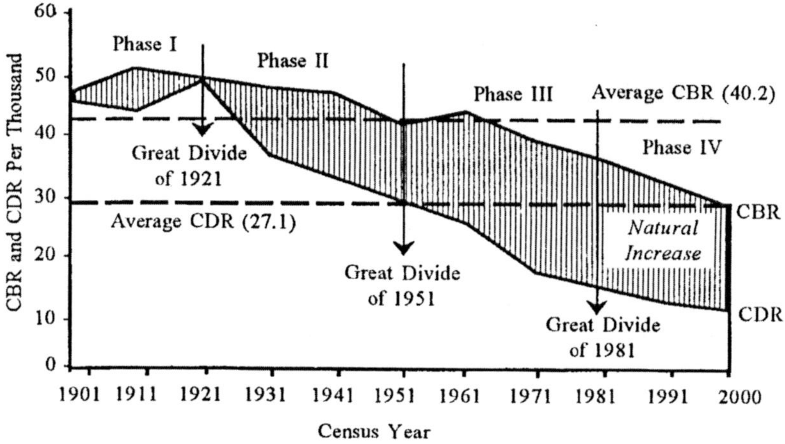


**Fig. 2.2:** India : Crude Birth Rates and Crude Death Rates, 1901-2001

1000. By 1981, while CDR declined to 14 per thousand, the CBR decreased to only 34 per thousand. Therefore, the year 1951 set the trend of rapid population growth, as the gap between CBR and CDR started increasing at an alarming rate, being more than 20 per thousand (Table 2.2 & Fig. 2.2.). Consequently, the third phase of population growth in India is characterized by a clearly marked increase in growth rate as well as in the size of population (Table 2.1 & Fig. 2.1.) and is often referred to as the *period of population explosion*. The explanatory factors were improved health, sanitation, food and nutrition.

**Table 2.2:** Natural Growth Rate (NGR) of Population, 1901-2000

*(Per Thousand)*

| *Census Year* | *Crude Birth Rate (CBR)* | *Crude Death Rate (CDR)* | *Natural Growth Rate (NGR)* |
|---|---|---|---|
| 1901 | 45.8 | 44.4 | 1.4 |
| 1911 | 49.2 | 42.6 | 6.6 |
| 1921 | 48.1 | 47.2 | 0.9 |
| 1931 | 46.2 | 36.3 | 9.9 |
| 1941 | 45.2 | 31.2 | 14.0 |
| 1951 | 40.0 | 27.4 | 12.6 |
| 1961 | 41.7 | 22.8 | 18.9 |
| 1971 | 36.9 | 14.9 | 22.0 |
| 1981 | 33.9 | 12.5 | 21.4 |
| 1991* | 29.5 | 9.8 | 19.7 |
| 2000 | 25.8 | 8.5 | 17.3 |

*Sources*: (i) Census of India, *Handbook of Population Statistics* (1988), Table 35, p. 99.
(ii) Registrar General, India (1999), *Compendium of India's Fertility and Mortality Indicators, 1971-1997*, Table 1, p. 3.
(iii) Registrar General, India (2001), *Sample Registration System Bulletin*, Vol. 35, No. 2, Table I, p. I.
* Excludes Jammu & Kashmir due to non-receipt of returns.

*Phase IV: 1981-2001*

The year 1981 took India into the fourth phase of high growth of population with definite signs of slowing down. Both CBR and CDR have shown declining trend in the post-1981 period. However, 1991 census figures indicate that the decline in fertility was getting established, while the decline in mortality was decelerating. That is why, the decade 1981-91 recorded a marginal decline of 0.81 per cent in the growth rate making the year 1981 as the third great divide in the demographic history of India. However, the decadal growth rate during 1991-2001, has registered the sharpest decline since Independence. It has declined from 23.86 per cent for 1981-91 to 21.34 per cent for the period 1991-2001, a decrease of 2.52 percentage points. The average exponential growth rate for the corresponding period declined from 2.14 per cent per annum to 1.93 per cent per annum. This implies that as a result of the combination of population momentum and somewhat impeded fertility, although India continues to grow in size, its pace of net addition is on the decrease. It seems that the country has now reached the take off stage in its demographic evolution.

The expansion of health care facilities during the last two decades in India has also brought down the infant mortality rate (IMR) by a considerable degree particularly in the urban areas. Thus, the efforts to control the death rates have produced better results than checking the birth rate. It has led to an increase of younger population in the reproductive age group which, in turn, has further raised the number of births. Perhaps, this could be taken care by the increase in the marriage age reducing the rates of married couples in this age group. However, it still poses a serious question as to what went wrong with Indian family planning programme in so far as checking the birth rate was concerned. A number of explanations can be offered in this connection. But it is a fact that the family planning programme in India has not been fully welcomed by the masses. A deeper analysis at the regional scale of the associated variables can provide useful understanding of the causes and consequences of the family planning programmes. One may, however, obtain from a number of studies that regional variations in literacy rates, distribution of scheduled castes, religious composition, standards of living, and also the physical size of the states have had a strong bearing on the differential fertility rates in India. Furthermore, personal factors like age at marriage, age at the first birth and spacing between the subsequent births, social status and practice in family planning methods, etc., also contributed to differential fertility rates and are also associated with living conditions, education, etc.

## Population Growth: A Spatial Analysis

Population growth needs to be viewed not only in the context of increase in numbers, but also within the broader perspective of patterns in different states of India. It is well known from the experiences of the developed countries that the course of secular demographic transition has been marked by pronounced regional contrasts. Not all inhabitants of different sub-regions of a country were affected by the progress of changes in their living conditions and they also remained oblivious of new ideas and values simultaneously.

An analysis of the population growth patterns at the state level in India will help as a first step towards understanding the direction in which the population and population-related studies should develop. The influence of contextual factors and the patterns of population growth, therefore, are to be evaluated at the state-level to ascertain the nature of correlations.

Although, there has been a universal growth of population in the country, yet the wide regional variations in the rate of population growth have been experienced at the state/union territory level (Map 2.1). The highest growth has been recorded by Nagaland (64.41 per cent) and the lowest by Kerala (9.42 per cent) (Table 2.3). The states that recorded the growth rate higher than the national average (21.34 per cent) were as many as 15 out of 28 in the country. These included Nagaland (64.41 per cent), Mizoram (29.18 per cent), Arunachal Pradesh (26.21 per cent), Meghalaya (29.94 per cent), Manipur (30.02 per cent), Jammu & Kashmir (29.04 per cent), Sikkim (32.98 per cent), Rajasthan (28.33 per cent), Haryana (28.06 per cent), Madhya Pradesh (24.34 per cent), Maharashtra (22.57 per cent), Uttar Pradesh (25.80 per cent), Bihar (28.33 per cent), Jharkhand (23.19 per cent), and Gujarat (22.48 per cent).

By comparison, the growth rate lower than the national average (21.34 per cent) was recorded by thirteen states. Out of these thirteen states, only four southern states, *viz*. Kerala (9.42 per cent), Tamil Nadu (11.19 per cent), Andhra Pradesh (13.86 per cent) and Goa (14.89 per cent) experienced growth rate below 15 per cent. This is because of: (i) out- migration due to severe population pressure and paucity of resources, and (ii) the declining trend of rate of natural increase. The decline in the rate of natural increase in these states was attributable to a significant fall in the birth rate which was the result of rising age at marriage of girls and increasing awareness about small sized families.

From amongst the union territories, Daman & Diu recorded the highest growth rate of 55.59 per cent and is followed by Dadra & Nagar Haveli (59.20 per cent), Delhi (46.31 per cent), Chandigarh (40.33 per cent) and Andaman & Nicobar Islands (26.94 per cent). On the other hand, Lakshadweep with 17.19 per cent growth rate was at the other end of the scale and was followed by Pondicherry (20.56 per cent). It is interesting to note that out of the seven, five union territories have

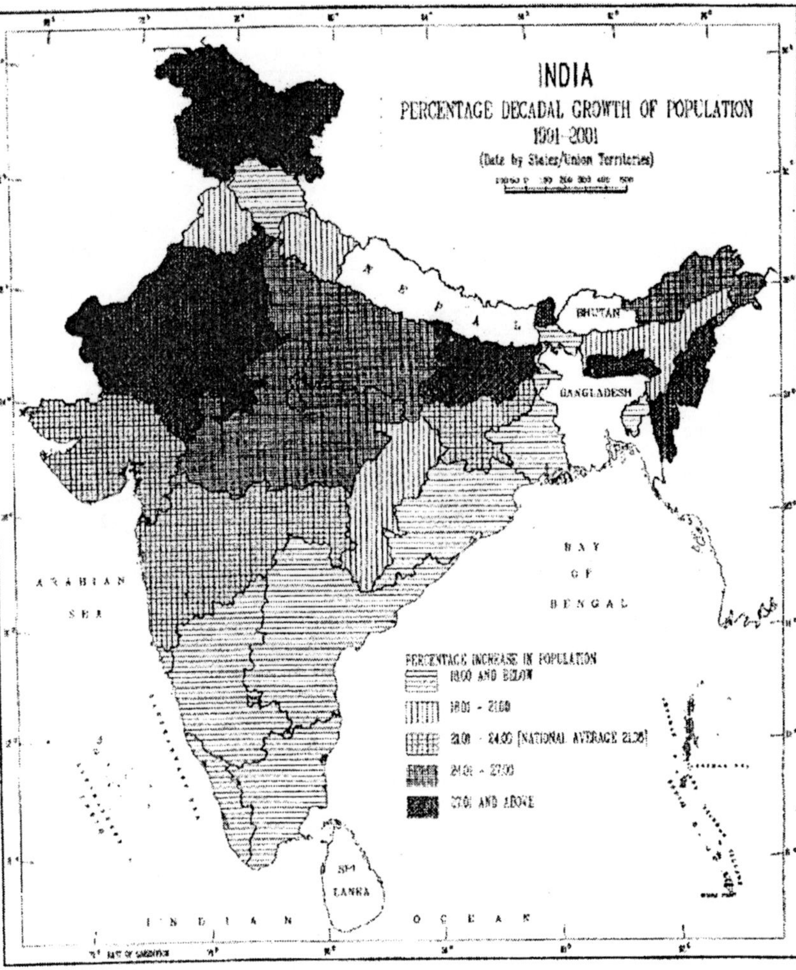


**Map 2.1 :** India: Percentage Decadal Growth of Population, 1991-2001 (Data by States/ Union Territories)

recorded the growth rate above national average (21.34 per cent) mainly because of their urban character. The analysis of growth rates of states starting from the decade 1951-1961 tells the real story of population growth in India. It took four decades even for Kerala to reach a decadal growth of less than 10 per cent from a high growth rate of 26.29 per cent during 1961-71. Tamil Nadu also took 40 years to reduce its growth from a high of 22.30 per cent during 1961-1971 to 11.19 per cent during

**Table 2.3:** India: Change in Growth Rate of Population, 1981-2001

| *Country/ State/ Union Territory* | *Growth Rate (Per cent)* | | *Change in Growth Rate (Per cent)* |
|---|---|---|---|
| | *1981-1991* | *1991-2000* | |
| **INDIA** | **23.86** | **21.34** | **-2.52** |
| *States* | | | |
| Tripura | 34.30 | 15.74 | −18.56 |
| Arunachal Pradesh | 36.83 | 26.21 | −10.63 |
| Mizoram | 39.70 | 29.18 | −10.51 |
| Andhra Pradesh | 24.20 | 13.86 | −10.33 |
| Chhatisgarh | 25.73 | 18.06 | −7.67 |
| West Bengal | 24.73 | 17.84 | −6.89 |
| Assam | 24.24 | 18.85 | −5.39 |
| Bihar | 23.38 | 28.43 | −5.05 |
| Uttaranchal | 24.23 | 19.20 | −5.03 |
| Kerala | 14.32 | 9.42 | −4.90 |
| Tamil Nadu | 15.39 | 11.19 | −4.20 |
| Orissa | 20.06 | 15.94 | −4.12 |
| Karnataka | 21.12 | 17.25 | −3.87 |
| Himachal Pradesh | 20.79 | 17.53 | −3.26 |
| Maharashtra | 25.73 | 22.57 | −3.16 |
| Meghalaya | 32.86 | 29.94 | −2.93 |
| Madhya Pradesh | 27.24 | 24.34 | −2.91 |
| Goa | 16.08 | 14.89 | −1.19 |
| Punjab | 20.81 | 19.76 | −1.05 |
| Jharkhand | 24.03 | 23.19 | −0.84 |
| Rajasthan | 28.44 | 28.33 | −0.11 |
| Uttar Pradesh | 25.55 | 25.80 | +0.25 |
| Haryana | 27.41 | 28.06 | +0.65 |
| Manipur | 29.29 | 30.02 | +0.73 |
| Gujarat | 21.19 | 22.48 | +1.29 |
| Sikkim | 28.47 | 32.98 | +4.51 |
| Nagaland | 56.08 | 64.41 | +8.33 |
| *Union Territories* | | | |
| Andaman & N. Islands | 48.70 | 26.94 | −21.76 |
| Pondicherry | 33.64 | 20.56 | −13.08 |
| Lakshadweep | 28.47 | 17.19 | −11.28 |
| Delhi | 51.45 | 46.31 | −5.14 |
| Chandigarh | 42.16 | 40.33 | −1.84 |
| Dadra & Nagar Haveli | 33.57 | 59.20 | +22.63 |
| Daman & Diu | 28.62 | 55.59 | +26.97 |

*Source*: Census of India (2001), *Provisional Population Totals*, Paper-1 of 2001, Series-1, India, Statement 4, pp. 42-43.

*Notes*:
(i) The population of India includes the estimated population of entire Kachchh district, Morvi, Maliya-Miyana and Wankaner talukas of Rajkot district, Jodiya taluka of Jamnagar district of Gujarat state and entire Kinnaur district of Himachal Pradesh where population enumeration of Census of India, 2001, could not be conducted due to natural calamities.
(ii) The population of Himachal Pradesh includes estimated population of entire Kinnaur district, where the population enumeration of Census of India, 2001, could not be conducted due to natural calamity.
(iii) The population of Gujarat includes estimated population of entire Kachchh district, Morvi, Maliya-Miyana and Wankaner talukas of Rajkot district and Jodiya taluka of Jamnagar district where the population enumeration of Census of India, 2001, could not be conducted due to natural calamity.

1991-2001. The growth rate in Bihar has shown an upward swing during 1991-2001 and the growth rates in Rajasthan, Uttar Pradesh, and Madhya Pradesh are now at a level where Kerala and Tamil Nadu were forty years ago. Even if it takes four decades for these four states to reach the present levels achieved by Kerala and Tamil Nadu, it seems it would be difficult for India to achieve a stable population by 2045. Therefore, it is imperative that some bold and path breaking initiatives are taken in reversing the trends of growth in these states, which at this stage do not show perceptible signs of abatement. Andhra Pradesh, however, has apparently shown an impressive fall in decadal growth rate by over 10 percentage points within a short span of a decade and this success story does inspire confidence that it should be possible to cross all hurdles to achieve sharp declines in population growth.

Change in growth rate between two latest decades of 1981-91 and 1991-2001 is another important indicator which is useful in determining, whether population growth rate has increased, declined or remained the same. Viewed in the spatial context, as many as 21 states, out of 28 in the country, recorded a decline in their growth rate in comparison to the previous decade (Table 2.3). The percentile decline ranged between the maximum of 18.56 per cent in Tripura to the minimum of 0.11 in Rajasthan. Since these 21 states together account for 66.70 per cent of the country's total population, it is no mean an achievement. What is significant to note in this regard is that even the states like Rajasthan, Jharkhand, and Madhya Pradesh recorded a decline in their growth rate in comparison to the previous decade, though marginally. There are as many as 16 states where the decline is above the national average of –2.52 per cent. These states are Tripura (–18.56 per cent), Arunachal Pradesh (–10.63 per cent), Mizoram (–10.51 per cent), Andhra Pradesh (–10.33 per cent), Chhatisgarh (–7.67 per cent), West Bengal (–6.89 per cent), Assam (–5.39 per cent), Uttaranchal (–5.03 per cent), Kerala (–4.90 per cent), Tamil Nadu (–4.20 per cent), Orissa (–4.12 per cent), Karnataka (–3.87 per cent), Himachal Pradesh (–3.26 per cent), Maharashtra (–3.16 per cent), Meghalaya (–2.93 per cent) and Madhya Pradesh (–2.91 per cent). Thus, the so called four BIMARU (Bihar, Madhya Pradesh, Rajasthan, and Uttar Pradesh) states have landed themselves into two different categories. While Madhya Pradesh earned the distinction of having recorded a decline (–2.91 per cent) in its growth rate of higher order than the national average, Rajasthan has recorded only a marginal decline (–0.11 per cent) in its growth rate (less than the national average). On the other hand, while Uttar Pradesh has only a marginal increase (+0.25 per cent), Bihar has experienced an increase (+5.05 per cent) of high order in its growth rate. During the inter-censal period of 1991-2001, a decline of more than five percentage points in decadal growth rate from the previous census decade was recorded for the states of Andhra Pradesh, West Bengal, Arunachal Pradesh, Delhi, Mizoram, Tripura, Assam, Uttaranchal and Chhatisgarh, and also for the union territories of Lakshadweep, Pondicherry and Andaman and Nicocbar Islands. These twelve states and union territories together account for 22.61 per cent of the country's population. In fact, among the major states, Andhra Pradesh has registered the sharpest drop of 10.33 percentage points during the said period followed by Chhatisgarh (7.67) and West Bengal (6.89). Jammu and Kashmir, Himachal Pradesh, Punjab, Meghalaya, Orissa, Madhya Pradesh, Maharashtra, Karnataka, Goa, Kerala and Tamil Nadu and the union territory of Chandigarh have shown a decline of one to five percentage points in their growth rates during 1991-2001 as compared to 1981-1991. These twelve states and union territories together account for 37.54 per cent of total population. The number of states and union territories with percentage decadal growth below 21 per cent, the current national average, has increased substantially from six in 1981-1991 to 15 in the decade 1991-2001, whereas the number of states/union territories with percentage decadal growth more than 21 per cent has reduced significantly from 29 to 20. More significantly, the sum total of the population of the states and union territories that registered less than the national growth rate has shown an impressive increase from about 17 per cent in 1991 to 42 per cent in 2001.

Examined at the district level, the regional disparities get further sharpened. Within the same state there may be districts experiencing slow growth of population as well as high growth of population (Map 2.2.). Out of the total of 593 districts, 58 districts have recorded less than 10 per cent growth rate during 1991-2001. Out of 58 districts that have registered decadal growth rate of less than 10 per cent, as many as 20 are in Tamil Nadu and 11 in Kerala. Andhra Pradesh and Karnataka have five and four districts respectively in this category. By contrast, there are 19 districts in the country which have registered high growth rate of more than 50 per cent. Among them as many as five belong to Nagaland and four to Delhi.

During the decade 1991-2001, Wokha district in Nagaland has the highest decadal growth rate (95.01 per cent), and is followed by the districts of Daman (83.49 per cent) in Daman and Diu; Senapati (81.96

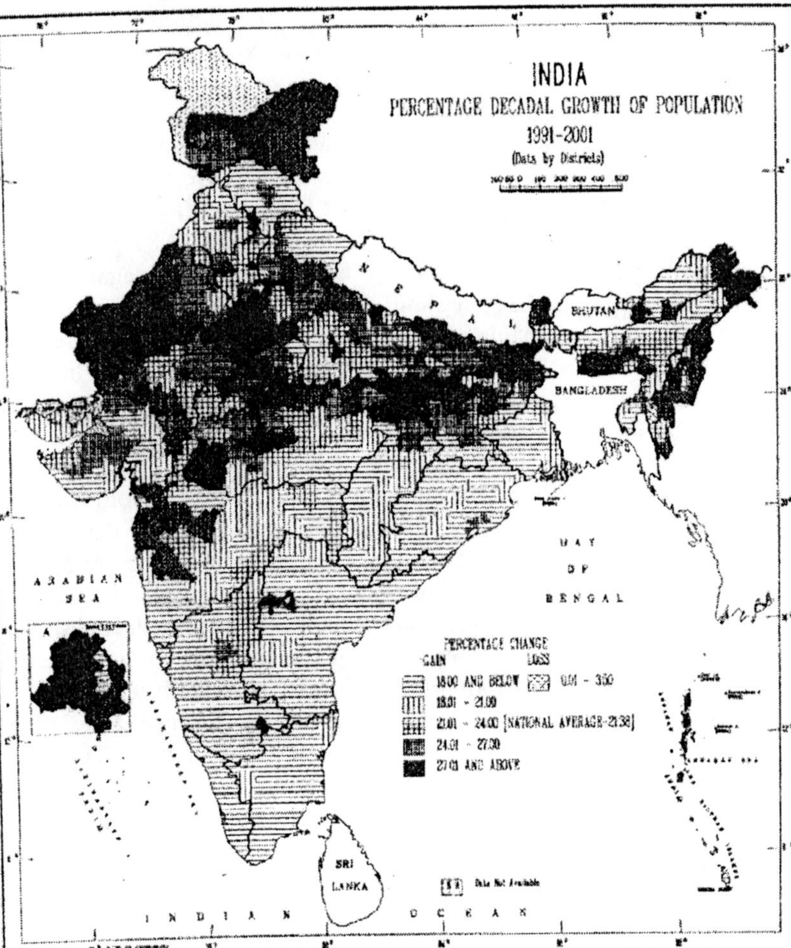


**Map 2.2 :** India : Percentage Decadal Growth of Population, 1991-2001 (Data by Districts)

per cent) in Manipur; Tuensang (78.10 per cent), Mon (73.42 per cent) and Dimapur (73.30 per cent) in Nagaland; Chandel (72.80 per cent) in Manipur; Papum Pore (67.21 per cent) in Arunachal Pradesh; North-East (62.52 per cent) and South-West (61.20 per cent) in Delhi.

Thus, four districts of Nagaland find place in the top ten slots of the districts with the highest growth rate. Among the districts in major states, the highest decadal growth of 54.86 per cent has been recorded in Thane district of Maharashtra, followed by Panchkula (51.16 per cent) and Faridabad (48.47 per cent) in Haryana.

By comparison, Mamit district in Mizoram has recorded the lowest growth rate (–3.50 per cent). It is followed by the districts of Central (–1.91 per cent) and New Delhi (2.47 per cent) in Delhi; Almora (3.14 per cent) in Uttaranchal; Sindhudurg (3.55 per cent) in Maharashtra; Pathanamthitta (3.72 per cent) in Kerala; Garhwal (3.87 per cent) in Uttaranchal; Kolkata (4.11 per cent) in West Bengal; Sivaganga (4.32 per cent) and Theni (4.33) in Tamil Nadu. Thus, Delhi and Tamil Nadu have the districts of having two districts each among the ten districts that have registered lowest decadal growth rate during 1991-2001.

The pattern of growth across the country during 1991-2001 is more discernible in Map. 2.2; which clearly depicts the district-wise percentage decadal growth of population during 1991-2001. The higher growth rates are visible in almost the entire Indo-Gangetic plain from Haryana in the west and extending upto northern Bengal. High growths are also observed in regions north of Satpura ranges, spreading across the Malwa Plateau, entire Rajasthan including the Great Indian Desert, western Maharashtra and parts of north-east. Relatively low growth is observed in regions lying south of Satpura ranges in the west, running across Godavari Basin and spreading through the Chhatisgarh plains, Chota Nagpur plateau and up to the western part of West Bengal and Orissa. Very low growth rates are observed in Punjab, Uttaranchal and in major part of the regions south of the Deccan plateau.

In addition to the differential fertility and mortality rates, the high differential growth rates of districts within the states/union territories can arise from differential levels of in-migrations or out-migrations which may be the result of economic development or otherwise. Certain districts may also have been influenced by recent drought and other natural calamities leading to temporary out-migration and in-migration of population. Districts being much smaller units than the states are relatively more sensitive to changes in population growth. It would, therefore, not be appropriate at this stage to comment and draw any definite conclusions based on these statements, about the possible changes in fertility or mortality levels as factors of differential growths in the districts.

## DISTRIBUTION AND DENSITY OF POPULATION

The analysis of population distribution and density holds immense significance for population geographers, as its successful understanding holds the key to the analysis of entire demographic character of an area.

**Distribution of Population**

Some of the typical characteristics of India's population and its distribution that carry wide range political, social and economic implications, both at national and international levels include: huge population base (1027 million in 2001), ethnic multiplicity and rural bias and unevenness in its distribution. (Chandna, 2000).

The most distinguishing feature of India's population is its huge size. The 2001 census reveals a massive total of 1027 million. It is more than the total population of five most populous countries, after China and India, of the world, if put together. These are U.S.A. (281.4 million), Indonesia (212.1 million), Brazil (170.1 million), Pakistan (156.5 million) and Russia (146.9 million). It shows that India's total population is more than three and a half times than U.S.A. and about five times than that of Indonesia, the third and fourth most populous countries in the world respectively. During 1991-2001, the population of India has increased by a whopping 180.6 million. This absolute addition to the population during the decade 1991-2001 is more than the estimated population of Brazil, the fifth most populous country in the world.

Unevenness of distribution is another most significant feature of India's population. On one hand, the population of India is highly concentrated in some pockets such as highly urbanized and industrialized areas and areas of high agricultural productivity, while on the other hand, there are virtually demographic deserts in high mountains, arid lands, thickly forested areas and some remote corners of the country. These wide regional contrasts in population distribution have been observed both at macro (state) and micro (district) levels. As far as macro level is concerned, Uttar Pradesh is by far the most populous state in the country with more than 166 million people living here, which is more than the population of Pakistan, the sixth most populous country in the world. The combined population of Uttar Pradesh and Uttaranchal (until recently a part of Uttar Pradesh) is greater than the population of Brazil. Nineteen states now have a population of over ten million. On the other extreme, there are eight states and union territories in the country that are yet to reach the one million mark. Almost half of the country's population lives in five states, namely, Uttar Pradesh, Maharashtra, Bihar, West Bengal and Andhra Pradesh. While Uttar

Pradesh and Maharashtra have held on to the first two positions in terms of their ranking in 2001 as compared to 1991, Bihar has moved on to take the third position from its fifth position pushing West Bengal and Andhra Pradesh now to the fourth and fifth spots respectively.

Another typical feature of India's population distribution is that of its concentration in rural areas from the very beginning of the present century (Table 2.4). Over three-fourths (76.6 per cent) of the country's total population even today is concentrated in the countryside. The Indian rural populace, by and large, unlike that in the West, lived in hamlets and agglomerated settlements of varying sizes. Dispersed habitations were often met with only in hilly regions of the Himalayas, Kerala (Spate and Learmonth, 1954) and semi-arid areas (Muthiah, 1987). There were about 575,000 rural settlements (villages) in the country, half of which had a population of less than 500 each. Only in 1835 villages, the population size crossed 10,000 mark (Muthiah, 1987). The spread of population into widely distributed large number of settlements (over half a million) carries its own impediments as far as the socio-economic development of the country is concerned. The chief impediment associated with such a pattern of distribution is the heavy expenditure on developing an infrastructure for speedy economic growth, rapid social advancement, efficient system of distribution and provision of amenities, for good living in each of the rural settlement.

**Table 2.4:** India: Distribution of Population by Rural-Urban Residence, 1901-1991

| *Census Year* | *Population as Per cent to Total* | |
|---|---|---|
| | *Rural* | *Urban* |
| 1901 | 89.15 | 10.85 |
| 1911 | 89.71 | 10.29 |
| 1921 | 88.82 | 11.18 |
| 1931 | 88.01 | 11.99 |
| 1941 | 86.14 | 13.86 |
| 1951 | 82.71 | 17.29 |
| 1961 | 82.03 | 17.97 |
| 1971 | 80.09 | 19.91 |
| 1981* | 76.66 | 23.34 |
| 1991** | 74.29 | 25.71 |

*Source*: Computed from, Census of India (1991), *Final Population Totals: Brief Analysis of Primary Census Abstract*, Paper 2 of 1992, Series-1, India, p. 86.

* Includes the projected population of Assam.

** Includes the projected population of Jammu & Kashmir.

Since the mainstay of India's economy continues to be agriculture, the factors that govern distribution of population in the country are those that promote good agriculture. The availability of cultivable land, depth of soil, fertility of soil, depth of underground watertable, availability of water for irrigation are, thus, some of the factors that have guided the distribution pattern of population in the country. In the absence of any spectacular spurts in the country's urban/industrial development, the recently observed redistribution tendencies still reflect the hold of all such factors on the distributional pattern of Indian population. That is why, the areas that have been recently reclaimed for agricultural purposes, the areas where intensification of agriculture has significantly enhanced the supporting capacity of the land and the areas where plantations have been extended, all have witnessed large scale in-migration of agricultural families from the crowded areas (Chandna, 2000).

## Density of Population

Density of population, generally expressed in terms of persons per square kilometre or per square mile of land area, is a significant measure of degree of population concentration. As per 2001 census, India has an average density of 324 persons per square kilometre (Table 2.5) which is about eight times the average density (less than 40 persons/km$^2$) of

**Table 2.5:** India: Density of Population, 1901-2001

| *Census Year* | *Density of Population (Persons/km$^2$)* |
|---|---|
| 1901 | 77 |
| 1911 | 82 |
| 1921 | 81 |
| 1931 | 90 |
| 1941 | 103 |
| 1951 | 117 |
| 1961 | 142 |
| 1971* | 177 |
| 1981** | 216 |
| 1991** | 267 |
| 2001** | 324 |

*Source*: Census of India (2001), *Provisional Population Totals*, Paper-1 of 2001, Series-1, India, Statement 14, p. 73.

* While working out the density of India, Jammu & Kashmir has been excluded as comparable figures of area and population are not available for that state.

** The density has been worked out on comparable data.

the world as a whole. India, thus, is considered to be one of the most densely populated countries of the world.

The most striking feature of India's density of population is that, it has been consistently increasing since 1901 except in 1921 when the density fell by one point to 81 persons per sq. km. In a span of hundred years, India's population density has increased by almost four times, from 77 to 324 persons per sq. km. The persons living in per sq. km. has increased by 21.3 per cent in 2001 as compared to 1991.

High increase in the density of population is a matter of great concern as it puts immense pressure on our natural resources. Also it may adversely affect the quality of life. Due to difference in climatic conditions, availability of resources etc., the states and union territories of our country largely varied in terms of density. (Table 2.6) It is, therefore, essential to analyze the variations across the states and union territories.

From amongst various states in the country, West Bengal is still the most thickly populated, where population density has gone up from 767 in 1991 to 904 persons per $km^2$ in 2001. However, Bihar with 880 persons per $km^2$ is now the second highest densely populated state pushing Kerala (819) to the third spot in terms of ranking. The continuous drifting of Kerala from first position in 1981 to second in 1991 and at third in 2001 in terms of density of population is mainly due to its controlled growth of population. The other seven states that have displayed higher density of population than the national average (324) are Uttar Pradesh (689), Punjab (482), Tamil Nadu (478), Haryana (477), Goa (363), Assam (340) and Jharkhand (338) (Map 2.3).

At the other end of the scale is Arunachal Pradesh which among various states has the lowest density of only 13 persons per $km^2$. Although, there are 18 states which experience density of population lower than the national average (324 persons per $km^2$), but three states, besides Arunachal Pradesh, are having the low density of less than 100 persons per $km^2$. These are Mizoram (42), Sikkim (76) and Jammu & Kashmir (99). Thus, the states having low density are either the hill states or have a large proportion of mountainous areas.

As far as union territories are concerned in terms of density of population, all the union territories, except Andaman and Nicobar Islands (43), have a higher density than the national average of 324 persons per $km^2$. Delhi with a density of 9294 persons is the most densely populated union territory of the country. Most of the union territories are generally highly urbanized and hence display high degree of

**Table 2.6**: India: Density of Population, 1991 and 2001

| *Country/State/Union Territory* | *Density (Persons/km²)* | |
|---|---|---|
| | *1991* | *2001* |
| **INDIA** | **267** | **324** |
| *States* | | |
| West Bengal | 757 | 904 |
| Bihar | 685 | 880 |
| Kerala | 749 | 819 |
| Uttar Pradesh | 548 | 689 |
| Punjab | 403 | 482 |
| Tamil Nadu | 429 | 478 |
| Haryana | 372 | 477 |
| Goa | 316 | 363 |
| Assam | 286 | 340 |
| Jharkhand | 274 | 338 |
| Maharashtra | 257 | 314 |
| Tripura | 263 | 304 |
| Andhra Pradesh | 242 | 275 |
| Karnataka | 235 | 275 |
| Gujarat | 211 | 258 |
| Orissa | 203 | 236 |
| Madhya Pradesh | 158 | 196 |
| Rajasthan | 129 | 165 |
| Uttaranchal | 133 | 159 |
| Chhatisgarh | 130 | 154 |
| Nagaland | 73 | 120 |
| Himachal Pradesh | 93 | 109 |
| Manipur | 82 | 107 |
| Meghalaya | 79 | 103 |
| Jammu & Kashmir | 77 | 99 |
| Sikkim | 57 | 76 |
| Mizoram | 33 | 42 |
| Arunachal Pradesh | 10 | 13 |
| *Union Territories* | | |
| Delhi | 6352 | 9294 |
| Chandigarh | 5632 | 7903 |
| Pondicherry | 1683 | 2029 |
| Lakshadweep | 1616 | 1894 |
| Daman & Diu | 907 | 1411 |
| Dadra & Nagar Haveli | 282 | 449 |
| Andaman & Nicobar Islands | 34 | 43 |

*Source*: Census of India (2001), *Provisional Population Totals*, Paper-1 of 2001, Series-1, India, Statement 15, pp. 75-76.

*Note*: States and Union Territories are arranged in descending order of density of population for 2001.

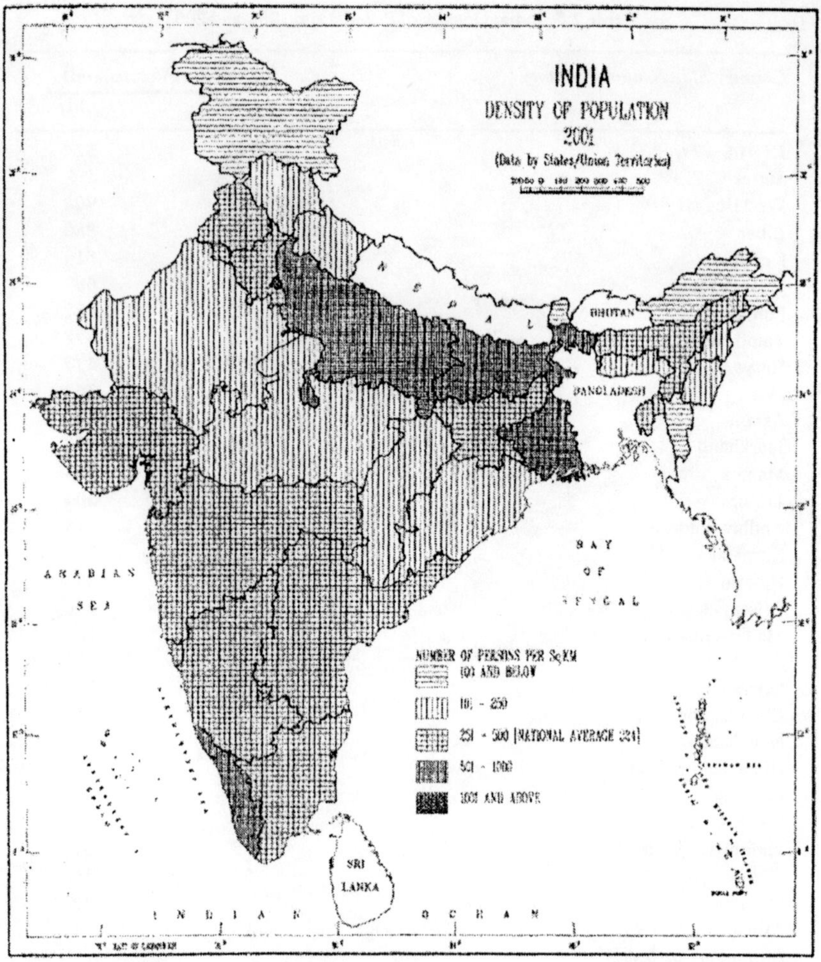


**Map 2.3 :** India : Density of Population, 2001 (Data by States / Union Territories)

population concentration. The sparsely populated union territory of Andaman & Nicobar Islands consists of a large number of widely spread, poorly connected islands which are distantly located from the mainland (Chandna, 2000).

At the district level, wide regional varieties in the density of population are bound to occur in a vast country like India with a large variety of surface configuration and resource potential (Map 2.4). Out of the total of 593 districts, 294 districts experienced density of population

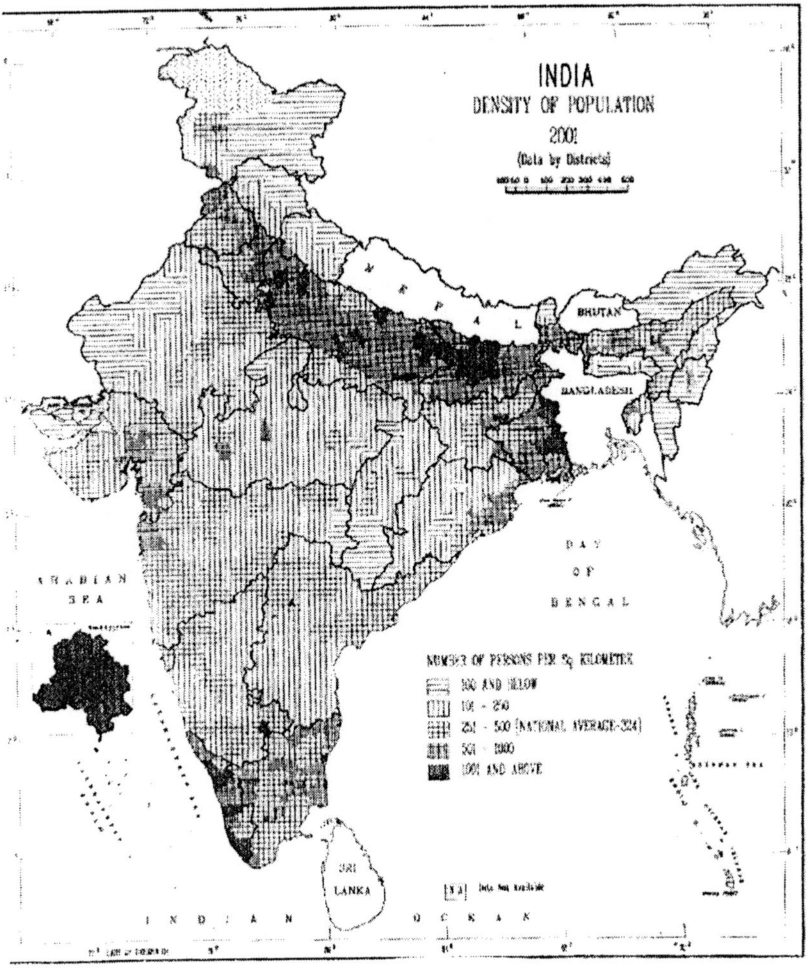


**Map 2.4 :** India : Density of Population, 2001 (Data by Districts)

higher than the national average of 324 persons per km², while one district of Dhaulpur in Rajasthan is at par with the national average. The North East district in Delhi has the highest population density in the country with 29,395 persons per km². This is followed by the districts of Central (25,760) in Delhi; Kolkata (24,760) in West Bengal; Chennai (24,231) in Tamil Nadu; East (22,637) in Delhi; Mumbai (21,190) and Mumbai (Suburban) (19,255) in Maharashtra; Hyderabad (16,988) in Andhra Pradesh; and West (16,431) and North (12,996) in Delhi. These top 10 most densely populated districts of the country together account for three per cent of the country's total population and are characterized with a very high density of population more than 10,000 persons per $km^2$. Because, all these districts are either fully urban or highly urbanized.

As depicted in Map 2.4, the pressure on land in the entire Indo-Gangetic plain extending upto Hoogly basin in the east is quite evident. Thus, it can be stated that the largest most conspicuous area of high density of population is constituted by the so called Hindi heartland covering large parts of Uttar Pradesh and Bihar alongwith adjacent areas of Haryana in the west and West Bengal in the east. Largely, the densities here are rural except in the east and the west where urban industrial developments of some consequence had resulted in select urban concentrations (Sadasyuk, 1971). The region is marked by extensive availability of large levelled, deep alluvium-filled plain with most productive soils and favourable rainfall conditions. In fact, it is a paradox to find poor agriculture in this belt which otherwise possesses conditions conducive to good agriculture. Poor water management, *inter alia* has been considered to be responsible for poor agricultural development in this belt (Chandna and Kant, 1985). The rural over-population in large parts of the heartland (Singh, 1971) has resulted in out-migration of landless labourers from north Bihar and eastern Uttar Pradesh to agriculturally prosperous areas of Punjab, Haryana and Assam. The eastern and western margins of this large belt of high density have, of course, witnessed some super-imposition of industrial concentrations of sugar industry in western Uttar Pradesh and jute textiles in West Bengal. Thus, the pressure of population in the central more rural parts of the belt is higher than that in its extremes (Bhutani, 1995).

The Tamil Nadu uplands and Malabar coast in the south together constitute another large contiguous region of high density. Within this belt, the Malabar coastal areas and highly urbanized district of Madras have comparatively higher density. A density of more than 1000 persons per square kilometre is met within the coastal areas of Kerala where highly intensive agriculture is the mainstay of economy. In the interior, plantation agriculture (coffee, tea and rubber) and industries associated with these plantation crops contributed to the high density of population. The Kaveri delta and the adjacent districts in the north-eastern parts of Tamil Nadu upland plain, have high densities associated with the developments in the field of agriculture and dispersal of household industries, respectively. This part of peninsular India has urban development of relatively high order. Madras, as the pivotal point alongwith Coimbatore, Madurai, Tuticorin, constituted one of the oldest city system of the country accounting for great economic activity in the region (Sadasyuk, 1971).

Apart from these two major areas, the agriculturally developed areas of Mahanadi delta, Godavari delta, Bari and Bist doabs and highly urbanized districts of Greater Bombay, Hyderabad, Bangalore, Delhi and Chandigarh, Ahmedabad, Kheda and Indore also displayed high densities.

On the other end of the scale, Lahul & Spiti district of Himachal Pradesh has the lowest density of population (2 persons/km$^2$) in the country. It is followed by the districts of Leh (Ladakh) (3) in Jammu & Kashmir; Dibang Valley (4), Upper Siang (5) and Upper Subansiri (8) in Arunachal Pradesh; Kargil (8) in Jammu & Kashmir; Lower Subansiri (10) and West Kameng (10) in Arunachal Pradesh; North (10) in Sikkim; and Lohit (13) in Arunachal Pradesh. It is interesting to note that out of the bottom 10 districts having extremely low density of population, 6 districts are found in Arunachal Pradesh alone. Moreover, extremely low densities of less than 50 persons per km$^2$ are typical of the frontier zones having land border with Pakistan, China and Myanmar. These frontier zones suffered from serious physiographic handicaps such as water logging in Rann of Katchchh in Gujarat, desert conditions in Rajasthan and mountainous terrain in rest of the border districts. It is interesting to note that wherever such physical handicaps were overcome such as that in Ganganagar in Rajasthan and Amritsar, Firozepur, Gurdaspur in Punjab, the densities shot up. Thus, by and large, border location coupled with physico-socio-cultural handicaps were responsible for keeping the densities extremely low.

## POPULATION COMPOSITION

The composition of population, or the population structure, refers to those aspects of population which may be measured, however, inadequately (Clark, 1972). The individual characteristics to which composition generally refers include sex, age, marital status, place of birth, mother tongue, education, vital rates, occupation, labour force status and households, including relationship to the head of household (United Nations, 1949). But among these various components of population composition, sex composition, age composition and economic composition hold a prime place for population geographers (Chandna, 2000).

## Sex Composition

Sex composition of the human population is one of the basic demographic characteristics, which is extremely vital for any meaningful demographic analysis. Indian census has the tradition of bringing out disaggregated information by sex on various aspects of population. The first and foremost is the simple count of males and females. A change in sex composition largely reflects the underlying socio-economic and cultural patterns of a society in different ways. Sex ratio, defined here as the number of females per 1000 males in the population, is an important social indicator to measure the extent of prevailing equity between males and females in a society at a given point of time. It is mainly the outcome of the interplay of sex differentials in mortality, sex-selective migration, sex ratio at birth and at times the sex differential in population enumeration.

The study of sex ratio in a population is also important because (i) the analysis of the sex ratio can help in drawing several inferences regarding the dynamics of demographic phenomena; (ii) it affects the labour supply through marriage and fecundity (fertility). If the proportion of males is higher than that of females, more workers will be available; (iii) it has bearing upon the fertility rate, morality rate, marriage rate and even on the rate of migration directly. Shryock *et al.* (1976) also recognized the profound effect of the proportion of two sexes upon the other demographic elements like population growth, marriage rates, occupational structure, etc.

According to Census of India, 2001, the sex ratio stands at 933 for the country as a whole. This is a welcome improvement from the 1991 census, which had recorded 927 females per 1000 males. However, right from the beginning of census operations, the sex ratio in India had always remained unfavourable to females. Moreover, barring some hiccups, it has shown a long-term declining trend. The sex ratio at the beginning of the twentieth century was 972 and thereafter showed continuous decline until 1941. In 1951, there was a marginal increase of one point, but thereafter it again dropped for two consecutive decades to reach 930 in 1971. In fact, between 1961-1971, the country saw the sharpest decline of 11 points in the sex ratio. Thereafter, it has fluctuated marginally around 930 in successive censuses (Table 2.7 and Fig. 2.3).

Table 2.7 reveals that the sex ratio in India has suffered a consistent decline all through the twentieth century except during the decades of 1941-51, 1971-81 and 1991-2001. Several reasons are adduced to

**Table 2.7:** India: Sex Ratio, 1901-2001

| *Census Year* | *Females per 1000 Males* |
|---|---|
| 1901 | 972 |
| 1911 | 964 |
| 1921 | 955 |
| 1931 | 950 |
| 1941 | 945 |
| 1951 | 946 |
| 1961 | 941 |
| 1971 | 930 |
| 1981 | 934 |
| 1991 | 927 |
| 2001 | 933 |

*Source*: Census of India (2001), *Provisional Population Totals*, Paper-1 of 2001, Series-1, India, Statement 18, p. 85.

*Notes*: (i) For 1991 the interpolated figures for Jammu & Kashmir have been used.

(ii) While working out the sex ratio for India for the year 2001, the estimated population of entire Kachchh district, Morvi, Maliya-Miyana and Wankaner talukas of Rajkot district, Jodiya taluka of Jamnagar district of Gujarat state and entire Kinnaur district of Himachal Pradesh have been used, as the population enumeration of Census of India, 2001, could not be conducted due to natural calamities.

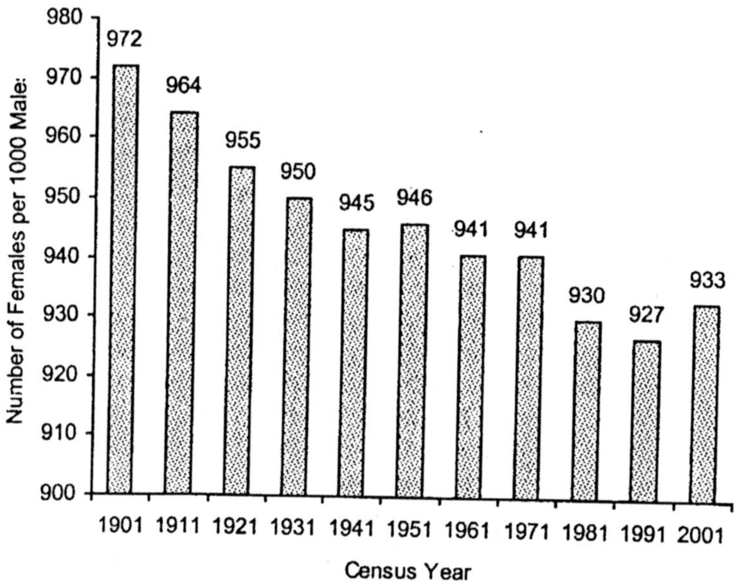


**Fig. 2.3** : India : Sex Ratio, 1901-2001

explain the consistently low levels of sex ratio and their further decline in the country. However, some of the important reasons attributed to this declining trend in sex ratio of India are: (i) neglect of the girl child resulting in their higher mortality at younger ages, (ii) high maternal mortality, (iii) sex-selective female abortions, (iv) female infanticide, and (v) change in sex ratio at birth.

Viewed in its regional perspective, there is a phenomenal diversity in sex ratio among the states and union territories of India (Map 2.5). From amongst the states, Kerala with a sex ratio of 1058 is the only state in the country which has excess of females over males (Table 2.8). This is mainly because Kerala has been one of the most densely populated states of the country which has been experiencing male-selective out-migration to other parts of the country for employment since long. Moreover, it has a sizeable proportion of Christian population and highest literacy rates in the country, which together may have contributed to a low female mortality rate. The states that display more or less balanced sex ratio include Chhatisgarh (990), Tamil Nadu (986), Manipur (978), Andhra Pradesh (978), Meghalaya (975), Orissa (972) and Himachal Pradesh (970). Although the states of Chhatisgarh, Tamil Nadu, Manipur, Meghalaya and Orissa have experienced a continuous declining trend in sex ratio over the decades in twentieth century, Himachal Pradesh is the only state that has shown a considerable improvement in sex ratio from 884 in 1901 to 970 in 2001. This is mainly because of male-selective out-migration as well as declining female mortality in the state. The other states with sex ratio higher than the national average of 933 in 2001 are Uttaranchal (964), Karnataka (964), Goa (960), Tripura (950), Jharkhand (941), Mizoram (938) and West Bengal (934).

At the other end of the scale is Haryana with lowest sex ratio of 861 females per 1000 males mainly because of the increasing trend of female foetal abortions on the basis of sex-determination tests as well as a strong preference to have a son at the cost of female child. The other states with fairly large paucity of females are Punjab (874), Sikkim (875), Uttar Pradesh (898), Jammu & Kashmir (900), Arunachal Pradesh (901), Nagaland (909), Madhya Pradesh (920), Bihar (921), Gujarat (921), Rajasthan (922), Maharashtra (922) and Assam (932), all of which have a sex ratio lower than the national average (933).

From amongst the union territories, Pondicherry, like Kerala, is the only union territory in India which has excess of females over males (1001 females per 1000 males) and is followed by Lakshadweep (947). Both these union territories displayed relatively high sex ratio, higher

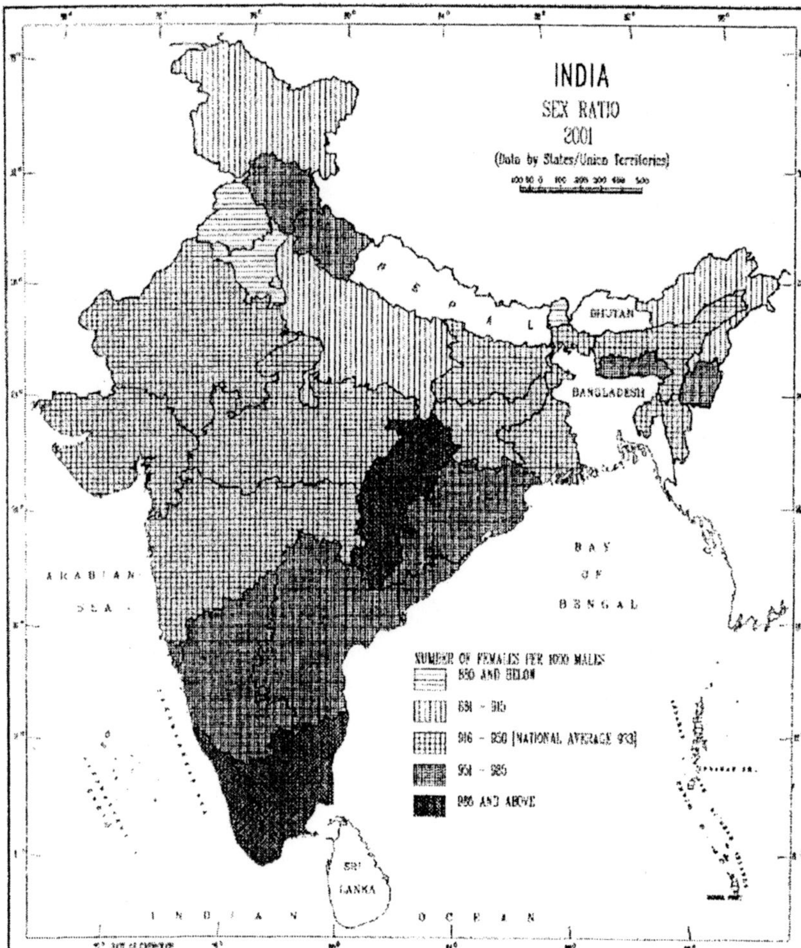


**Map 2.5 :** India: Sex Ratio 2001 (Data by States/Union Territories)

than the national average (933).

By contrast, Daman & Diu with a sex ratio of only 709 displayed the highest paucity of females in the country mainly because of male-selective in-migration. It is followed by Chandigarh (773), Dadra & Nagar Haveli (811), Delhi (821), and Andaman & Nicobar Islands (846). It is interesting to note that out of seven union territories, five have a sex ratio lower than the national average. Chandigarh and Delhi are highly urbanized union territories where among other factors, male-selective in-migration is a

**Table 2.8:** India: Sex Ratio, 1991 and 2001

| *Country/State/Union Territory* | *Females per 1000 Males* | |
|---|---|---|
| | 1991 | 2001 |
| **INDIA** | **927** | **933** |
| *States* | | |
| Kerala | 1036 | 1058 |
| Chhatisgarh | 985 | 990 |
| Tamil Nadu | 974 | 986 |
| Andhra Pradesh | 972 | 978 |
| Manipur | 958 | 978 |
| Meghalaya | 955 | 975 |
| Orissa | 971 | 972 |
| Himachal Pradesh | 976 | 970 |
| Karnataka | 960 | 964 |
| Uttaranchal | 936 | 964 |
| Goa | 967 | 960 |
| Tripura | 945 | 950 |
| Jharkhand | 922 | 941 |
| Mizoram | 921 | 938 |
| West Bengal | 917 | 934 |
| Assam | 923 | 932 |
| Maharashtra | 934 | 922 |
| Rajasthan | 910 | 922 |
| Bihar | 907 | 921 |
| Gujarat | 934 | 921 |
| Madhya Pradesh | 912 | 920 |
| Nagaland | 886 | 909 |
| Arunachal Pradesh | 859 | 901 |
| Jammu & Kashmir | NA | 900 |
| Uttar Pradesh | 876 | 898 |
| Sikkim | 878 | 875 |
| Punjab | 882 | 874 |
| Haryana | 865 | 861 |
| *Union Territories* | | |
| Pondicherry | 979 | 1001 |
| Lakshadweep | 943 | 947 |
| Andaman & Nicobar Islands | 818 | 846 |
| Delhi | 827 | 821 |
| Dadra & Nagar Haveli | 952 | 811 |
| Chandigarh | 790 | 773 |
| Daman & Diu | 969 | 709 |

*Source*: Census of India (2001), *Provisional Population Totals*, Paper-1 of 2001, Series-1, India, Statement 19, pp. 92-94.

*Notes*: (i) While working out sex ratio of child population for 1991 census in the age group 0-6 and population aged 7 and above for India, the population in the age group 0-6 and population aged 7 and above of areas of Gujarat and Himachal Pradesh affected by natural calamities have been excluded.

(ii) To make the data comparable with Census of India, 2001, the proportion of child population for 1991 census in the age group 0-6 and population aged 7 and above shown against Gujarat excludes the population data of entire Kachchh district, Morvi, Maliya-Miyana and Wankaner talukas of Rajkot district, Jodiya taluka of Jamnagar district of Gujarat state where population enumeration of Census of India, 2001, could not be conducted due to natural calamity.

(iii) States and Union territories are arranged in descending order of sex ratio for 2001.

plausible reason in explaining the striking deficiency of females. Similarly, the union territory of Andaman & Nicobar Islands, which displayed sex ratio of 846 females per 1000 males, may have witnessed male-selective in-migration. Another typical feature of sex ratio in Andaman & Nicobar Islands is a significant improvement over the decades in twentieth century. In 1901, the sex ratio in Andaman & Nicobar Islands was desperately low at 318 females per 1000 males, which was one-third of the national average (972), but also the lowest among the states and union territories and remained lowest throughout the demographic history of India upto 1981 when it increased to 760. During pre-Independence period, the improvement in sex ratio was gradual and it reached to 574 in 1941. This was mainly because of the repressive policy of the British government, when freedom fighters from the mainland of India were used to send as prisoners there. In the absence of male-selective in-migration of prisoners during post-Independence era, the sex ratio improved significantly upto 846 in 2001. It is because this area is strategically important for the country where the in-migration of personnel from armed services has been on the increase.

One significant feature of 2001 census is that a total of 23 states and union territories register an overall increase in their sex ratio as compared to 1991 (Table 2.8). However, during the corresponding period the sex-ratio of the child population in the age group 0-6 has increased in only four states and one union territory. Furthermore, it has been observed that the number of states and union territories with sex ratio below national average has increased from 17 in 1991 to 18 in 2001 and the proportion of population has increased from 54 per cent to about 60 per cent. Inspite of the increase in the number and relative share in the total population, the overall sex ratio of the country has improved. What could be the possible reason for this? It can be observed that on the one hand, the proportion of population constituted by the highly populated BIMARU states *i.e.* Bihar, Madhya Pradesh, Rajasthan and Uttar Pradesh, has increased to 36 per cent in 2001 from 34 per cent in 1991 and on the other, they have been attributed with a sex ratio below the national average. Therefore, the increase in the overall sex ratio is possible due to the relative larger increase in the sex ratio of these four populous states.

The distribution pattern of sex ratio at the district level reveals more pronounced regional variations (Map 2.6). Out of the total of 593 districts, 324 districts display relatively high sex ratio more than the national average of 933 females per 1000 males. In other words, around

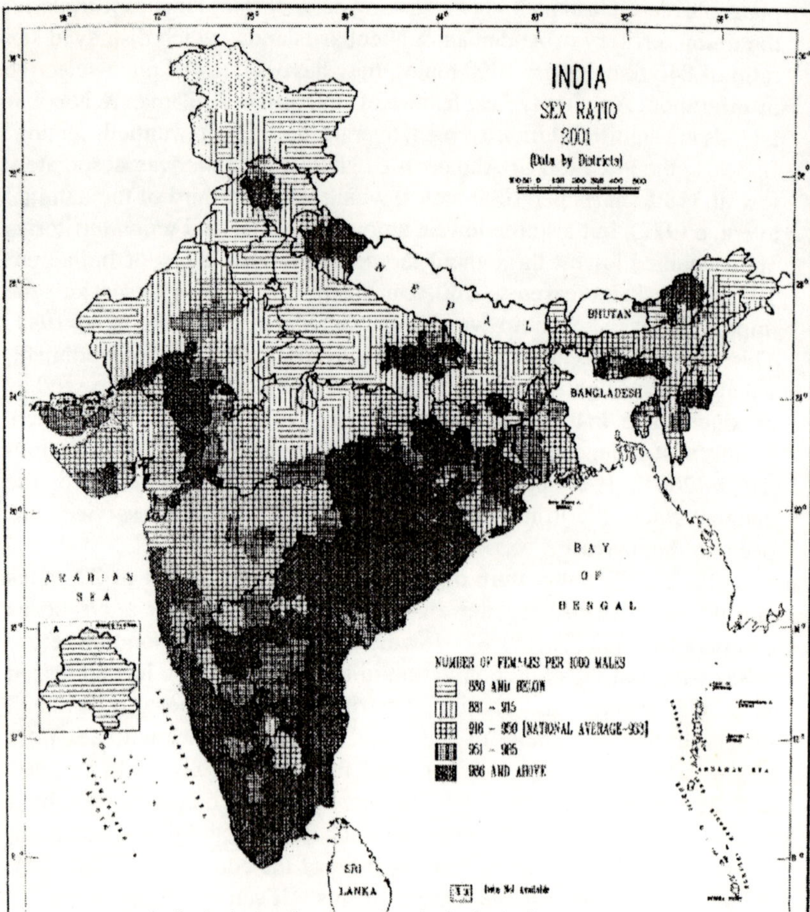


**Map 2.6 :** India : Sex Ratio, 2001 (Data by Districts)

55 per cent of the total districts record sex ratio above the national average. Four districts in the country are having the sex ratio equal to the national average. Of the 265 districts recording sex ratio below national average, as many as 23 districts have sex ratio less than 833. In other words, a further deficit of over a hundred women, compared to the low national average is found in these districts.

Mahe district of Pondicherry has the highest sex ratio of 1148 females per 1000 males and is followed closely by Almora district (1147) in Uttaranchal. Ratnagiri district in Maharashtra, which recorded the highest sex ratio in 1991, has slipped down to third place with 1135 females per 1000 males. It is followed by the districts of Udupi (1127) in Karnataka; Rudraprayag (1117) in Uttaranchal; Diu (1117) in Daman & Diu; Bageshwar (1110) and Garhwal (1104) in Uttaranchal; Hamirpur (1102) in Himachal Pradesh and Pathanamthitta (1094) in Kerala. It is interesting to note that though Kerala at the state level has recorded the highest sex ratio, only one of its districts *i.e.* Pathanamthitta squeezes to occupy the last spot in the first ten districts of India in ranking order in terms of highest sex ratio.

On the other hand, of the bottom ten districts having the extremely low sex ratio in the country, Daman district of Daman & Diu union territory stands at the lowest at 591 females per 1000 males. It is followed by the districts of West Kameng (749) in Arunachal Pradesh; North (752) in Sikkim; Chandigarh (773) in Chandigarh; Mumbai (774) in Maharashtra; South West (783), New Delhi (791) and South (797) in Delhi; Lahul & Spiti (804) in Himachal Pradesh; and Leh (Ladakh) (805) in Jammu & Kashmir. The very low sex ratios in the large metropolitan areas like Mumbai and Delhi could be influenced principally due to the inflow of male migrants seeking work in the industrial, commercial, construction, informal and the unorganized sectors of the economy.

Another significant feature of 2001 census is that there is a substantial increase in the number of districts, which displayed excess of females over males as compared to 1991. In all, there are 78 districts in 2001 as against 55 districts in 1991 in the country where the females outnumbered males. Although, these 78 districts are spread over 16 states/union territories, but the largest number of such districts is from Tamil Nadu (15) followed by Kerala (13), Uttaranchal (8), Chhatisgarh and Orissa with 7 districts each.

It is noteworthy that none of the districts in the southern part of the country, *i.e.*, Andhra Pradesh, Karnataka, Kerala, Tamil Nadu and Pondicherry have recorded a low sex ratio of less than 900 during the Census of India, 2001. A similar pattern emerges in case of the districts of Orissa and Chhatisgarh besides that of the north-eastern states of Manipur, Mizoram, Tripura and Meghalaya. On the other extreme, Uttar Pradesh has the largest number of districts (50), which have recorded sex ratio less than 900 and this accounts for 71 per cent of the total districts in the state and 31 per cent of the total of such districts at the national level. The majority of the districts in Punjab, Haryana and Delhi record sex ratio in this low range.

Districts having extremely low sex ratio of even less than 800 are spread over six states and union territories. Delhi contributes the largest share of three districts and is followed by Maharashtra, Chandigarh, Sikkim, Arunachal Pradesh and Daman & Diu with one district each.

The quantum of the change in sex ratio at the district level shows that 455 districts register an increase during this period, 11 districts have no change while 127 districts show a decline. Thus, around seventy five per cent districts either register the same or a higher sex ratio in the population for 2001 Census. It is further observed that 143 or around twenty five per cent of the districts in the country show an increase of twenty points or more in the sex ratio of the population during 1991-2001. In contrast, only twenty four districts constituting four per cent of the total number of districts register a steep decline of more than twenty points or more in their sex ratio during 1991-2001.

## Age Composition

The age composition of a population (sometimes called age structure or age distribution) is one of the most basic characteristics of a population. One cannot proceed very far in the study of population growth or migration without an examination of age composition. There is a functional relationship between age composition of a country and components of population change. The age composition, therefore, strongly influences the rate of growth and have profound effects on the social and economic conditions under which a population lives. The study of age composition enables us to determine the proportion of labour force in the total population. It is also helpful in finding out the dependency load. It indicates the approximate number of people who are attaining working age and retirement. Thus, an estimate may be made of the net addition to the working force for which new jobs are to be created. For understanding the further growth of population, it is necessary to know the age structure because it affects the marriage rate and reproductive performance of the population. Thus, on the basis of age composition, it is possible to know whether country has a progressive or regressive type of population.

The age composition of a population is determined basically by three factors *i.e.* fertility, mortality and migration. These factors are interdependent and any change in one of these may influence the other two. It is the fertility rate that determines the proportion of population in different age categories. One of the consequences of a high birth rate is that India's population has an age structure which is typical of the countries of less developed regions—a very broad base and a tapering top. In demographic terms, such an age structure is characterized with large proportion of "population in young age groups", which was 38.6 per cent in 1901 and increased to 41.9 per cent in 1971, but slightly decreased to 37.3 per cent in 1991 (Table 2.9). Such a higher child population in India is not only due to high birth rate but also because of recent decline in infant mortality. A high proportion of children only reflects a large proportion of unproductive consumers.

**Table 2.9:** India: Percentage Distribution of Population by Age & Sex, 1901-1991

| *Census Year* | *Age Group* | | | | | | | | |
|---|---|---|---|---|---|---|---|---|---|
| | *0-14* | | | *15-59* | | | *60+* | | |
| | *Total* | *Male* | *Female* | *Total* | *Male* | *Female* | *Total* | *Male* | *Female* |
| 1901 | 38.6 | 39.2 | 38.0 | 56.4 | 56.2 | 56.5 | 5.1 | 4.6 | 5.5 |
| 1911 | 38.5 | 38.8 | 38.1 | 56.4 | 56.4 | 56.4 | 5.2 | 4.8 | 5.5 |
| 1921 | 39.2 | 39.4 | 39.0 | 55.6 | 55.6 | 55.5 | 5.3 | 5.0 | 5.5 |
| 1931 | 40.0 | 40.0 | 40.0 | 56.0 | 56.1 | 55.8 | 4.1 | 3.9 | 4.2 |
| 1941 | 38.3 | 38.1 | 38.4 | 56.9 | 57.0 | 56.7 | 4.9 | 4.9 | 4.9 |
| 1951 | 37.5 | 37.1 | 37.9 | 56.9 | 57.4 | 56.3 | 5.7 | 5.5 | 5.8 |
| 1961 | 41.1 | 40.9 | 41.2 | 53.3 | 53.6 | 53.0 | 5.7 | 5.5 | 5.8 |
| 1971 | 41.9 | 41.9 | 41.9 | 52.2 | 52.2 | 52.1 | 6.0 | 5.9 | 6.0 |
| 1981 | 39.7 | 39.6 | 39.8 | 53.6 | 53.3 | 53.9 | 6.3 | 6.2 | 6.3 |
| 1991 | 37.3 | 37.1 | 37.4 | 55.5 | 55.4 | 55.5 | 6.8 | 6.8 | 6.8 |

*Sources*: (i) Census of India (1971), *Age Tables*, Paper-3 of 1977, Series-1, India, pp. 142-143.
(ii) Census of India (1981), *Population Projections for India*, 1981-2001, Paper-I, of 1984, Series-I, India, p. 10.
(iii) Census of India (1991), *State Profile 1991, India*, Registrar General and Census Commissioner, India, Table 7, pp. 28-29.

It is revealed from Table 2.9 that there is not much of change in the composition of population in broad age groups over the 90 years period. However, the proportion of population in the age group 60 and above was on continuous increase except in the year in 1931 when it decreased to 4.1 per cent from 5.1 per cent in 1901. According to 1991 census, 6.9 per cent of the population of India was aged 60 years and above. Despite the continuous increase of population in this age group, the existing figure (6.9 per cent) for India is relatively low as compared to more developed nations mainly because of high mortality incidence. Like the age group 0-14, this age group is also economically unproductive.

As a whole, 44 per cent of India's population depends on 56 per cent of the population in the economically active ages between 15 to 59, indicating that the "dependency ratio" is 78.6 per 100 persons of ages 15-59 which is very high as compared to more developed nations. A large proportion of the dependent population tends to reduce savings and investments, and inhibits the rate of economic and social advancement since a large proportion of the scarce resources are diverted towards consumption. Also, an increasingly larger number of persons continue to enter the working ages swelling the ranks of the unemployed. The present age structure is also conducive to higher population growth as bigger cohorts of males and females continue entering reproductive ages, especially since universal and early marriage is the pattern in India. This would tend to further aggravate the unemployment problem. To reduce the percentage of non-productive consumers, it is essential to bring down the birth rate.

## Economic Composition

Economic composition of population consists of working and non-working population, unemployed, underemployed, surplus labour, economically active and inactive populations and the like. An analysis of a population's economic composition unfolds the diverse economic, demographic and cultural attributes of an area which form the basis for region's social and economic development. Economic composition of population, therefore, deals mainly with the description of working force and its industrial composition.

### *Working Force*

The total population of a country may be divided into two categories *i.e. economically active population,* which is engaged in gainful economic activities like production of goods and services, and *economically non-active population*, which is engaged in activities like household duties in their own house or at the place of their relatives, retired personnel, inmates of institutions, students and those living on royalties, rents, dividends, pensions, etc. The economically active population of a country is also known as its *working force.* The study of working force is of immense significance for planning and development particularly for a country like India, where size of population is large and the country is experiencing economic transformation.

Instead of dividing the population into two categories of economically active and economically non-active population, the Indian census divides the entire population into two categories of *workers* and *non-workers*. The concept of worker was introduced, for the first time, in India, in 1961. According to the Census of India, "any person whose main activity was participation in any economically productive work either by his physical or by his mental activity was classified as worker" (Census of India, 1971). Thus, work involved not only actual work but also effective supervision and direction. Ever since the introduction of the concept in 1961, the definition of a worker in India has been changing from census to census. In 1961, any person who had worked for at least one hour a day on an average during the reference period was classified as worker. In 1971, if a person worked on any one of the days during the reference period of one week prior to the date of enumeration was considered as a worker provided his/her main activity was economically productive work. Thus, persons engaged primarily in household duties (housewives), those getting education (students), those receiving income without participating in any productive activity (pensioners, rent-receivers, thieves, pick-pocketers, prisoners, beggars, etc.) were classified as non-workers.

However, in 1981, the workers were divided into two groups of *main workers* [those who were engaged in any economically productive activity for six months (183 days) or more during the year] and *marginal workers* [those who had worked for less than six months (183 days) in the year]. The 1991 Census of India also adopted the aforesaid definitions. The working force in India, thus, comprises both the main workers as well as marginal workers and is computed as percentage of workers to total population.

The size of working force is determined by population growth and work participation rates *i.e.* proportion of working population to total population. Population growth depends upon fertility, mortality and migration, whereas work participation rates depend upon a variety of demographic, social and economic factors like fertility, mortality, migration, age composition, age of retirement, life expectancy, wage levels, household income, educational attainments, the availability of work and attitude towards work. Since these factors differ from one country to another and within each country from state to state and city to city, participation is subject to variation over regions and time (Suri, *et al.*, 1988).

According to 1991 census, there are a total of 314.13 million workers accounting for 37.50 per cent of the country's total population. Out of these, 285.93 million (34.18 per cent) are main workers and the remaining 28.20 million (3.32 per cent) are marginal workers. This leaves a huge population of 524.44 million (62.50 per cent) as non-workers indicating high dependency ratio. Thus, a little less than two-thirds of non-working population depends upon a little more than one-third of work force, which is not congenial to economic growth of the country. India's low percentage of working force is the outcome of her demographic, socio-cultural and economic structure. Among the major factors responsible for low percentage of work force are high birth rate and consequent large proportion of children below the age of 15, prejudices against females' education, mobility and employment, and incapability of the Indian economic structure to generate enough employment opportunities.

### *Composition of Working Force*

The composition of working force in an area varies both by sex and residence. One of the typical features of the Indian work force that differentiates the country from the developed world is wide disparity in the work participation rates (WPR) of males and females. While in case of developed countries, females are almost equal partners in the economic struggle, in case of India, the female participation in economically gainful activities is only nominal. As per 1991 census, while 51.6 per cent of the country's males were recorded as workers, the corresponding figure for the female population was only 21.3 per cent (Table 2.10). Thus, while one out of every two males in India was working, in case of females one out of every five females was working.

**Table 2.10:** India: Working Force by Sex and Residence, 1991*

| *Sex* | *Workers as per cent to Total Population* | | |
|---|---|---|---|
| | *Total* | *Rural* | *Urban* |
| Persons | 37.5 | 40.0 | 30.2 |
| Males | 51.6 | 52.5 | 48.9 |
| Females | 22.3 | 26.7 | 9.2 |

*Source*: Census of India (1991), *State Profile 1991, India*, Registrar General and Census Commissioner, India, Table-24, pp. 110-111.

* Excludes figures for Jammu & Kashmir where the 1991 census was not conducted due to disturbed conditions.

The patriarchal system of Indian society, age old prejudices against females' mobility, prejudices against their education, their relatively low status in the society, frequent child births, limited job opportunities for them, and limited desire on the part of the females themselves to participate in the economic struggle are the factors that have contributed to poor female participation in work in India (Kaur and Chandna, 1983). No wonder, the responsibility of earning the bread in India still lies on the masculine shoulders, while the females keep themselves occupied with the responsibility of baking the bread and looking after other domestic chores, which the Indian census does not consider economically productive work.

The incidence of participation in work also varied greatly among rural and urban populations. While 40 per cent of rural population in the country was recorded as worker, the corresponding figure for urban population was only 30.2 per cent (Table 2.10). The relatively low participation rate in urban areas was attributable to the difference in the nature of economy and society in the two areas. The nature of jobs in urban areas was such for which education and skill was a pre-requisite. Education, normally, delayed the entry into work force. Moreover, the urban population was socially and economically more awakened. In the countryside, the nature of economy was such that education and skill was of little relevance. Moreover, females and children could participate in various agricultural operations as well as in the household industry at home, as an associate worker. It added to the percentage of workers in the countryside (Bhutani, 1995).

Interestingly, the incidence of female participation in urban areas of India was much smaller than that in the countryside. While in rural areas one in every four females (26.7 per cent) was working, in urban areas approximately one in every eleven females (9.2 per cent) was working. This factor also contributed to the relatively low participation rates in the urban areas in comparison to the rural areas. The participation rates in urban areas of India would have been still lower but for a sizeable in-migration of workers from rural areas to urban areas.

### *Industrial Composition*

The industrial composition of Indian work force is overwhelmingly dominated by the primary sector consisting of 67.5 per cent main workers of the total population as against the national average of 34.1 per cent for all the three economic sectors (Table 2.11). Cultivators and

**Table 2.11:** India*: Work Participation Rate (WPR) for Main Workers by Sex and Residence, 1991

| *Country/State/Union Territory* | *Work participation rate (per cent)* | | | | | | | | |
|---|---|---|---|---|---|---|---|---|---|
| | *Total* | | | *Rural* | | | *Urban* | | |
| | *Person* | *Male* | *Female* | *Person* | *Male* | *Female* | *Person* | *Male* | *Female* |
| *Primary Sector (I+II+III+IV)* | 67.5 | 63.5 | 81.2 | 82.7 | 80.4 | 89.8 | 14.4 | 13.3 | 22.8 |
| I. Cultivators | 38.7 | 39.9 | 34.6 | 48.4 | 51.6 | 38.9 | 4.9 | 4.9 | 5.1 |
| II. Agricultural Labourers | 26.1 | 20.8 | 44.2 | 31.6 | 26.0 | 48.5 | 6.7 | 5.4 | 15.5 |
| III. Livestock, Forestry, Fishing, Hunting and Plantations, Orchards and Allied Activities | 2.1 | 2.1 | 2.1 | 2.2 | 2.3 | 2..1 | 1.7 | 1.8 | 1.5 |
| IV. Mining and Quarrying | 0.6 | 0.7 | 0.3 | 0.5 | 0.5 | 0.3 | 1.1 | 1.2 | 0.7 |
| *Secondary sector (V+VI)* | 11.9 | 13.2 | 8.0 | 6.8 | 7.2 | 5.5 | 30.1 | 30.9 | 24.9 |
| V. Manufacturing, Processing, Servicing and Repairs in: | | | | | | | | | |
| (A) Household Industry | 2.4 | 2.1 | 3.5 | 2.2 | 1.9 | 2.9 | 3.1 | 2.5 | 7.5 |
| (B) Other than Household Industry | 7.6 | 8.8 | 3.8 | 3.6 | 4.0 | 2.3 | 21.9 | 23.1 | 14.1 |
| VI. Constructions | 1.9 | 2.3 | 0.7 | 1.0 | 1.3 | 0.3 | 5.1 | 5.3 | 3.3 |
| *Tertiary Sector (VII+VIII+IX)* | 20.5 | 23.3 | 10.8 | 10.5 | 12.4 | 4.7 | 55.4 | 55.8 | 52.4 |
| VII. Trade and Commerce | 7.4 | 9.0 | 2.2 | 3.3 | 4.0 | 1.1 | 22.0 | 23.8 | 10.0 |
| VIII. Transport, Storage and Communications | 2.8 | 3.5 | 0.3 | 1.2 | 1.6 | 0.1 | 8.3 | 9.2 | 2.0 |
| IX. Other Services | 10.3 | 10.8 | 8.3 | 6.0 | 6.8 | 3.5 | 25.1 | 22.8 | 40.4 |
| *Total Main Workers (I-IX)* | 34.1 | 50.9 | 15.9 | 35.7 | 51.8 | 18.6 | 29.5 | 48.6 | 8.1 |

*Source:* Census of India (1991), *State Profile 1991, India,* Registrar General and Census Commissioner, India, Table 26, pp. 130-131.

* Excludes figures for Jammu & Kashmir where the 1991 census was not conducted due to disturbed conditions.

agricultural labourers together accounted for 64.8 per cent of our main workers. Cultivators alone claimed 38.7 per cent of the Indian main workers, while agricultural labourers accounted for above one-fourth (26.1 per cent) of the country's main workers. It not only establishes the primacy of agriculture in the country's economy but also exposes the incapability of the secondary sector of the country's economy to create jobs and absorb labour force (Chandna, 2000).

India's economy is still rural-based and 74.29 per cent of its population is living in rural areas. Out of a total of 285.9 million main workers, 222.2 million (77.72 per cent) were located in rural areas. Of rural main workers, 17.3 per cent engage themselves in non-agricultural pursuits, and 14.4 per cent of urban main workers engage themselves in agricultural occupations. Sex-wise, 77.72 per cent of male main workers and 87.07 per cent of female main workers in the country have been enumerated in the rural areas. However, the occupational structure of female main workers was more primary sector oriented than that of male main workers. Whereas, 36.5 per cent of male main workers were outside the primary sector, only 18.8 per cent of female main workers were outside the primary sector. Among females, the percentage of agricultural labourers was also significantly higher (44.2 per cent) than that of cultivators (34.6 per cent). It is because in most parts of rural India, bread-earning responsibility goes mainly to the males who do all kinds of agricultural work and the females are engaged to help in carrying out simple operations in the farms particularly at the sowing and harvesting time.

### *Decadal Changes in Working Force, 1981-91*

During 1981-91, there has been an obvious sectoral shift in the working force among states/union territories (Table 2.12).

Table 2.12 reveals that there has been loss in primary sector while work force in tertiary sector has increased. It is perhaps focusing on trend towards shifting of people's attitude. With increasing literacy and growing industrialization, tertiary sector is attracting more people. Moreover, there is sharp difference between rural-urban wage structure.

### *Primary Sector*

The general trend of a decreasing pattern is discernible in primary sector. However, four states and two union territories have recorded some

**Table 2.12:** India: Decadal Change in Work Participation Rate (WPR) for Main Workers by Sectors, 1981-1991

| *Country/State/ Union Territory* | *Work Participation Rate (Percent)* | | | | | | | | |
|---|---|---|---|---|---|---|---|---|---|
| | *Primary Sector* | | | *Secondary Sector* | | | *Tertiary Sector* | | |
| | *1981* | *1991* | *Change* | *1981* | *1991* | *Change* | *1981* | *1991* | *Chang* |
| **India*** | **69.41** | **67.37** | **-2.04** | **12.96** | **12.13** | **-0.83** | **17.63** | **20.50** | **+2.87** |
| *States* | | | | | | | | | |
| Andhra Pradesh | 72.47 | 71.25 | -1.22 | 11.49 | 10.48 | -1.01 | 16.04 | 18.27 | +2.23 |
| Arunachal Pradesh | 75.28 | 67.44 | -7.84 | 8.92 | 8.66 | -0.26 | 15.80 | 23.90 | +8.10 |
| Bihar | 81.51 | 82.36 | +0.85 | 7.18 | 4.64 | -2.54 | 11.31 | 13.00 | +1.69 |
| Goa | 39.36 | 32.29 | -0.07 | 20.52 | 21.98 | +1.46 | 40.12 | 45.73 | +5.61 |
| Gujarat | 62.83 | 59.76 | -3.07 | 16.88 | 17.86 | +0.98 | 20.29 | 22.38 | +2.09 |
| Haryana | 61.81 | 58.84 | -2.97 | 15.42 | 13.18 | -2.24 | 22.77 | 27.98 | +5.21 |
| Himachal Pradesh | 73.59 | 69.28 | -4.31 | 10.71 | 9.99 | -0.72 | 15.70 | 20.73 | +5.03 |
| Karnataka | 69.37 | 67.37 | -2.00 | 14.15 | 13.17 | -0.98 | 16.48 | 19.46 | +2.98 |
| Kerala | 51.65 | 48.02 | -3.63 | 18.86 | 18.17 | -0.69 | 29.49 | 33.81 | +4.32 |
| Madhya Pradesh | 78.98 | 77.54 | -1.44 | 9.43 | 8.37 | -1.06 | 11.59 | 14.09 | +2.50 |
| Maharashtra | 64.03 | 61.51 | -2.52 | 16.07 | 15.80 | 0.27 | 19.90 | 22.69 | +2.79 |
| Manipur | 69.60 | 70.00 | +0.40 | 13.35 | 9.66 | -3.69 | 17.05 | 20.34 | +3.29 |
| Meghalaya | 79.76 | 74.81 | -4.95 | 4.22 | 3.73 | -0.49 | 16.02 | 21.46 | +5.44 |
| Mizoram | 73.92 | 65.99 | -7.93 | 4.93 | 5.07 | +0.14 | 21.45 | 28.94 | +7.79 |
| Nagaland | 73.56 | 72.26 | +1.70 | 3.47 | 3.48 | +0.01 | 22.97 | 21.96 | -1.71 |
| Orissa | 77.93 | 75.83 | -2.10 | 8.04 | 7.51 | -0.53 | 14.03 | 16.66 | +2.63 |
| Punjab | 59.05 | 56.08 | -+2.97 | 15.20 | 14.84 | -0.36 | 25.76 | 29.08 | +3.33 |
| Rajasthan | 72.72 | 71.63 | -1.09 | 10.91 | 9.87 | -1.04 | 16.37 | 18.50 | +2.13 |
| Sikkim | 65.12 | 68.40 | +3.28 | 12.20 | 11.12 | -1.08 | 22.68 | 20.48 | -2.20 |
| Tamil Nadu | 63.88 | 61.81 | -2.07 | 17.01 | 16.18 | -0.83 | 19.11 | 22.01 | +2.90 |
| Tripura | 70.19 | 64.08 | -6.11 | 7.41 | 6.41 | -1.00 | 22.40 | 29.51 | +7.11 |
| Uttar Pradesh | 75.11 | 73.01 | -2.10 | 10.04 | 8.98 | -1.06 | 14.85 | 18.01 | +3.16 |
| West Bengal | 59.13 | 56.49 | -2.64 | 18.03 | 17.82 | -0.21 | 22.84 | 25.69 | +2.85 |
| *Union Territories* | | | | | | | | | |
| Andaman & N. Islands | 37.33 | 34.50 | -2.83 | 28.17 | 25.14 | -3.03 | 34.50 | 40.36 | +5.56 |
| Chandigarh | 2.96 | 4.46 | +1.50 | 25.71 | 27.82 | +2.11 | 71.33 | 67.72 | -3.61 |
| Dadra & Nagar Haveli | 74.85 | 71.81 | -3.04 | 15.41 | 16.13 | +0.72 | 9.74 | 12.06 | +2.32 |
| Daman & Diu | 48.19 | 37.32 | -10.87 | 22.93 | 25.40 | +2.47 | 28.88 | 37.28 | +8.40 |
| Delhi | 3.81 | 2.85 | -0.96 | 34.87 | 32.43 | -2.44 | 61.32 | 64.72 | +3.40 |
| Lakshadweep | 22.18 | 25.02 | +2.84 | 28.05 | 25.27 | -2.78 | 49.77 | 49.71 | -0.06 |
| Pondicherry | 45.80 | 39.24 | -6.56 | 22.75 | 19.19 | -2.76 | 31.45 | 40.77 | +9.32 |

*Source:* Census of India (1991), *Final Population Totals: Brief Analysis of Primary Census Abstract*, Paper 2 of 1992, Series-I, India, Table 4.4, pp. 169-175

* Excluding Assam and Jammu & Kashmir.

marginal increase. Amongst the states, the highest increase was recorded by Sikkim (3.28 per cent) followed by Nagaland (1.70 per cent), Bihar (0.85 per cent), and Manipur (0.40 per cent). The union territories of Lakshadweep and Chandigarh experienced an increase of 2.84 per cent and 1.50 per cent respectively. Loss in primary sector is again observed in the areas which are economically depressed regions.

*Secondary Sector*

Work force pattern in this sector has shown hardly any variation during the decade. Only a nominal increase is noticed in four states, *viz.*, Goa (1.46 per cent), Gujarat (0.98 per cent), Mizoram (0.14 per cent), Nagaland (0.01 per cent), and three union territories, *viz.*, Daman & Diu (2.47 per cent), Chandigarh (2.11 per cent) and Dadra & Nagar Haveli (0.72 per cent), while majority of the states show declining trend. The declining trend in this sector is an unhealthy situation for the economic environment of the country which will generate more unemployment in the coming decade.

*Tertiary Sector*

In this sector, there is gain in all the states and union territories except two states, *viz.*, Sikkim (–2.20 per cent), Nagaland (–1.71 per cent) and two union territories of Chandigarh (–3.61 per cent) and Lakshadweep (–0.06 per cent). All the states and union territories, thus, have recorded loss in primary sector except these four states /union territories where gain in primary sector has been experienced. The highest gain in tertiary sector has been recorded by Pondicherry (9.32 per cent), followed by Daman & Diu (8.40 per cent), Arunachal Pradesh (8.10 per cent), Mizoram (7.79 per cent) and Tripura (7.11 per cent).

In terms of areal spread at the district level, the work participation rate for main workers varies from the minimum of 21.08 per cent in Mahe district of Pondicherry to the maximum of 55.25 per cent in Tawang district of Arunachal Pradesh. Out of the total of 452 districts, 239 districts experienced work participation rate for main workers higher than the national average (34.10 per cent).

Being an agricultural country, there is an overwhelming majority of the districts in India which have more than two-thirds of their workers classified as primary workers. Out of the total of 452 districts, 302 districts display work participation rate for main workers in primary sector higher than the national average (67.53 per cent). There are 51 districts which have more than 85 per cent of their main workers in this sector, which are primarily concentrated in the Tarai area of Uttar Pradesh, northern Bihar, eastern Madhya Pradesh and a few in north-eastern states. Madhepura district of Bihar has the highest work participation rate (92.69 per cent) for main workers in primary sector, while Greater Bombay of Maharashtra has the lowest proportion of main workers (0.84 per cent). In general, it is noticed that highly urbanized districts have very low work participation rate for main workers in the primary sector.

On an average, 11.97 per cent of total main workers of the country are classified as secondary workers. The lowest percentage has been recorded by Senapati district of Manipur (1.01 per cent) and the highest by Nicobar (47.50 per cent) of Andaman & Nicobar Islands. The localized distribution of secondary workers is clear from the fact that there are 323 districts out of 452 districts that stay above the national average (11.97 per cent).

Higher proportion of tertiary main workers in the country is confined mainly to more urbanized districts of the country. The variation ranges from 5.95 per cent in Madhepura district of Bihar to 72.48 per cent in Hyderabad district of Andhra Pradesh which is followed by Calcutta (69.05 per cent), Chennai (68.36 per cent), Chandigarh (67.72 per cent), Delhi (64.72 per cent) and Mahe (62.42 per cent). There are 66 districts which have above 30 per cent of the workers in tertiary sector. Most of these districts fall in the state of Kerala, while others are spread all over the country. Majority of the districts (299) have the proportion of tertiary workers ranging from 10.01 to 20.00 per cent. A very low proportion (less than 10 per cent) of tertiary workers is seen among 47 districts located mainly in north-eastern Uttar Pradesh, Bihar and eastern Madhya Pradesh.

## CULTURAL COMPOSITION

The cultural composition of population involves literacy, religion, language, marital status and so on. Some of these cultural components may be discussed below:

### Religious Composition

Religion is one of the basic cultural characteristics of the population.

Religion's role in formulating and preserving a culture system has been well recognized. However, there are many ways in which the religion may reflect its influence on way of life of its adherents. Religion strongly influences the totality of way of life of its adherents through its impact upon their socio-cultural behaviour, economic expression, political ethos and legal institutions (Chandna, 2000).

Religion is certainly a factor of social diversification in India, and still the religious grip on the thinking process and human behaviour in India has not loosened. The study of religion is important to scholars of Indian demography because the religious sanctions, restrictions, and practices pertaining to marriage, reproduction, social mobility and migration persist; and a number of religious-cultural practices affect the mortality in the population. For example, taboos on sexual intercourse on certain auspicious days, pre-puberty marriage, and the *Satti Pratha* (which of course is no more in existence).

India is birth place of four major religions, *viz*., Hinduism, Buddhism, Jainism and Sikhism. The most dominant religion, however, is Hinduism. In addition to being the birth place of four major religions of the world, India has also embraced other world religions like Islam and Christianity.

In India, there have been large scale changes in the religious composition of population due to conversions from one-fifth to another. Spatial pattern of distribution of different religious groups had undergone drastic changes due to large scale migrations as a result of partition of India in 1947. Before partition, Hindus accounted for 66.5 per cent of the population of the sub-continent and Muslims 23.7 per cent (Census of India, 1941). With partition, large number of Muslims migrated from India to Pakistan and Bangladesh and Hindus migrated to India from these countries. Consequently, the proportion of these two religious communities in the total population changed. The percentage of Hindus increased to 84.1 per cent and that of Muslims fell to 9.8 per cent (Census of India, 1951). Since then, the percentage of Hindu population has fallen marginally, while that of Muslims has increased considerably. The percentage of Hindus had fallen from 84.1 per cent in 1951 to 82.41 per cent in 1991, while that of Muslims had increased from 9.8 per cent in 1951 to 11.67 per cent in 1991 (Table 2.13).

Table 2.13 reveals that Hindus form majority comprising 82 per cent of India's population. The second major religious community is Muslims with 11.67 per cent population and followed by Christians (2.17 per cent), Sikhs (2.00 per cent), Buddhists (0.66 per cent), and

Jains 0.40 per cent). During the census decade 1981-91, the religious composition of India has undergone a change, albeit a little. Hindus, Christians and Jains have decreased in proportion, while Muslims, Sikhs and Buddhists have increased. Demographers attribute the differential rate of growth of various religious communities to differential birth rate. The decadal growth rate of population is highest among Buddhists (35.98 per cent) and is followed by Muslims (32.76 per cent), Sikhs (25.48 per cent), and Hindus (22.78 per cent). By contrast, the lowest growth rate has been experienced by Jains (4.42 per cent) followed by Christians (16.89 per cent). Among the major six religions, sex ratio varies from 888 females per 1000 males among the Sikhs, to 994 among the Christians. In a country of diverse culture like India, sex ratio differentials by religion are important at societal level and may imply inter-religious marriages.

**Table 2.13**: India*: Decadal Variations and Sex Ratio of Population by Religion, 1981-1991

| *Religion* | *Per cent to Total Population* | | *Decadal Variation (Per cent) 1981-1991* | *Sex Ratio (Females per 1000 Males) 1991* |
|---|---|---|---|---|
| | *1981* | *1991* | | |
| Hindu | 83.09 | 82.41 | 22.78 | 925 |
| Muslim | 10.88 | 11.67 | 32.76 | 930 |
| Christian | 2.45 | 2.32 | 16.89 | 994 |
| Sikh | 1.96 | 1.99 | 25.48 | 888 |
| Buddhist | 0.71 | 0.77 | 35.98 | 952 |
| Jain | 0.48 | 0.41 | 4.42 | 946 |
| Others | 0.42 | 0.38 | 13.19 | 982 |

*Source*: Census of India (1991), *Religion*, Paper-I of 1995, India, Registrar General & Census Commissioner, India, pp. X-XV.

* Excludes Assam and Jammu & Kashmir.

Regionally, Hindus are in predominant majority in 20 states and 6 union territories out of a total of 25 states and 7 union territories respectively. The states and union territories where Hindus are in a minority are Jammu & Kashmir, Punjab, Meghalaya, Mizoram, Nagaland, and Lakshadweep respectively. In Jammu & Kashmir, Muslims constitute nearly 65.85 per cent of the population (as per 1981 census), while Meghalaya (64.6 per cent), Mizoram (85.7 per cent) and Nagaland (87.5 per cent) are dominated numerically by Christians. In Punjab, Sikhs with 63.0 per cent of the total population form the majority.

Lakshadweep is the only union territory where Muslims (94.3 per cent) dominate the scene.

Among the Buddhists, the largest number is concentrated in Sikkim which accounts for 27.15 per cent of the total population of India. The other states where Buddhists are found in a reasonably good number are Arunachal Pradesh (12.88 per cent), Mizoram (7.83 per cent), Maharashtra (6.39 per cent), and Tripura (4.65 per cent). Jains (0.40 per cent), like Buddhists (0.76 per cent), numerically account for less than one per cent of the total population and are spread all over the country especially in Rajasthan (1.28 per cent), Maharashtra (1.22 per cent), Gujarat (1.19 per cent), Madhya Pradesh (0.74 per cent), Karnataka (0.73 per cent), Haryana (0.21 per cent), Uttar Pradesh (0.13 per cent) and Tamil Nadu (0.12 per cent).

**Literacy**

Literacy greatly expands the range of human potentialities and is a worthwhile goal in its own right. Literacy is also an important driving force behind economic and social development, and it is a powerful influence that tends to reduce fertility and, therefore, helps to ameliorate India's pressing population problem. (Sharma and Retherford, 1993).

Literacy and education are reasonably good indicators of development in a society. Spread and diffusion of literacy is generally associated with essential traits of today's civilization such as modernization, urbanization, industrialization, communication and commerce. It forms an important input in the overall development of individuals enabling them to comprehend their social, political and cultural environment better and respond to it appropriately. Higher levels of education and literacy lead to a greater awareness and also contributes in improvement of economic conditions. It acts as a catalyst for social upliftment enhancing the returns on investments made in almost every aspect of development effort, be it population control, health, hygiene, environmental degradation control, empowerment of women and weaker sections of the society. Improved levels of literacy also are pre-requisites for acquiring various skills. (Banthia, 2001).

Literacy is one of the important social characteristics on which information is obtained of every individual in the census. For the purposes of census, "a person aged seven years and above, who can both read and write with understanding in any language, is treated as literate". A person, who can only read but cannot write, is not literate. In the censuses prior to 1991, children below five years of age were necessarily treated as illiterates.

The ability to read and write with understanding is not ordinarily achieved until one had some schooling or at least some time to develop these skills. It was, therefore, decided at the 1991 census that all children in the age group 0-6, will be treated as illiterate by definition and the population aged seven years and above only is to be classified as literate or illiterate. The same criterion has been retained at the Census of India, 2001, also. It is not mandatory that to be treated as literate, a person should have received any formal education or acquired any minimum educational standard. Literacy status can be acquired through adult literacy classes or by attending any non-formal educational system. Persons who are unfortunately blind and read in Braille are also treated as literates.

In censuses upto 1981, it was customary to work out the literacy rate taking into account the total population. Since literacy rate is more meaningful if the sub-population in the age group 0-6 is excluded from the total population, it was decided in 1991 to use the term literacy rate for the population relating to seven years and above. The same concept has been continued in the Census of India, 2001. The literacy rate taking into account the total population in the denominator has now been termed as *crude literacy rate.*

According to 2001 census of India, crude literacy rate of 55.30 per cent had grown from a low level of literacy of only 5.35 per cent at the beginning of twentieth century (Table 2.14). There has also been considerable improvement in both male and female crude literacy rates, although male literacy always had an edge over the female literacy. Table 2.14 reveals that despite the consistent improvement in crude literacy rates, the pace of literacy transition in India has been rather slow, when compared with advanced countries or when the target of universal literacy is considered. The crude literacy rate in India which was barely 5.35 per cent in 1901 could be increased only to 9.50 per cent in 30 years by 1931. During this period, the country suffered from frequent natural calamities in the form of epidemics of plague, smallpox, influenza, and cholera, famines, droughts, etc. warranting lot of attention of the administration.

The crude literacy rate further improved sharply to 16.10 per cent during 1931-41, recording an increase of 6.60 percentage points. It was because once the havoc played by the natural calamities was put under check, the processes of economic development and social advancement started receiving greater attention of the administration.

**Table 2.14:** India: Crude Literacy Rates by Sex, 1901-2001

| *Census Year* | *Crude Literacy Rate (Per cent)* | | |
|---|---|---|---|
| | *Persons* | *Males* | *Females* |
| 1901 | 5.35 | 9.83 | 0.60 |
| 1911 | 5.92 | 10.56 | 1.05 |
| 1921 | 7.16 | 12.21 | 1.81 |
| 1931 | 9.50 | 15.59 | 2.93 |
| 1941 | 16.10 | 24.90 | 7.30 |
| 1951 | 16.67 | 24.95 | 7.93 |
| 1961 | 24.02 | 34.44 | 12.95 |
| 1971 | 29.45 | 39.45 | 18.69 |
| 1981 | 36.23 | 46.89 | 24.82 |
| 1991 | 42.84 | 52.74 | 32.17 |
| 2001 | 55.30 | 64.13 | 45.84 |

*Source:* Census of India (2001), *Provisional Population Totals*, Paper-I of 2001, Series-I, India, Statement 30, p. 114.

*Notes* (i) Figures of 1901, 1911, 1921, 1931 are for undivided India.
(ii) Figures for 1981 excludes Assam as 1981 Census could not be conducted in this state due to disturbed conditions.
(iii) Figures for the 1951 and 1991 Censuses do not include Jammu and Kashmir, as no census was held in the state.
(iv) Figures for 2001 do not include figures of entire Kachchh district, Morvi, Maliya-Miyana and Wankaner talukas of Rajkot district, Jodiya taluka of Jamnagar district of Gujarat state and entire Kinnaur district of Himachal Pradesh where population enumeration of Census of India, 2001 could not be conducted due to natural calamities.

The improvement in literacy during 1941-51 was barely visible with gains of only 0.57 percentage points, perhaps due to the implications of World War II as well as the partition of India in 1947.

In post-Independence period, there has been a more rapid growth in crude literacy rate. It has grown more than three times from 16.67 per cent in 1951 to 55.30 per cent at the Census of India, 2001. The crude literacy rate crossed the significant milestone of fifty per cent in the current census.

The jump of 12.46 percentage points between 1991 and 2001 compares extraordinarily with the decadal literacy growth of previous decades since 1901. It is for the first time since 1901 that an increase in two digit percentage points during 1991-2001, has occurred in case of all the three categories of persons, males and females. The male crude literacy has moved forward by 11.39 percentage points from 52.74 per cent to 64.13 per cent and among females it has gone up by 13.67 percentage points from 32.17 per cent in 1991 to 45.84 in 2001.

In pre-Independence period, the male crude literacy rate increased from 9.83 per cent in 1901 to 24.90 per cent in 1941, whereas the corresponding increase in female crude literacy rate was from 0.60 per cent to 7.30 per cent. In post-Independence era, the crude literacy rate of males has gone up by almost forty per cent. The corresponding increase among females is thirty eight per cent.

Independence in 1947 provided the real impetus to literacy in the country. The administration in free India started paying more attention to social advancement. Large number of schools were opened in rural areas, apart from upgrading the existing schools. Similarly, the post-Independence period also witnessed multiplication of institutions of higher education *e.g.* colleges, universities, research institutes, etc. In 1947, the country had only 20 universities and 591 colleges including 132 professional colleges with a total enrolment of more than 2.3 lakh students, which increased to a total of 229 universities and 8,529 colleges including 1,770 professional colleges with a total enrolment of more than 59 lakh students in 1997 (Government of India, 1997). All these factors have, thus, been responsible for the improvement in the pace of change in literacy rates.

Literacy rates are, however, more meaningful if the segment of population compulsorily treated as illiterate by definition is excluded from the total population. Table 2.15 presents the literacy rates for the country since 1951. While literacy rates in this table for the 1951, 1961 and 1971 censuses relate to the population aged five years and above, those for the 1981, 1991 and 2001 relate to the population aged seven years and above. The literacy rate for the country as a whole in 2001, works out to 65.38 per cent for the population aged seven years and above. The corresponding figures for males and females are 75.85 and 54.16 per cent respectively. Thus, three-fourth of the male and more than half of the female population aged seven years and above are literate in the country today. India has continued its inexorable march in improving its literacy rate by recording a jump of 13.17 percentage points from 52.21 in 1991 to 65.38 in 2001. The increase in literacy rates in males and females are in the order of 11.72 and 14.87 percentage points respectively. Thus, the increase in literacy rates observed during 1991-2001 in respect of persons, males as well as females have been the highest recorded in comparison to earlier decades since 1951 except in case of males during 1951-61. This improvement in literacy rate augurs well for the country and needs not only to be sustained but requires a fillip particularly in the case of the fairer sex.

The gap in male-female literacy rates of 18.30 percentage points in 1951, increased to 26.62 in 1981, but since then there are unmistakable signs of improvement. Thus, in 1991, this gap was marginally reduced to 24.84 and in 2001 it has further gone down to 21.70 percentage points. These declines are bound to be slow initially as a result of the continuing past legacy of a large number of adult illiterate women.

**Literacy Differentials**

Indian literacy is characterized by striking differentials not only between one part of the country to another but also between males and females, between rural and urban populations and between various caste-based sub-groups. Such contrasts are the manifestation of the differences in the socio-economic background of the concerned area/population. A brief analysis of these literacy differentials is essential for a comprehensive understanding of the process of literacy transition taking shape in the country.

*Male-Female Differentials*

The most notable feature of Indian literacy is that the females always lagged far behind the males in terms of literacy rates. While 75.85 per cent of the males are recorded as literate in 2001, the corresponding figure for females is only 54.16 per cent (Table 2.15). Females in India have for long been confined to the four walls of the house and have been subjects to various prejudices. Moreover, there were not many opportunities for them to participate in the family's economic struggle. Added to it were the factors of general poverty, low status of women, prevailing early marriage, especially among the rural girls, resulting in a very high incidence of drop-outs (Chandna, 2000). All these factors have been responsible for wide male-female literacy differentials in India. Though, the disparities in male-female literacy rates occurred both in rural and urban areas, yet these were more pronounced in the countryside. Sagar (1984), attributed relatively low male-female literacy differentials in urban areas to (i) better status of women, (ii) availability of educational institutions equally for males and females, and (iii) better standards of living in urban areas. However, with increasing socio-economic awareness and with literacy among females increasingly becoming a matrimonial necessity, the male-female literacy differentials, in India, are narrowing down, though only steadily.

**Table 2.15: India: Literacy Rates by Sex, 1951-2001**

| *Census Year* | *Per Cent Literates to Total Population* | | | *Male-Female Differential* |
|---|---|---|---|---|
| | *Persons* | *Males* | *Females* | |
| 1951 | 18.33 | 27.16 | 8.86 | 18.30 |
| 1961 | 28.30 | 40.00 | 15.35 | 25.05 |
| 1971 | 34.45 | 45.96 | 21.97 | 23.98 |
| 1981 | 43.57 | 56.38 | 29.76 | 26.62 |
| 1991 | 52.21 | 64.13 | 39.29 | 24.84 |
| 2001 | 65.38 | 75.85 | 54.16 | 21.70 |

*Source*: Census of India (2001), *Provisional Population Totals*, Paper-I of 2001, Series-I, India, Statement 31, p. 115.

*Notes* (i) Literacy rates for 1951, 1961 and 1971 Censuses related to population aged 5 years and above. The rates for 1981, 1991 and 2001 census relate to the population aged 7 years and above.

(ii) The literacy rates for 1981 excludes Assam where the 1981 census could not be conducted. The 1991 census literacy rates excludes Jammu & Kashmir where the 1991 census could not be conducted due to disturbed conditions.

(iii) The 2001 Census literacy rates exclude entire Kachchh district, Morvi, Maliya-Miyana and Wankaner talukas of Rajkot district, Jodiya taluka of Jamnagar district of Gujarat state and entire Kinnaur district of Himachal Pradesh where population enumeration of Census of India, 2001, could not be conducted due to natural calamities.

The relatively high rate of increase in female literacy is related to the increasing educational facilities, particularly for the females (Government of India, 1985), increasing standards of living, increasing value of female education for matrimony (Chandna, 2000) and increasing availability of female teachers in rural areas, waning prejudices against females' education and increasing degree of socio-economic awareness. As there was a positive correlation between male literacy and female literacy, the increasing male literacy rates also stimulated female's literacy (Sagar, 1990).

### *Regional Differentials*

Among the various states and union territories of India, there are wide regional variations in the levels of literacy as per 2001 census (Map 2.7) Kerala with 90.92 per cent of its population as literate has the distinction of having highest literacy in the country. It also continues to occupy the top position in the country, both in male literacy with 94.20 per cent and female literacy with 87.86 per cent (Table 2.16). It is followed by Mizoram (88.49 per cent), Goa (82.32 per cent), Maharashtra (77.27

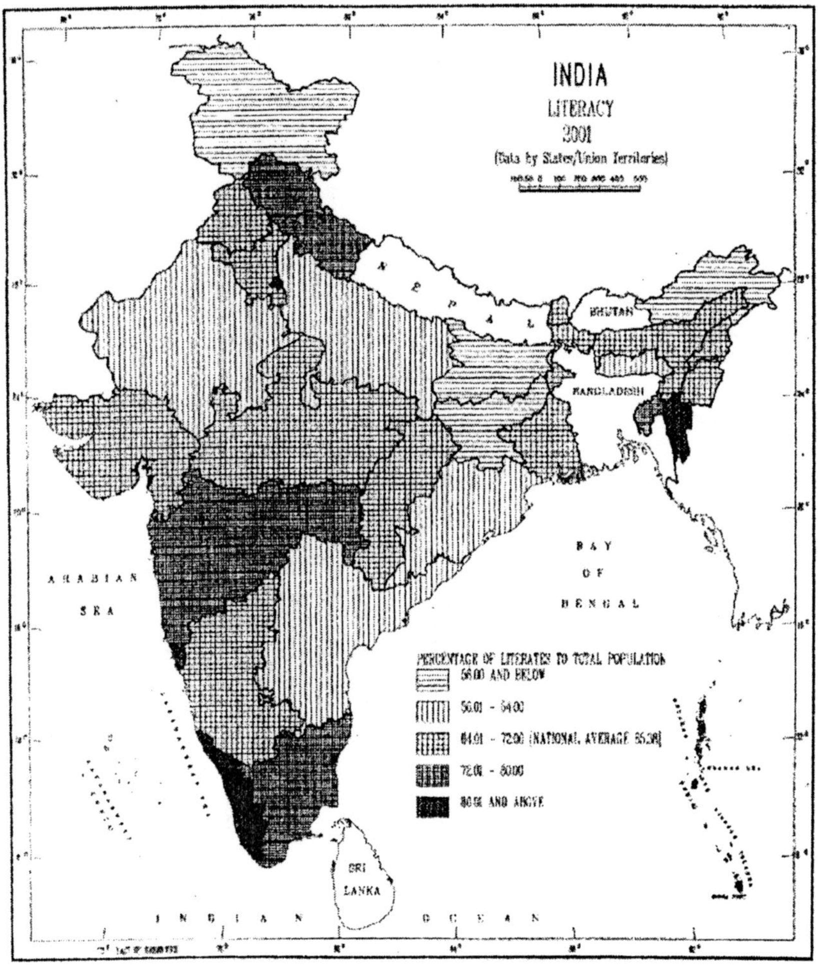


**Map 2.7 :** India : Literacy, 2001 (Data by States / Union Territories)

per cent), Himachal Pradesh (77.13 per cent), Tripura (73.66 per cent), Tamil Nadu (73.47 per cent), Uttaranchal (72.78 per cent), and so on. Thus, 16 out of 28 states have recorded literacy rates higher than the national average (65.38 per cent).

Bihar with 47.53 per cent of its population as literate is at other end of the scale, not only in case of total literacy rate but also for male literacy (60.32 per cent) and female literacy (33.57 per cent). The other states that have literacy rates below the national average are Jammu

**Table 2.16:** India: Literacy Rates by Sex, 2001

| *Country/State/ Union Territory* | *Per cent Literates to Total Population* | | |
|---|---|---|---|
| | *Persons* | *Males* | *Females* |
| **INDIA*** | **65.38** | **75.85** | **54.16** |
| *States* | | | |
| Kerala | 90.92 | 94.20 | 87.86 |
| Mizoram | 88.49 | 90.69 | 86.13 |
| Goa | 82.32 | 88.88 | 75.51 |
| Maharashtra | 77.27 | 86.27 | 67.51 |
| Himachal Pradesh | 77.13 | 86.02 | 68.08 |
| Tripura | 73.66 | 81.47 | 65.41 |
| Tamil Nadu | 73.47 | 82.33 | 64.55 |
| Uttaranchal | 72.28 | 84.01 | 60.26 |
| Gujarat | 69.97 | 80.50 | 58.60 |
| Punjab | 69.95 | 75.63 | 63.55 |
| Sikkim | 69.68 | 76.73 | 61.46 |
| West Bengal | 69.22 | 77.58 | 60.22 |
| Manipur | 68.87 | 77.87 | 59.70 |
| Haryana | 68.59 | 79.25 | 56.31 |
| Nagaland | 67.11 | 71.77 | 61.92 |
| Karnataka | 67.04 | 76.29 | 57.45 |
| Chhatisgarh | 65.18 | 77.86 | 52.40 |
| Assam | 64.28 | 71.93 | 56.03 |
| Madhya Pradesh | 64.11 | 76.80 | 50.28 |
| Orissa | 63.61 | 75.95 | 50.97 |
| Meghalaya | 63.31 | 66.14 | 60.41 |
| Andhra Pradesh | 61.11 | 70.85 | 51.17 |
| Rajasthan | 61.03 | 76.46 | 44.34 |
| Uttar Pradesh | 57.36 | 70.23 | 42.98 |
| Arunachal Pradesh | 54.74 | 64.07 | 44.24 |
| Jammu & Kashmir | 54.46 | 65.75 | 41.82 |
| Jharkhand | 54.13 | 67.94 | 39.38 |
| Bihar | 47.53 | 60.32 | 33.57 |
| *Union Territories* | | | |
| Lakshadweep | 87.52 | 93.15 | 81.56 |
| Chandigarh | 81.76 | 85.65 | 76.65 |
| Pondicherry | 81.49 | 88.89 | 74.13 |
| Andaman & N. Islands | 81.18 | 86.07 | 75.29 |
| Daman & Diu | 81.09 | 88.40 | 70.37 |
| Dadra & Nagar Haveli | 60.03 | 73.32 | 42.99 |
| Delhi | — | 87.37 | 75.00 |

*Source:* Census of India (2001), *Provisional Population Totals*, Paper-I of 2001, Series-I, India, Statement 32, pp. 117-188

*Notes:* (i) The 2001 census literacy rates exclude entire Kachchh district, Morvi, Maliya-Miyana and Wankaner talukas of Rajkot district, Jodiya taluka of Jamnagar district of Gujarat state and entire Kinnaur district of Himachal Pradesh where population enumeration of Census of India, 2001, could not be conducted due to natural calamities.

(ii) The literacy rates for Himachal Pradesh have been worked out by excluding entire Kinnaur district, as population enumeration of Census of India, 2001, could not be conducted due to natural calamity.

(iii) The literacy rates for Gujarat have been worked out by excluding entire Kachchh district, Morvi, Maliya-Miyana and Wankaner talukas of Rajkot district and Jodiya taluka of Jamnagar district of Gujarat state where population enumeration of Census of India, 2001, could not be conducted due to natural calamity.

and Kashmir (54.46 per cent) in north; Rajasthan (61.03 per cent) in west; Andhra Pradesh (61.11 per cent) in south; Madhya Pradesh (64.11 per cent), Chhatisgarh (65.18 per cent) and Uttar Pradesh (57.36 per cent) in central; Jharkhand (54.13 per cent) and Orissa (63.61 per cent) in east; and Arunachal Pradesh (54.74 per cent), Meghalaya (63.31 per cent) and Assam (64.28 per cent) in the north-east parts of the country.

From amongst the union territories, Dadra and Nagar Haveli with 60.63 per cent of its population as literate is the only union territory which has literacy rate below the national average (65.38 per cent). Dadra and Nagar Haveli is entirely rural territory unlike other unions territories most of which are highly urbanized. Lakshadweep continued to display the highest literacy rate of 87.52 per cent. It was followed closely by Delhi (81.82 per cent), Andaman & Nicobar Islands (81.18 per cent), and Daman & Diu (81.09 per cent). Chandigarh (81.76 per cent), and Pondicherry (81.49 per cent). Chandigarh which in 1981 had the first position among union territories with 74.8 per cent literacy has been deprived of its distinction by Lakshadweep which has improved its literacy from 68.4 per cent in 1981 to 79.2 per cent in 1991. Lakshadweep, because of its strategic location, has attracted highly educated defence personnel, thereby raising the literacy rate. Chandigarh, on the other hand, has attracted unskilled and uneducated workers during the decade as fallout of the rehabilitation programme of the labour colony dwellers, which has adversely affected its literacy rate.

The states and union territories, which have literacy rates below the national average (65.38 per cent) in respect of all the three categories *i.e.* persons, males and females are Arunachal Pradesh, Andhra Pradesh, Bihar, Dadra and Nagar Haveli, Jammu and Kashmir, Jharkhand and Uttar Pradesh (Table 2.16).

Broadly speaking, the literacy rates are low in areas with backward agricultural economy, low degree of urbanization, considerable proportion of Muslim population, a fairly long spell of feudal rule in the past and still a caste-ridden society. By comparison, the areas with high literacy are those which have coastal location, high degree of urbanization, more diversified economy, considerable proportion of Christian population, greater agricultural prosperity, and an early start of modern education (Chandna, 2000).

The regional differentials in literacy rates become sharper and show wider range of variations when examined at the district level (Map 2.8). Out of the total of 593 districts, about fifty per cent *i.e.* 294 districts have recorded literacy rate above the national average (65.38 per cent).

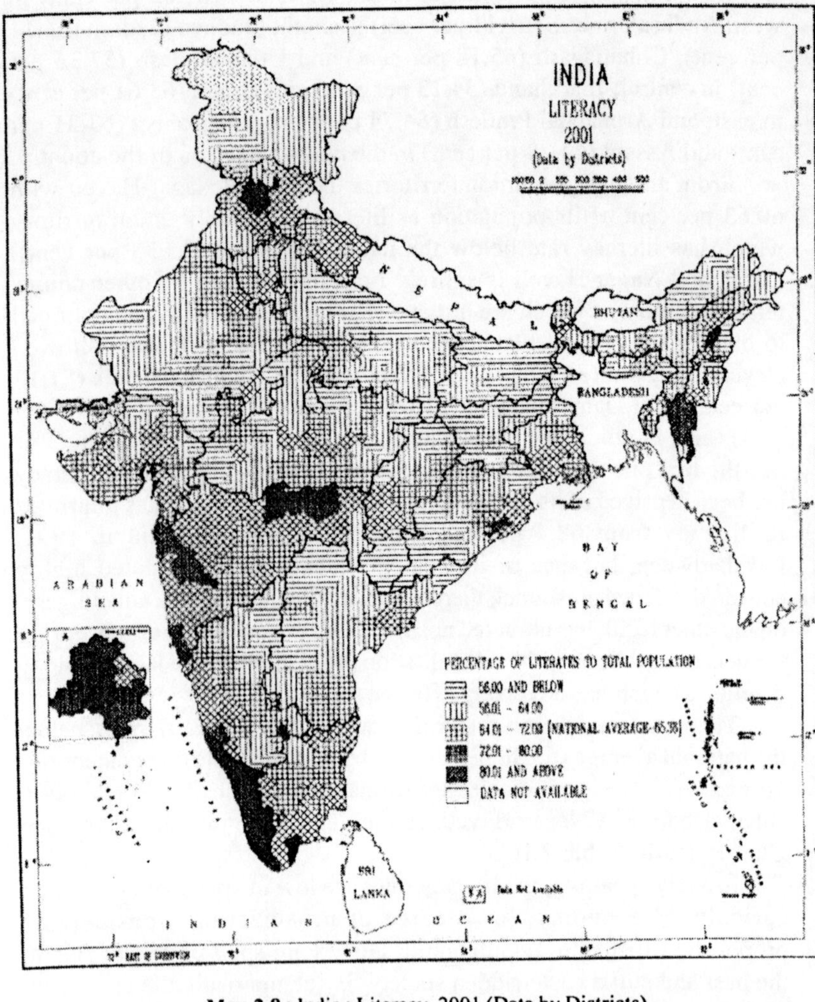


**Map 2.8 :** India : Literacy, 2001 (Data by Districts)

The district of Aizawl in Mizoram recording 96.44 per cent of its population as literate has the distinction of being the most literate district of the country. By contrast, Dantewada district in Chhatisgarh with 30.01 per cent of its population as literate is the least literate district in the country. The ratio of 1:3 between the least and the most literate districts speaks volumes of the contrasting socio-economic conditions prevailing in the country. Out of the thirteen districts having literacy rate more than 90 per cent, eight are from Kerala, four from Mizoram and one from Pondicherry. Thus, nine out of top thirteen districts are concentrated in southern India and four in north-east India. Broadly speaking, south India was more literate than north India. Within south India, the coastal areas were more literate than the interiors and between the coastal regions the western coast was more literate than the eastern coast. Within north India, parts of Punjab plains in the north-west and Christian dominated hill states in the north-east have higher literacy than the rest of the areas.

The bottom ten districts with lowest literacy rates are scattered in central and eastern India. Four of them are in Bihar, two each in Orissa and Uttar Pradesh and one each in Chhatisgarh and Jharkhand. Six districts, *viz.*, Dantewada district of Chhatisgarh, Pakaur district of Jharkhand, Malkangiri district of Orissa, Balrampur district of Uttar Pradesh, Kishanganj and Araria districts of Bihar are common in bottom ten districts of all the three categories, *viz.*, persons, males and females. The above-mentioned districts are the most critical districts which will require special attention. Infact, most of these districts have a large number of illiterates waiting to be converted into literates. Further, it is observed that many of these districts have also added a large number of illiterates during 1991-2001 which, perhaps, suggests that a large number of children and adolescents who should have been attending school were possibly not doing so.

Among males, the highest literacy rate has been recorded in Mahe district of Podicherry (97.6 per cent) and as observed in case of persons Dantewada district of Chhatisgarh (39.6 per cent) records the lowest male literacy rate. It has been observed that out of the total of 591 districts, 318 districts have reported male literacy rates above the national average of 75.85 per cent.

Among the females, the literacy rate varies considerably between 96.1 per cent in Aizawl district of Mizoram and 18.5 per cent in Kishanganj district of Bihar. It is observed that there are 277 districts with female literacy rates above the national average of 54.2 per cent. There are two districts in the country with the female literacy rate below 20 per cent. One of them is Kishanganj (18.5 per cent) in Bihar and the other Shravasti (18.8 per cent) in Uttar Pradesh.

## SCHEDULED CASTES AND SCHEDULED TRIBES

For the purpose of special benefits to uplift the social, economic and political status of certain castes, the President of India is empowered to declare, through public notification, any caste or tribe or part thereof as *Scheduled Caste* or *Scheduled Tribe*, as the case may be. Therefore, under the Indian Constitution, Scheduled Castes and Scheduled Tribes mean such castes, races or tribes or parts of or groups within castes, races or tribes as are declared by the President of India to be *Scheduled Castes* under Article 341 and *Scheduled Tribes* under Article 342 of the Constitution (Census of India, 1991).

## Scheduled Castes

The scheduled castes in each state/union territory are enumerated as per the list of such castes mentioned in the Presidential Order "The Scheduled Castes and Scheduled Tribes Lists (Modification Order 1956)" as amended from time to time. No Scheduled Caste has been listed in the state of Nagaland and union territories of Andaman & Nicobar Islands and Lakshadweep as per this Presidential Order (Census of India, 1991).

The scheduled castes population as per 1991 census (excluding Jammu & Kashmir where 1991 census could not be held due to disturbed conditions) was 138.2 million, accounting for 16.48 per cent of the total population. During the decade 1981-91, they experienced a growth rate of about 31 per cent (from about 106 million in 1981 to about 139 million in 1991), as against 22.4 per cent by the non-scheduled caste sections put together, thus far outdoing the latter in demographic dynamism. As a consequence, their proportion to total population of the country has increased from 15.7 per cent in 1981 to 16.5 per cent in 1991. This massive growth is attributable to (a) their birth rate staying at a high level, well above 40 per 1000 which is much higher than the national average for the total population, (b) death rate declining rapidly with medical facilities extending all over the country, and (c) a slight improvement in their economic conditions. During the preceding decade of 1971-81 too, their growth rate was staggeringly high—32.4 per cent, as against 23.4 per cent in the case of non-scheduled caste population, raising their share in the total population from 14.8 per cent in 1971 to 15.7 per cent in 1981. During 1961-71, the growth rates of the scheduled caste and non-scheduled caste populations were practically the same—24.1 per cent and 24.9 per cent respectively, though for different reasons. It seems that 1971 is the take-off year in the recent history of population growth of the scheduled castes. Apparently, this important segment of

Indian society is in the early second stage of demographic transition which characteristically experiences explosive growth.

If the recent trend of their birth rates staying at a high level and death rates declining consistently continues, which is very likely, the scheduled castes are sure to maintain an explosive growth rate in the years to come, further raising their proportion to the country's total population. This development is only expected since it is a truism that socially and economically backward groups, particularly those which stand very low in their accomplishments in literacy and education, generally suffer from a time lag in their passage through different phases of demographic transition as compared to those sections of the society which are better placed in socio-economic progress (Gosal, 1997).

Regionally, Punjab with 28.31 per cent scheduled castes population occupies the first position among the Indian states (Table 2.17). It is followed by Himachal Pradesh (25.34 per cent), West Bengal (23.62 per cent), Uttar Pradesh (21.05 per cent), Haryana (19.75 per cent), Tamil Nadu (19.18 per cent) and Rajasthan (17.29 per cent). Thus, only 7 states out of 24 are having percentage of scheduled castes higher than the national average (16.48 per cent). The other states which have sizeable proportion of scheduled castes population but below the national average are Karnataka (16.38 per cent), Tripura (16.36 per cent), Orissa (16.20 per cent), Andhra Pradesh (15.93 per cent), Bihar (14.55 per cent), Madhya Pradesh (14.55 per cent) and Maharashtra (11.09 per cent). By contrast, Mizoram has the lowest proportion of scheduled castes population accounting for only 0.10 per cent of the total population of the state. It is followed closely by Arunachal Pradesh (0.47 per cent), Meghalaya (0.51 per cent), and Manipur (2.02 per cent). It shows that majority of north-eastern states have a very low percentage of scheduled castes because of the dominance of tribal population in these states.

From amongst the union territories, Delhi has the highest proportion of scheduled castes (19.05 per cent). It is followed by Chandigarh (16.51 per cent) and Pondicherry (16.25 per cent). By comparison, Dadra & Nagar Haveli has the lowest percentage of scheduled castes population (1.97 per cent) and is followed by Daman and Diu with 3.83 per cent of the total population.

In terms of absolute numbers, Uttar Pradesh has the highest of 29.3 million scheduled castes population, followed by West Bengal (16.1 million), Bihar (12.6 million), Tamil Nadu (10.7 million), Andhra Pradesh (10.6 million), Madhya Pradesh (9.6 million), Maharashtra (8.8 million), Rajasthan (7.6 million), Karnataka (7.4 million), Punjab

**Table 2.17: India: Distribution of Scheduled Castes and Scheduled Tribes Population, 1991**

| *Country/State/ Union Territory* | *Population (in Millions)* | | | *Per cent to Total Population* | |
|---|---|---|---|---|---|
| | *Total* | *Scheduled Castes* | *Scheduled Tribes* | *Scheduled Castes* | *Scheduled Tribes* |
| **INDIA*** | **838.6** | **138.2** | **67.8** | **16.78** | **8.08** |
| *States* | | | | | |
| Punjab | 20.3 | 5.7 | NA | 28.31 | NA |
| Himachal Pradesh | 5.1 | 1.3 | 0.2 | 25.34 | 4.22 |
| West Bengal | 68.1 | 16.1 | 3.8 | 23.62 | 5.59 |
| Uttar Pradesh | 139.1 | 29.3 | 0.3 | 21.05 | 0.21 |
| Haryana | 16.5 | 3.3 | NA | 19.75 | NA |
| Tamil Nadu | 55.09 | 10.7 | 0.6 | 19.18 | 1.03 |
| Rajasthan | 44.0 | 7.6 | 5.5 | 17.29 | 12.44 |
| Karnataka | 45.0 | 7.4 | 1.9 | 16.38 | 4.26 |
| Tripura | 2.8 | 0.5 | 0.9 | 16.36 | 30.95 |
| Orissa | 31.7 | 5.1 | 7.0 | 16.20 | 22.21 |
| Andhra Pradesh | 66.5 | 10.6 | 4.2 | 15.93 | 6.31 |
| Bihar | 86.4 | 12.6 | 6.6 | 14.55 | 7.66 |
| Madhya Pradesh | 66.2 | 9.6 | 15.4 | 14.55 | 23.27 |
| Maharashtra | 78.9 | 8.8 | 7.3 | 11.09 | 9.27 |
| Kerala | 29.1 | 28.9 | 0.3 | 9.92 | 1.10 |
| Gujarat | 41.3 | 3.1 | 6.2 | 7.41 | 14.92 |
| Assam | 22.4 | 1.7 | 2.9 | 7.40 | 12.82 |
| Sikkim | 0.4 | 0.02 | 0.09 | 5.93 | 22.36 |
| Goa | 1.2 | 0.02 | 0.0004 | 2.08 | 0.03 |
| Manipur | 1.8 | 0.04 | 0.6 | 2.02 | 34.41 |
| Meghalaya | 1.8 | 0.01 | 1.5 | 0.51 | 85.53 |
| Arunachal Pradesh | 0.9 | 0.004 | 0.6 | 0.47 | 63.66 |
| Mizoram | 0.7 | 0.001 | 0.7 | 0.10 | 94.75 |
| Nagaland | 1.2 | NA | 1.1 | NA | 87.70 |
| *Union Territories* | | | | | |
| Delhi | 9.4 | 1.8 | NA | 19.05 | NA |
| Chandigarh | 0.6 | 0.1 | NA | 16.51 | NA |
| Pondicherry | 0.8 | 0.1 | NA | 16.25 | NA |
| Daman & Diu | 0.1 | 0.004 | 0.01 | 3.83 | 11.54 |
| Dadra & Nagar Haveli | 0.1 | 0.003 | 0.10 | 1.97 | 78.99 |
| Andaman & Nicobar Islands | 0.3 | NA | 0.03 | NA | 9.54 |
| Lakshadweep | 0.05 | NA | 0.05 | NA | 93.15 |

*Source:* Census of India (1991), *Union Primary Census Abstract for Scheduled Castes and Scheduled Tribes*, Paper I of 1993, Series-I, India, Table-1, p.11.

NA = "No Scheduled Caste/Scheduled Tribe has been listed in the state/union territory.

* Excludes figures of Jammu & Kashmir where 1991 census was not held.

(5.7 million), Orissa (5.1 million), Haryana (3.3. million), Gujarat (3.1. million), Kerala (2.9 million) and Assam (1.7 million). Uttar Pradesh and West Bengal together have one-third of the scheduled castes population of India.

At the district level, the regional variations in the distribution of scheduled castes population are more pronounced. Out of the total of 452 districts, 197 districts are having scheduled castes population more than the national average (16.48 per cent). The highest proportion (51.57 per cent) of scheduled castes population is found in the Kooch Behar district of West Bengal, whereas, West Khasi Hills district of Meghalaya has the lowest (0.01 per cent). In Punjab, Faridkot and Jalandhar; in Uttar Pradesh, Sonbhadra and in West Bengal, South Twenty-Four Parganas and Kooch Behar districts are having more than 34 per cent scheduled castes population.

In parts of Punjab, Himachal Pradesh, western Uttar Pradesh, Gangetic West Bengal and some parts of coastal Tamil Nadu, 24.01-34.00 per cent of the total population is categorized as scheduled castes population. In the range of 17.01-24.00, there are 137 districts, while in the range of 10.01-17.00 per cent, there are 132 districts. Barring a few districts of western coastal region and north-eastern states, these are spread all over the country.

Eighty-three districts of the country have a scheduled castes population ranging between 3.01 and 10.00 per cent, while in 44 districts it is below 3.00 per cent. These are mainly concentrated over the north-eastern states, Gujarat, parts of Madhya Pradesh and Bihar and along the western coast.

## Scheduled Tribes

As in the case of Scheduled Castes, the Scheduled Tribes are also listed in each state/union territory separately under the Presidential Order "The Scheduled Castes and Scheduled Tribes Lists (Modification Order 1956)" as amended from time to time. No Scheduled Tribe has been listed in Haryana, Punjab, Chandigarh, Delhi and Pondicherry as per this Presidential Order (Census of India, 1991).

The scheduled tribes population as per 1991 census (excluding Jammu & Kashmir where 1991 census could not be held due to disturbed conditions) was 67.76 million, constituting 8.08 per cent of the total population. During the decade 1981-91, scheduled tribes experienced a growth rate of 25.67 per cent (from about 53.8 million in 1981 to about

67.8 million in 1991), as against 22.4 per cent by the non-scheduled castes sections put together, thus marginally outdoing the latter in demographic dynamism. As a consequence, their proportion to total population of the country has marginally increased from 7.83 per cent in 1981 to 7.95 per cent in 1991.

The spatial distribution of scheduled tribes is markedly different from that of scheduled castes. Because scheduled tribes have a tendency of clustering and concentrating in remote areas like hilly and forested tracts of the country, whereas scheduled castes show a very high concentration on the fertile lands like Indo-Gangetic plain and the coastal plains where they work as agricultural labourers. Among the various states and union territories of India, there are wide regional variations in the distribution of tribal population. Mizoram with 94.75 per cent scheduled tribes population occupy the first position among the states of India (Table 2.17). The other states with predominantly scheduled tribes population are Nagaland (87.70 per cent), Meghalaya (85.53 per cent) and Arunachal Pradesh (63.66 per cent). Manipur and Tripura also have substantial proportion of population as scheduled tribes, the respective proportions being 34.41 and 30.95 per cent. The other states which have proportion of scheduled tribes above the national average (8.08 per cent) are Madhya Pradesh (23.27 per cent), Sikkim (22.36 per cent), Orissa (22.21 per cent), Gujarat (14.92 per cent), Assam (12.82 per cent), Rajasthan (12.44 per cent) and Maharashtra (9.27 per cent). By contrast, Goa has the lowest proportion of scheduled tribes population accounting for only 0.03 per cent of the total population of the state. It is closely followed by Uttar Pradesh (0.21 per cent), Tamil Nadu (1.03 per cent) and Kerala (1.10 per cent). The other states having proportion of scheduled tribes population below the national average (8.08 per cent) are Himachal Pradesh (4.22 per cent), Karnataka (4.26 per cent), West Bengal (5.59 per cent), Andhra Pradesh (6.31 per cent) and Bihar (7.66 per cent).

From amongst the union territories, Lakshadweep has the highest proportion of scheduled tribes (93.15 per cent) and is followed by Dadra & Nagar Haveli (78.99 per cent). The other two union territories of Daman & Diu (11.54 per cent) and Andaman & Nicobar Islands (9.54 per cent) also have the proportion of scheduled tribe population more than the national average (8.08 per cent).

In terms of absolute numbers, Madhya Pradesh has the highest of 15.4 million scheduled tribes population, followed by Maharashtra (7.3 million), Orissa (7.0 million), Bihar (6.6 million), Gujarat (6.2 million),

Rajasthan (5.5. million), Andhra Pradesh (4.2 million), West Bengal (3.8 million), Assam (2.9 million), Karnataka (1.9 million), Meghalaya (1.5 million) and Nagaland (1.1 million). All other states and union territories together have a little over 4 million scheduled tribes population (Table 2.17).

At the district level, the regional variations in the distribution of scheduled tribes population are more pronounced. Out of the total of 452 districts, 138 districts are having scheduled tribes population more than the national average (8.08 per cent). The highest proportion (98.11 per cent) of scheduled tribes population is found in West Khasi Hills district of Meghalaya, whereas there are 17 districts in Uttar Pradesh, Madhya Pradesh and Bihar, which constitute only 0.01 per cent scheduled tribes population.

In India, there are 29 districts, where more than 75.01 per cent of the total population is scheduled tribes. Among them, 24 districts are in the north-eastern states and the remaining 5 districts are Lahul and Spiti, The Dangs, Dadra and Nagar Haveli, Jhabua and Lakshadweep.

In the ranges of 35.01-75.00 and 15.01-35.00 per cent there are 43 and 47 districts respectively. Besides the districts of north-eastern states, these districts form a continuous region spreading over the states of Rajasthan, Gujarat, Maharashtra, Madhya Pradesh, Orissa, West Bengal and Andhra Pradesh.

Seventy four districts in the country are in the range of 5.01-15.00 per cent, while other 87 districts are in the range of 1.01-5.00 per cent. one hundred seventeen districts in the Gangetic plain, Tamil Nadu, Kerala, Karnataka and Gujarat have very low scheduled tribes population, even less than one per cent.

## CONCLUDING REMARKS

1. India, with 1027 million people as per 2001 census, is the second largest populous country next to China. It consists about 16.7 per cent of the population of the world living on only 2.4 per cent of the total land area of the world. Since, the annual rate of population growth happens to be 1.9 per cent during 1991-2001, the absolute addition of 180.6 million people to the population during this decade is more than the estimated population of Brazil, the fifth most populous country in the world.
2. India has had a very chequered demographic history, more so during

the twentieth century. A perusal of population data for this period reveals that there have been significant demographic divides like the census years of 1921, 1951 and 1981 resulting into four distinct phases of population growth from 1901 to 2001. These are: (a) very slow growth (1901-1921), (b) steady growth (1921-1951), (c) rapid high growth (1951-1981), and (d) high growth with definite signs of slowing down.

Spatially, the highest growth of population has been recorded by Nagaland (64.41 per cent) and the lowest by Kerala (9.42 per cent). The states that recorded the growth rate higher than the national average (21.34 per cent) were as many as 15 out of 28 in the country. From amongst the union territories, Daman & Diu recorded the highest growth rate of 55.59 per cent. On the other hand, Lakshadweep with 17.19 per cent growth rate was at the other end of the scale. It is interesting to note that out of the seven, five union territories have recorded the growth rate above national average (21.34 per cent) mainly because of their urban character

During the decade 1991-2001, out of the total of 593 districts, 58 districts have recorded less than 10 per cent growth rate. By contrast, there are 19 districts in the country which have registered high growth rate of more than 50 per cent. Wokha district in Nagaland has the highest decadal growth rate (95.01 per cent), whereas Mamit district in Mizoram has recorded the lowest growth rate (–3.50 per cent).

3. As per 2001 census, India has an average density of 324 persons per km$^2$, which is about eight times the average density (less than 40 persons/ km$^2$) of the world as a whole. From amongst various states in the country, West Bengal is still the most thickly populated, where population density has gone up from 767 in 1991 to 904 persons per km$^2$ in 2001. At the other end of the scale is Arunachal Pradesh which among various states has the lowest density of only 13 persons per km$^2$. All the union territories, except Andaman and Nicobar Islands experiencing lowest density of 43 persons per km$^2$, have a higher density than the national average of 324 persons per km$^2$. Delhi with a density of 9294 persons is the most densely populated union territory of the country.

At the district level; out of the total of 593 districts, 294 districts experienced density of population higher than the national average of 324 persons/km$^2$. The North-East district in Delhi has the highest population density in the country with 29,395 persons/ km$^2$. On the other hand, Lahul & Spiti district of Himachal Pradesh has the lowest density of population (2 persons/km$^2$) in the country.

4. According to Census of India (2001), the sex ratio stands at 933 females per 1000 males for the country as a whole. This is a welcome improvement from the 1991 census, which had recorded 927 females per 1000 males. However, right from the beginning of census operations, the sex ratio in India has been adverse to females. The sex ratio in 1901 was 972 and thereafter has suffered a consistent decline all through the twentieth century except during the decades of 1941-1951, 1971-1981 and 1991-2001. Some of the important reasons attributed to this declining trend in sex ratio of India are: (i) neglect of the girl child resulting in their higher mortality at younger ages, (ii) high maternal mortality, (iii) sex-selective female abortions, (iv) female infanticide, and (v) change in sex ratio at birth.

   Viewed in its regional perspective, from amongst the states, Kerala with a sex ratio of 1058 is the only state in the country, which has excess of females over males. This is mainly because of that it has a sizeable proportion of Christian population and highest literacy rates in the country, which together may have contributed to a low female mortality rate. At the other end of the scale is Haryana with lowest sex ratio of 861 females per 1000 males mainly because of the increasing trend of female foetal abortions on the basis of sex - determination tests as well as a strong preference to have a son at the cost of female child.

   From amongst the union territories, Pondicherry, like Kerala, is the only union-territory in India, which has excess of females over males (1001 females per 1000 males). By contrast, Daman & Diu with a sex ratio of only 709 displayed the highest paucity of females in the country mainly because of male-selective in-migration.

   At the district level, out of the total of 593 districts, 324 districts display relatively high sex ratio more than the national average of 933 females per 1000 males. Mahe district of Pondicherry has the highest sex ratio of 1148 females per 1000 males and is followed closely by Almora district (1147) in Uttaranchal. On the other hand, Daman district of Daman & Diu union territory stands at the lowest at 591 females per 1000 males. One of the significant features of 2001 census is that there is a substantial increase in the number of districts, which displayed excess of females over males as compared to 1991. In all, there are 78 districts in 2001, as against 55 districts in 1991 in the country where the females outnumbered males.

5. In tune with most of the developing countries, India too displayed high dependency ratio, where a little less than two-thirds of non-working population depends upon a little more than one-third of workforce. One of the typical features of the Indian workforce that differentiates the country from the developed world is wide disparity in the work participation rates (WPR) of males and females. As per 1991 census, while 51.6 per cent of the country's males were recorded as workers, the corresponding figure for the female population was only 21.3 per cent. Thus, while one out of every two males in India was working, in case of females one out of every five females was working.

   The industrial composition of Indian workforce is overwhelmingly dominated by the primary sector consisting of 67.5 per cent main workers of the total population as against the national average of 34.1 per cent for all the three economic sectors. Cultivators and agricultural labourers together accounted for 64.8 per cent of our main workers. It shows that two out of every three workers were still engaged in agricultural pursuits.

   In terms of spatial spread at district level, the work participation rate for main workers varies from the minimum of 21.08 per cent in Mahe district of Pondicherry to the maximum of 55.25 per cent in Tawang district of Arunachal Pradesh. Out of the total of 452 districts, 239 districts experienced work participation rate for main workers higher than the national average (34.10 per cent). Being an agricultural country, there is an overwhelming majority of the districts in India, which have more than two-thirds of their workers, classified as primary workers.

6. In India, there have been drastic changes in the religious composition of population due to large scale migration as a result of partition of India in 1947. As per 1991 census, Hindus form majority comprising 82 per cent of India's population and followed by Muslims (11.67 per cent), Christians (2.17 per cent), Sikhs (2.00 per cent), Buddhists (0.66 per cent), and Jains (0.40 per cent).

   Regionally, Hindus are in predominant majority in 20 states and 6 union-territories. Muslims, with 65.85 per cent of the population are in majority in Jammu & Kashmir, while Meghalaya (64.6 per cent), Mizoram (85.7 per cent), and Nagaland (87.5 per cent) is dominated numerically by Christians. In Punjab, Sikhs with 63.0 per cent of the total population form the majority. Lakshadweep is the only union territory where Muslims (94.3 per cent) dominate the scene. Among the Buddhists, the largest number is concentrated in Sikkim which accounts for 27.15 per cent of the total population of India. Jains (0.40 per cent), like Buddhists (0.76 per cent), numerically account for less than one per cent of the total population and are spread all over the country, but highest proportion is found in Rajasthan (1.28 per cent).

7. Independence in 1947 provided the real impetus to literacy in the country. The crude literacy rate has grown more than three times from 16.67 per cent in 1951 to 55.30 per cent at the Census of India, 2001. Similarly, more than three-fold increase has been noticed in effective literacy rate which increased from 18.33 per cent in 1951 to 65.38 per cent in 2001. So, the literacy rate for the country as a whole in 2001, works out to 65.38 per cent for the population aged seven years and above. The corresponding figures for males and females are 75.85 and 54.16 per cent respectively. Thus, three-fourths of the male and more than half of the female population aged seven years and above are literate in the country today.

   The most notable feature of Indian literacy is that the females always lagged far behind the males in terms of literacy rates. While 75.85 per cent of the males are recorded as literate in 2001, the corresponding figure for females is only 54.16 per cent. This is mainly because females in India have for long been confined to the four-walls of the house and have been subject to various prejudices.

   Regionally, 16 out of 28 states have recorded literacy rates higher than the national average (65.38 per cent). Kerala with 90.92 per cent of its population as literate has the distinction of having highest literacy in the country. It also continues to occupy the top position in the country both in male literacy with 94.20 per cent and female literacy with 87.86 per cent. Bihar with 47.53 per cent of its population as literate is at other end of the scale, not only in case of total literacy rate but also for male literacy (60.32 per cent) and female literacy (33.57 per cent).

   From amongst the union territories, Dadra and Nagar Haveli with 60.63 per cent of its population as literate is the only union territory which has literacy rate below the national average (65.38 per cent). By contrast, Lakshadweep continued to display the highest literacy rate of 87.52 per cent. Lakshadweep, because of its strategic location, has attracted highly educated defence personnel, thereby raising the literacy rate.

   At the district level, out of the total of 593 districts, 294 districts have recorded literacy rate above the national average (65.38 per cent). The district of Aizawl in Mizoram recording 96.44 per cent of its population as literate has the distinction of being the most literate district of the country. By contrast, Dantewada district in Chhatisgarh with 30.01 per cent of its population as literate is the least literate district in the country.

Broadly speaking, the literacy rates are low in areas with backward agricultural economy, low degree of urbanization, considerable proportion of Muslim population, a fairly long spell of feudal rule in the past and still a caste-ridden society. By comparison, the areas with high literacy are those, which have coastal location, high degree of urbanization, more diversified economy, considerable proportion of Christian population, greater agricultural prosperity, and an early start of modern education.

8. The scheduled castes population as per 1991 census (excluding Jammu & Kashmir) was 138.2 million, accounting for 16.48 per cent of the total population. During the decade 1981-91, they experienced a growth rate of about 31 per cent as against 22.4 per cent by the non-scheduled castes put together, thus far outdoing the latter in demographic dynamism.

   Regionally, only 7 states out of 24 are having percentage of scheduled castes higher than the national average (16.48 per cent). Punjab with 28.31 per cent scheduled castes population occupies the first position among the Indian states. By contrast, Mizoram has the lowest proportion of scheduled castes population accounting for only 0.10 per cent of the total population of the state.

   From amongst the union territories, Delhi has the highest proportion of scheduled castes (19.05 per cent). On the other hand, Dadra & Nagar Haveli has the lowest percentage of scheduled castes population (1.97 per cent).

   At the district level, out of the total of 452 districts, 197 districts are having scheduled castes population more than the national average (16.48 per cent). The highest proportion (51.57 per cent) of scheduled castes population is found in the Kooch Behar district of West Bengal, whereas West Khasi Hills district of Meghalaya has the lowest (0.01 per cent).

9. The scheduled tribes population as per 1991 census (excluding Jammu & Kashmir) was 67.76 million, constituting 8.08 per cent of the total population. During the decade 1981-91, scheduled tribes experienced a growth rate of 25.67 per cent as against 22.4 per

cent by the non-scheduled castes sections put together.

At the state level, Mizoram with 94.75 per cent scheduled tribes population occupy the first position among the states of India. By contrast, Goa has the lowest proportion of scheduled tribes population accounting for only 0.03 per cent of the total population of the state. From amongst the union territories, Lakshadweep has the highest proportion of scheduled tribes (93.15 per cent) and is followed by Dadra & Nagar Haveli (78.99 per cent).

At the district level, out of the total of 452 districts, 138 districts are having scheduled tribes population more than the national average (8.08 per cent). The highest proportion (98.11 per cent) of scheduled tribes population is found in West Khasi Hills district of Meghalaya, whereas there are 17 districts in Uttar Pradesh, Madhya Pradesh and Bihar, which constitute only 0.01 per cent scheduled tribes population.

# 3

# SEX RATIO

Sex ratio is one of the best indicators of status of women in the society. In view of the partly contrasting and partly complementary roles of the two sexes in the economy and society, the study of their ratio to each other becomes of great interest to a population geographer. Sex ratio is an index of the socio-economic conditions prevailing in an area and is a useful tool for regional analysis (Franklin, 1956). In itself, the sex ratio is a function of three basic factors of sex ratio at birth, differential in mortality of the two sexes at different stages of life and sex-selectivity among the migrants (Clarke, 1960). In its own turn, sex ratio has a profound effect on other demographic elements like growth of population, marriage rates, occupational structure, etc. (Shyrock, 1976). The knowledge of sex ratio helps in understanding the employment and consumption patterns, social needs and psychological characteristics of a community. Equally significant is the relationship between change in sex ratio, on the one hand and the trends in socio-economic life of a region, on the other. It reveals the changes in birth and mortality pattern of the two sexes and their migrational behaviour. Thus, sex ratios are fundamental to the geographic analysis of an area, for they are not only important features of the landscape but also influence the other demographic elements significantly and as such provide additional means and materials for analysing regional landscape (Trewartha, 1953).

The numerical measurement of sex composition of a population is often expressed in terms of ratio. However, the method of expressing the ratio is not universal and this ratio is calculated differently in different countries. For instance, in USA, the sex ratio is expressed in terms of number of males per hundred females whereas, in New Zealand, the sex ratio is generally calculated as number of females per hundred males. However, in India, it is calculated in terms of number of females per thousand males and is expressed as under:

$$Pf/Pm \times 1000$$

where *Pf* is the number of females and *Pm* represents the number of males.

## Sex Ratio in India: A Temporal Analysis, 1901-2001

Right from the beginning of census operations, the sex ratio in India has been adverse to women. Moreover, barring some hiccups, it has shown a long term declining trend. The sex ratio at the beginning of the twentieth century was 972 and thereafter showed continuous decline until 1941 (Table 3.1).

**Table 3.1:** India: Sex Ratio, 1901-2001

| *Census Year* | *Females per 1000 males* |
|---|---|
| 1901 | 972 |
| 1911 | 964 |
| 1921 | 955 |
| 1931 | 950 |
| 1941 | 945 |
| 1951 | 946 |
| 1961 | 941 |
| 1971 | 930 |
| 1981 | 934 |
| 1991 | 927 |
| 2001 | 933 |

*Source:* Census of India (2001), *Provisional Population Totals*, Paper-I of 2001, Series-I, India, Statement 18, p. 85.

Notes: (i) For 1991 the interpolated figures for Jammu & Kashmir have been used.
(ii) While working out the sex ratio for India for the year 2001, the estimated population of entire Kachchh district, Morvi, Maliya-Miyana and Wankaner talukas of Rajkot district, Jodiya taluka of Jamnagar district of Gujarat state and entire Kinnaur district of Himachal Pradesh have been used, as the population enumeration of Census of India, 2001, could not be conducted due to natural calamities.

Table 3.1 reveals a fall in the sex-ratio from 972 to 964 in the decade of 1901-11. During this decade, in addition to famine, there were plague and malaria. The fall in the ratio was attributed to female mortality from these diseases, which was far in excess of the male deaths from famine. The sex ratio declined further to 955 by 1921 due to plague which continued from the previous decade and the outbreak of influenza epidemic which was specially fatal to women and more particularly to young married women. It continued to register decline from decade to decade except in the decade 1941-51, in which partition may have contributed to higher losses and wastage of male lives in certain tracts counter-balancing the continuing diminution of the sex-ratio in others (Mitra, 1979). After 1951, it again dropped for two consecutive decades to reach 930 in 1971. In fact, between 1961-71, the country saw the sharpest decline of 11 points in the sex ratio. However, during 1971-81, a slight improvement of 4 points (from 930 in 1971 to 934 in 1981) is noticed in contrast to the declining trend. Some of the demographers in India thought that this rise in sex-ratio may be due to the improvement brought in the status of women as well as mortality conditions leading to the higher expectancy of life of females especially during 70's decade. But, this upward trend is upset by the results of the sex ratio of 1991 census which has revealed a further decline of 7 females making it 927 females per 1000 males in India. According to Census of India (2001), the sex ratio stands at 933 for the country as a whole. This is a welcome improvement over the 1991 census and needs to be maintained in future.

It is interesting to note that the sex ratio in India has suffered a consistent decline all through the twentieth century except during the decades of 1941-51, 1971-81 and 1991-2001. Some of the reasons attributed to this declining trend in sex ratio of India are: greater neglect of females especially at the earlier ages, differences in sex ratio at birth, premature cohabitation and child-bearing coupled with unskilled mid-wifery, male sex-preference and discrimination of female sex, female infanticide, uneven sex migration patterns, hard work for females particularly among lower income groups which constitute the bulk of the population, high female mortality expressed in the form of female foetal, infant and maternal mortalities and general female mortality, the increasing trend of female foetal abortions on the basis of sex-determination tests, greater undercount of females in the census enumerations, the predominance of male sex among the acceptors of family planning as well as among the low birth rate communities, general adverse conditions of climate, nutrition, ventilation and house accommodation, and other social, economic, psychological and communal problems of females in the society due to the poor status of women, and the like (Reddy, 1996).

## INDIA: RURAL-URBAN DIFFERENTIALS IN SEX RATIO, 1901-91

The rural-urban differentials in sex ratio in India were the result of sex-selectivity among the rural-urban migrants in the past. More males than the females moved from rural areas to urban areas. Such as rural-urban migration takes place due to push and pull forces operating in the two areas. However, the male-selective influx into urban areas is the result of (i) prejudice against female employment and mobility, (ii) scarcity of jobs suitable for females, and (iii) high cost of living and problem of housing in urban centres which discourage and compel many male migrants to leave their families behind. Moreover, the joint family system prevailing in rural areas facilitates male-selective migration as the male migrant is assured of the safety and security of his family left behind (Krishan and Chandna, 1973). Thus, the rural-urban differential in sex ratio was largely the product of male-selectivity in rural-urban migration. This was in contrast to the excess of females among the rural-urban migrants in case of Western countries. Right from the beginning of twentieth century since 1901, the sex ratio in India had always remained unfavourable to females not only in rural areas but also in urban areas (Table 3.2 and Fig. 3.1). However, urban areas were characterized with excessive deficiency of women than their rural counterparts which was in contrast to the Western countries where the urban sex ratios were more in favour of females.

Table 3.2 reveals that the rural areas witnessed a continuous decline in sex ratio since 1901. The decline of 13 points between 1981-91 is a matter of serious concern. The main reason for this is male-biased birth rates (or masculinity at birth) and high mortality rate among females (due to their neglect) at almost all ages.

**Table 3.2:** India: Sex Ratio by Rural-Urban Residence, 1901-91

| *Census Year* | *Females Per 1000 Males* | | | *Rural-Urban Differential* |
|---|---|---|---|---|
| | *Total* | *Rural* | *Urban* | |
| 1901 | 972 | 979 | 910 | 69 |
| 1911 | 964 | 975 | 872 | 103 |
| 1921 | 955 | 970 | 846 | 124 |
| 1931 | 950 | 966 | 838 | 128 |
| 1941 | 945 | 965 | 831 | 134 |
| 1951 | 946 | 965 | 860 | 105 |
| 1961 | 941 | 963 | 845 | 118 |
| 1971 | 930 | 949 | 858 | 91 |
| 1981 | 935 | 952 | 880 | 72 |
| 1991 | 927 | 939 | 894 | 45 |

*Source*: Census of India (1991), *Final Population Totals: Brief Analysis of Primary Census Abstract*, Paper 2 of 1992, Series-I, India, Table 2.2, p.102.

**Table 3.3:** India: Decadal Change in Sex Ratio by Rural-Urban Residence, 1901-91

| *Census Decade* | *Decadal Change in Sex Ratio* | | *Rural-Urban Differential* |
|---|---|---|---|
| | *Rural* | *Urban* | |
| 1901-11 | -4 | -38 | +34 |
| 1911-21 | -5 | -26 | +21 |
| 1921-31 | -4 | -8 | +4 |
| 1931-41 | -1 | -7 | +6 |
| 1941-51 | 0 | +29 | -29 |
| 1951-61 | -2 | -15 | +13 |
| 1961-71 | -14 | +13 | -27 |
| 1971-81 | +2 | +21 | -19 |
| 1981-91 | -13 | +15 | -28 |

*Source*: Calculated from, Census of India (1991), *Final Population Totals: Brief Analysis of Primary Census Abstract*, Paper 2 of 1992, Series-I, India, Table 2.2, pp.102-105.

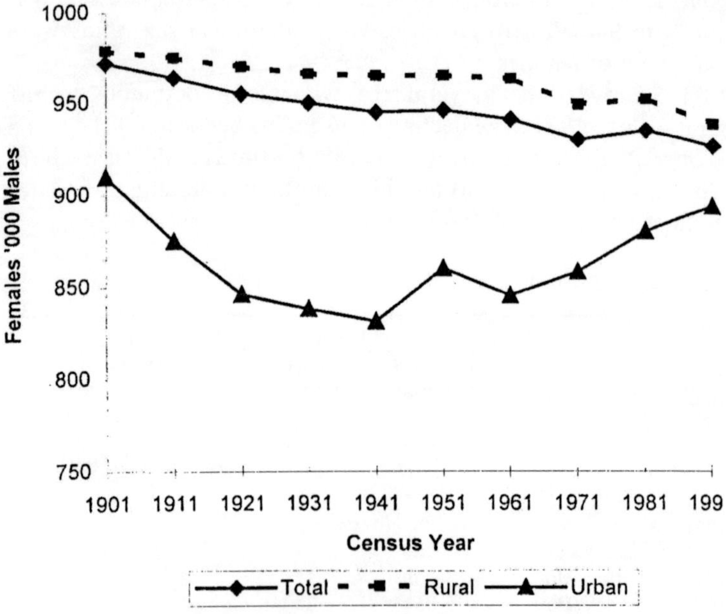


**Fig. 3.1**: India : Sex Ratio by Rural-Urban Residence, 1901-91

On the other hand, the urban sex ratio was 910 in 1901 and decreased continuously and reached 831 till 1941. But, it increased to 860 in 1951, as a result of the influx of Muslim women to the towns for security reasons, at the time of partition. They migrated later on either to Pakistan or to some other parts of the country. Consequently, the urban sex ratio again decreased 15 points and reached 845 in 1961. More male migrants from villages to cities also led to a decline of urban sex-ratio. But, after that it continuously increased and reached 894 in 1991. The reasons for this increase in sex-ratio are family migration to urban areas and improvement in living conditions, with the availability of medical facilities has led to greater survival of both males and females. Moreover, certain social change leading to somewhat greater attention towards the girl child in recent years in urban areas also increased urban sex ratio to some extent.

The increase in urban sex ratio and decline in rural sex-ratio after 1961 are compensatory to each other and the resultant rural-urban differential decreased 27 points in 1961-71, 19 points in 1971-81 and 28 points in 1981-91 (Table 3.3 and Fig. 3.2).

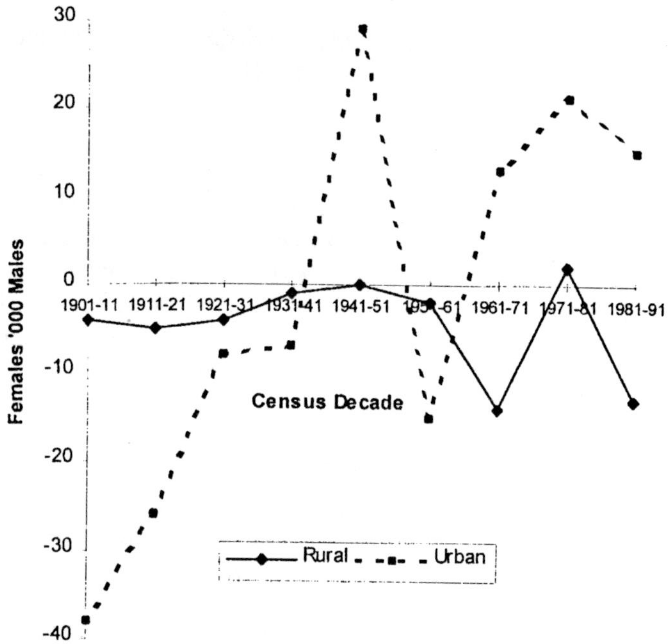


**Fig. 3.2:** India: Decadal Change in Sex Ratio by Rural-urban Residence, 1901-1991

The rural-urban differential declined from an all time high of 134 in 1941 to 45 in 1991 (Table 3.2). The main reasons for this considerable fall in differential over the period 1901-91 has been due to both increasing urban sex ratio and decreasing rural sex ratio. The decrease in rural sex-ratio from 979 (1901) to 939 (1991), which is almost for a century can be explained in terms of faster fall in male mortality rate in rural areas than female mortality rates and family out-migration. Secondly, the rapid development of transport and communication has somewhat put breaks on the phenomenal migration from rural to urban areas, by facilitating the probability of commuting from surrounding areas. This factor has reduced the influence of factor of male-selective migration. The increase in urban sex ratio from 845 in 1961 to 894 in 1991 is a result of increase in status of women, better health and medical facilities, bringing down the female mortality rates in urban areas. This shows that the rural-urban differential is on a continuous decline at a varying rate.

**India: Trend of Rural-Urban Differentials in Sex Ratio, 1901-1991**

The areal differences in sex ratio reflect the variations in social attitudes of the populations. The sex ratio is comparatively high among advanced societal groups where the level of status of women is high. However, despite the prevailing differentials in sex ratio between rural and urban areas as well as their inter-state variations, there have been noticeable trends in sex ratio decline during the last one century. As Table 3.4 indicates, the decline in differentials have been observed in more than half of the states, though its degree varied. In 1901, the maximum and minimum sex ratio in rural areas was 1113 in Mizoram and 836 in Punjab with a difference of 277 females per 1000 males. In 1991, the maximum rural sex ratio was 1037 females per 1000 males in Kerala, while the minimum was 864 females per 1000 males in Haryana, giving a difference of 173 females per 1000 males.

Similarly, the maximum urban sex ratio in 1901 was 1048 in Tamil Nadu while the minimum was 423 in Nagaland, making a difference of 625 females per 1000 males. In 1991, the maximum urban sex ratio was 1034 in Kerala and minimum was 728 in Arunachal Pradesh. This caused a difference of 306 females per 1000 males. Thus, as a whole, the sex ratio is showing a declining trend which is caused by a decline in the maximum and increase in minimum sex ratios and by reducing the difference between them.

One redeeming feature of sex composition of India's population is that the regional disparity has got squeezed over time (Table 3.5). In 1901, the urban sex ratio's coefficient of variability (65.37 per cent) was much higher than rural (31.46 per cent) implying that urban sex ratio had a greater variation and inconsistency. However, in 1991, not only both the areas displayed a decline in disparity, coefficient of variability being 7.81 per cent in rural and 8.70 per cent in the urban areas, but a tremendous decline in disparity within urban areas was noticeable.

Among the various states of India (Table 3.6), Nagaland was noted for the largest difference (166 females per 1000 males) in average of its rural (917 females per 1000 males) and urban (749 females per 1000 males) sex ratio. The large differential was related to an unusually low sex ratio and the rural being close to national average (938). Male selective migration from rural to urban areas explains this phenomenon.

Himachal Pradesh was also noted for a large differential in average rural (990) and urban (831) sex ratio. The functional structure of towns, most of which were administrative centres, along with recency of migration to them are responsible for this situation. In Arunachal Pradesh, too, rural-urban differential (152) is high with rural and urban sex ratios as 880 and 728 respectively. Among the union territories, the maximum rural-urban differential (148) in sex ratio is found in Dadra and Nagar Haveli.

On the other hand, lowest rural-urban differential (+3) in sex ratio is found in Kerala where females in both rural (1037) and urban (1034) areas exceed males. Matrilineal society in Kerala and relatively high level of status of females account for it.

Eight out of 32 states and union territories have urban sex ratio more than rural. These in ascending order of states are Haryana (–4), Tripura (–16), Mizoram (–20) and Manipur (–24) and among union territories are Pondicherry (–15), Delhi (–23), Daman & Diu (–102) and Chandigarh (–178).

On the basis of the trend of rural-urban differential (Map 3.1), all the states and union territories can be divided in five categories (Table 3.7).

**Table 3.4:** India: Sex Ratio by Rural-Urban Residence, 1901-91

*(Females per '000 Males)*

| *Country/ States/Union Territory* | *1901* | | | *1951* | | | *1971* | | | *1991* | | |
|---|---|---|---|---|---|---|---|---|---|---|---|---|
| | *Total* | *Rural* | *Urban* | *Total* | *Rural* | *Urban* | *Total* | *Rural* | *Urban* | *Total* | *Rural* | *Urban* |
| India | **972** | **979** | **910** | **946** | **965** | **860** | **930** | **949** | **858** | **927** | **938** | **894** |
| *States* | | | | | | | | | | | | |
| Andhra Pradesh | 985 | 983 | 999 | 986 | 985 | 987 | 977 | 983 | 949 | 972 | 977 | 959 |
| Arunachal Pradesh | DNA | DNA | DNA | DNA | DNA | DNA | **861** | **881** | **457** | **859** | 880 | **728** |
| Assam | 919 | 929 | 576 | 868 | 878 | 663 | 896 | 912 | 744 | 923 | 934 | 838 |
| Bihar | 1054 | 1057 | 997 | 990 | 1001 | 842 | 954 | 971 | 807 | 911 | 921 | 844 |
| Goa | 1091 | DNA | DNA | **1128** | **1145** | **1017** | 981 | **1025** | 864 | 967 | 993 | 930 |
| Gujarat | 954 | 951 | 965 | 952 | 964 | 920 | 934 | 951 | 893 | 934 | 949 | 907 |
| Haryana | 867 | 861 | 908 | 871 | 877 | 845 | 867 | 870 | 853 | 865 | **864** | 868 |
| Himachal Pradesh | 884 | 899 | 800 | 912 | 932 | 664 | 958 | 976 | 749 | 976 | 990 | 831 |
| Karnataka | 983 | 984 | 976 | 966 | 974 | 941 | 957 | 971 | 913 | 960 | 973 | 930 |
| Kerala | 1004 | 1008 | 953 | 1028 | 1033 | 992 | **1016** | 1020 | **997** | **1036** | **1037** | **1034** |
| Madhya Pradesh | 990 | 995 | 937 | 967 | 975 | 907 | 941 | 956 | 868 | 931 | 943 | 893 |
| Maharashtra | 978 | 1003 | 862 | 941 | 1000 | 807 | 930 | 985 | 820 | 934 | 972 | 875 |
| Manipur | 1037 | 1038 | 1036 | 1036 | 1039 | **633** | 980 | 980 | 980 | 958 | 951 | 975 |
| Meghalaya | 1036 | 1047 | 725 | 966 | 991 | 683 | 937 | 971 | 764 | 955 | 966 | 910 |
| Mizoram | **1113** | **1113** | DNA | 1041 | 1049 | 845 | 946 | 947 | 936 | 921 | 912 | 932 |
| Nagaland | 973 | 997 | **423** | 999 | 1005 | 739 | 871 | 928 | 472 | 886 | 917 | 749 |
| Orissa | 1037 | 1039 | 967 | 1022 | 1029 | 881 | 988 | 1002 | 845 | 971 | 988 | 866 |
| Punjab | **832** | **836** | 804 | **844** | **854** | 807 | 865 | **868** | 856 | 882 | 888 | 868 |
| Rajasthan | 905 | 898 | 947 | 921 | 919 | 928 | 911 | 919 | 875 | 910 | 919 | 879 |
| Sikkim | 916 | 916 | DNA | 907 | 912 | 686 | 863 | 884 | 681 | 879 | 892 | 750 |
| Tamil Nadu | 1044 | 1043 | **1048** | 1007 | 1014 | 986 | 978 | 990 | 951 | 974 | 981 | 960 |
| Tripura | 874 | 887 | 595 | 904 | 909 | 836 | 943 | 944 | 935 | 945 | 942 | 958 |
| Uttar Pradesh | 937 | 940 | 917 | 910 | 925 | 820 | 879 | 889 | 821 | 879 | 884 | 860 |
| West Bengal | 945 | 994 | 650 | 865 | 939 | 660 | 891 | 942 | 751 | 917 | 940 | 858 |
| *Union Territories* | | | | | | | | | | | | |
| A & N Islands | **318** | **318** | DNA | **625** | 654 | DNA | **644** | **671** | 558 | 818 | 837 | **769** |
| Chandigarh | 771 | 771 | DNA | 781 | 781 | DNA | 749 | 686 | 756 | **790** | **632** | 810 |
| D & N Haveli | 980 | 980 | DNA | 946 | 946 | DNA | 1007 | 1007 | DNA | 952 | 965 | 817 |
| Daman & Diu | 995 | DNA | DNA | **1125** | **1110** | **1151** | **1099** | **1104** | **1090** | 969 | 922 | **1024** |
| Delhi | 862 | 916 | 817 | 768 | 837 | **754** | 801 | 825 | 798 | 827 | 807 | 830 |
| Lakshadweep | **1063** | **1063** | DNA | 1043 | 1043 | DNA | 978 | 978 | DNA | 943 | 959 | 930 |
| Pondicherry | DNA | DNA | DNA | 1030 | 1030 | DNA | 989 | 984 | 996 | **979** | **970** | 985 |
| Coefficient of Variability | **24.06** | **31.46** | **65.37** | **10.92** | **10.04** | **47.71** | **9.12** | **9.30** | **31.85** | **5.78** | **7.81** | **8.70** |

*Source:* Census of India (1991), *Final Population Totals: Brief Analysis of Primary Census Abstract,* Paper 2 of 1992, Series-I, India, Table 2.2, pp. 102-105.
DNA–Data Not Available.

**Table 3.5**: India: Spatial Disparities in Sex Ratio, 1901-91

| *Census Year* | *Coefficient of Disparity* (Per cent)* | | |
|---|---|---|---|
| | *Total* | *Rural* | *Urban* |
| 1901 | 24.06 | 31.46 | 65.37 |
| 1951 | 10.92 | 10.04 | 47.71 |
| 1971 | 9.12 | 9.30 | 31.85 |
| 1991 | 5.78 | 7.81 | 8.70 |

*Source:* Calculated from, Census of India (1991), *Final Population Totals: Brief Analysis of Primary Census Abstract*, Paper 2 of 1992, Series-I, India, Table 2.2, pp. 102-105.

* Coefficient of disparity has been taken as synonymous with the coefficient of variability. State-wise data have been used for its calculation with the formula: $\sigma/Mean \times 100$.

## Category and Nomenclature

1. Areas with rural sex ratio higher than urban in 1901 as well as in 1991 with increasing differential trend.
2. Areas with rural sex ratio higher than urban in 1901 as well as in 1991 with declining differential trend.
3. Areas with urban sex ratio higher than rural in 1901 as well as in 1991 with declining differential trend.
4. Areas with urban sex ratio higher than rural in 1991 but reverse was true in 1901 with declining differential trend.
5. Areas with rural sex ratio higher than urban in 1991 but reverse was true in 1901 with increasing differential trend.

### *1. Areas with Rural Sex Ratio Higher than Urban in 1901 as well as in 1991 with Increasing Differential Trend*

The states where rural sex ratio has always been higher than urban with increasing differential trend are Himachal Pradesh (+56), Orissa (+50), Karnataka (+35), Bihar (+17) and Uttar Pradesh (+1). In all these sates, rural sex ratio is much more than the total sex ratio of these states. The main reason is sex selectivity among migrants. A large number of males in these states migrate to nearby states and urban areas in search of employment. Therefore, the sex ratio in rural areas increases in comparison to urban.

**Table 3.6**: India: Rural-Urban Differential in Sex Ratio, 1901-91

| *Country/State/Union Territory* | *Rural-Urban Differential* | |
|---|---|---|
| | *1991* | *1901* |
| **India** | **45** | **69** |
| *States* | | |
| Nagaland | 166 | 574 |
| Himachal Pradesh | 155 | 99 |
| Arunachal Pradesh | 152 | — |
| Sikkim | 142 | — |
| Orissa | 122 | 72 |
| Maharashtra | 97 | 141 |
| Assam | 96 | 353 |
| West Bengal | 82 | 344 |
| Bihar | 77 | 60 |
| Goa | 63 | — |
| Meghalaya | 56 | 322 |
| Madhya Pradesh | 50 | 58 |
| Karnataka | 43 | 8 |
| Gujarat | 42 | –14 |
| Rajasthan | 40 | 49 |
| Uttar Pradesh | 24 | 23 |
| Tamil Nadu | 21 | –5 |
| Punjab | 20 | 32 |
| Andhra Pradesh | 18 | –16 |
| Kerala | 3 | 55 |
| Haryana | –4 | –47 |
| Tripura | –16 | 292 |
| Mizoram | –20 | — |
| Manipur | –24 | 2 |
| *Union Territories* | | |
| Dadra & Nagar Haveli | 148 | — |
| Andaman & N. Islands | 68 | — |
| Lakshadweep | 29 | — |
| Pondicherry | –15 | — |
| Delhi | –23 | 99 |
| Daman & Diu | –102 | — |
| Chandigarh | –178 | — |

*Source:* Calculated from, Census of India (1991), *Final Population Totals: Brief Analysis of Primary Census Abstract*, Paper 2 of 1992, Series-I, India, Table 2.2, pp. 102-105.

*Note:* States and union territories are arranged in descending order of rural-urban differential, 1991.

### 2. *Areas with Rural Sex Ratio Higher than Urban in 1901 as well as in 1991 with Declining Differential Trend*

One-third of the states and union territories fall in this category. The

**Table 3.7**: India: Trend of Rural-Urban Differentials in Sex Ratio, 1901-91

| *Rural-Urban Differential Categories* | | | | |
|---|---|---|---|---|
| *1* | *2* | *3* | *4* | *5* |
| Himachal Pradesh (+56) | Nagaland (–408) | Haryana (–43) | Tripura (–308) | Gujarat (+56) |
| Orissa (+50) | Meghalaya (–266) | | Delhi (–122) | Andhra Pradesh (+34) |
| Karnataka (+35) | West Bengal (-262) | | Manipur (–26) | Tamil Nadu (+26) |
| Bihar (+17) | Assam (–257) | | | |
| Uttar Pradesh (+1) | Kerala (–52) | | | |
| | Maharashtra (–44) | | | |
| | Punjab (–12) | | | |
| | Rajasthan (–9) | | | |
| | Madhya Pradesh (–8) | | | |

*Source:* Calculated from, Census of India (1991), *Final Population Totals: Brief Analysis of Primary Census Abstract,* Paper 2 of 1992, Series-I, India, Table 2.2, pp. 102-105.

states where rural sex ratio is higher than urban in 1901 as well as in 1991, but with declining rural-urban differential trend are Nagaland (–408), Meghalaya (–266), West Bengal (–262), Assam (–257), Kerala (–52), Maharashtra (–44), Punjab (–12), Rajasthan (–9) and Madhya Pradesh (–8). Most of these states fall in northern half of India. The decline in differential is quite sharp in the eastern hill states of Nagaland, Meghalaya, Assam and in adjoining state of West Bengal. In all these states, rural sex ratio is above national average and the urban are below or near to the national average except in Nagaland, where urban sex ratio witnessed a sharp increase, which reduced the gap between rural and urban sex ratios.

The improvement in urban sex ratio of these states is due to the availability of better medical, health and sanitation facilities, which reduced the mortality rate among women to some extent in pre-natal and post-natal stages. Besides, the better transportation and communication network and availability of employment in cottage and small scale industries within the rural areas for young unemployed population have reduced the rural-urban male-selective migration.

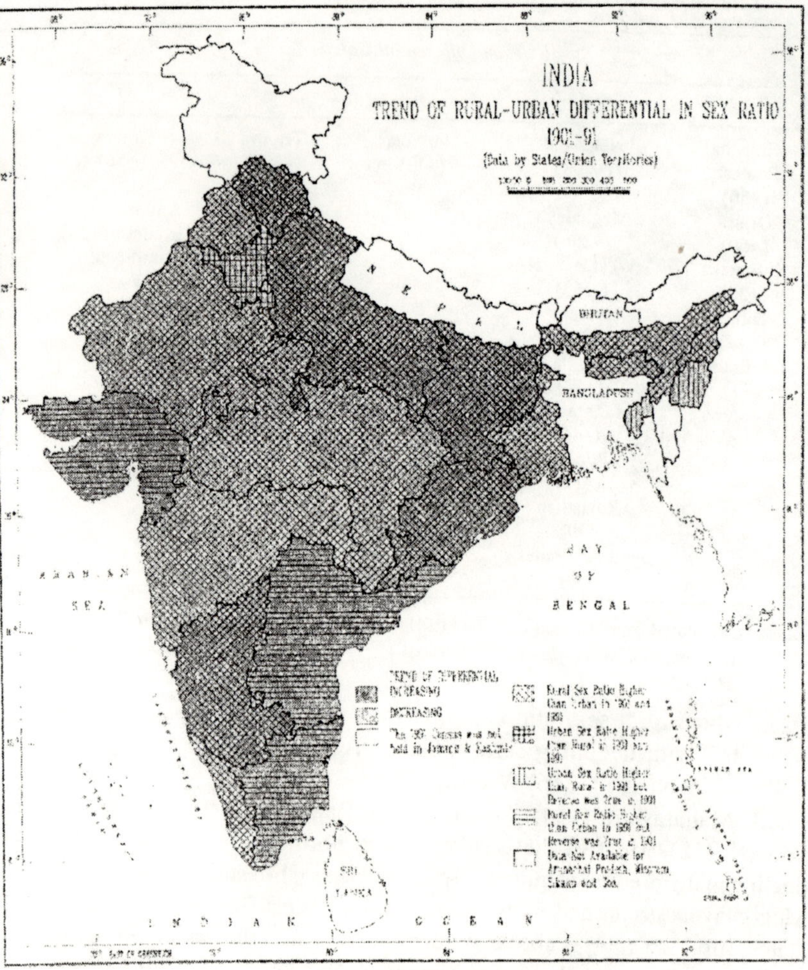


**Map 3.1:** India: Trend of Rural-Urban Differential in Sex Ratio, 1901-91
(Data by States / Union Territories)

*3. Areas with Urban Sex Ratio Higher than Rural in 1901 as well as in 1991 with Declining Differential Trend*

The only state falls in this category is Haryana (–43). This is the state where there is excessive deficiency of females per thousand males. An unusually low sex ratio at birth and a higher rate of mortality among females explain this phenomenon.

The gap between rural and urban sex ratio in Haryana is decreasing but it is still in favour of urban areas. Family migration to urban places has been predominant, notwithstanding male-selective migration to industrial towns like Faridabad township, Ballabhgarh, Gurgaon, Bahadurgarh, Sonipat, Yamunanagar and university towns like Hissar, Rohtak and Kurukshetra (Krishan & Chandna, 1973).

The rural character of small towns and preponderance of family migration to large towns have been the major factors to keep rural and urban sex ratios in Haryana quite close to each other and thereby give a decreasing trend of differential.

*4. Areas with Urban Sex Ratio Higher than Rural in 1991 and Reverse was True in 1901 with Decline in Differential Trend*

The states of Tripura (–308), Manipur (–26) and the union territory of Delhi (–122) experienced this phenomenon. In these two states and the union territory, urban sex ratio became higher than rural with tremendous decline in female mortality rates in urban areas as compared to the rural. In Delhi, particularly, intense commuting from as far a distance of 100 kms around has replaced male-selective migration. The rural-urban differential is showing a declining trend. In Tripura, both the rural and urban sex ratios improved, though the increase was about 7 times more in urban sex ratio in comparison to rural. But in case of Delhi, the sex ratio declined in rural and increased in urban areas. The decline in rural areas (–109) was much sharper than the increase in urban (+13) sex ratio. In Manipur, both the rural and urban sex ratio declined (–87 and –61 respectively) and this decline was sharper in rural areas.

*5. Areas with Rural Sex Ratio Higher than Urban in 1931 but Reverse was True in 1901 with Increasing Differential Trend*

Gujarat (+56), Andhra Pradesh (+34) and Tamil Nadu (+26) are the states where the differential has increased in favour of rural areas in 1991 as compared to 1901. With increase in female literacy rates, availability of transportation, medical facilities, drinking water and sanitation facilities in rural areas, the physical and social conditions of women have improved. All this increased the life expectancy of women at all ages in rural areas too. With improvement in women's status, the sex ratio declined at a very slow rate in rural areas such as in Andhra Pradesh, rural sex ratio decline was –6. In comparison to this urban sex ratio decline was 40 points. Similarly in Gujarat, sex ratio declined 2 points in rural areas and by 58 points in urban areas between 1901 and 1991. But the case of Tamil Nadu is somewhat different where both rural and urban areas experienced a great decline *i.e.* 62 and 88 points respectively between 1901-1991. Though the sex ratio declined in both the rural and urban areas between 1901 and 1991 but the fall in urban sex ratio was much faster and thereby gives increasing rural-urban differential trend.

**India: Spatial Patterns of Rural-Urban Differentials in Sex Ratio, 1991**

Rural-urban differentials in sex-ratio in India are a matter of serious concern because the overall sex ratio (927) has declined rapidly in 1991, in comparison to 1981 (934) (Table 3.2). Similarly, the rural sex ratio has also declined, but the urban sex ratio has modified itself to some extent, and the resultant rural-urban differential in sex ratio declined. As can be seen from the map of India (Map 3.2), there are wide regional variations in rural-urban differentials. The maximum differential is found in Nagaland (0.028), whereas it is minimum in Haryana (0.001) (Table 3.8).

When rural-urban differential index was correlated with some indicators for major states of India (Table 3.9), it was observed that it correlated negatively with rural female mortality rate and road density.

On the other hand, rural-urban differential is correlated positively with urban female mortality rate, rural male mortality rate and rural female literacy rate. As the urban female and rural male mortality decreases, the rural-urban differential will also decrease. Similarly, as the transportation network strengthens, male migration to urban areas will change to commuting and rural-urban differential would decline.

The lower sex ratio of the urban areas, in general, is mainly attributable to the fact that opportunities for female employment in Indian towns and cities are very low and the cost of living in urban areas is much higher than in rural areas. Faced with these handicaps, the working male members usually decide to leave their families in their villages, while they go to the cities for work themselves. However, the sex ratio

**Table 3.8:** India: Rural-Urban Differential Indices of Sex Ratio, 1991

| *Country/State/Union Territory* | *Differential Index* |
|---|---|
| **India** | **–0.006** |
| *States* | |
| Manipur | +0.003 |
| Mizoram | +0.003 |
| Punjab | +0.003 |
| Tripura | +0.002 |
| Haryana | +0.001 |
| Kerala | +0.000 |
| Andhra Pradesh | –0.002 |
| Tamil Nadu | –0.002 |
| Uttar Pradesh | –0.003 |
| Gujarat | –0.005 |
| Karnataka | –0.005 |
| Rajasthan | –0.005 |
| Madhya Pradesh | –0.007 |
| Meghalaya | –0.007 |
| Goa | –0.008 |
| Bihar | –0.011 |
| West Bengal | –0.011 |
| Maharashtra | –0.013 |
| Assam | –0.014 |
| Orissa | –0.016 |
| Himachal Pradesh | –0.022 |
| Sikkim | –0.024 |
| Arunachal Pradesh | –0.028 |
| Nagaland | –0.028 |
| *Union Territories* | |
| Chandigarh | +0.042 |
| Daman & Diu | +0.012 |
| Delhi | +0.004 |
| Pondicherry | +0.002 |
| Lakshadweep | –0.004 |
| Andaman & Nicobar Islands | –0.012 |
| Dadra & Nagar Haveli | –0.021 |

of towns and cities varies a great deal in accordance with their functions, types of industries, possibilities of female employment, sex ratio of the general population of the regions in which they are located and the social traditions of the people concerned. There is less sex-selectivity in the migration to urban areas in south India, probably because here the women enjoy a better status in society than in most other areas of the country. Also, the cottage industries, which are important in south Indian

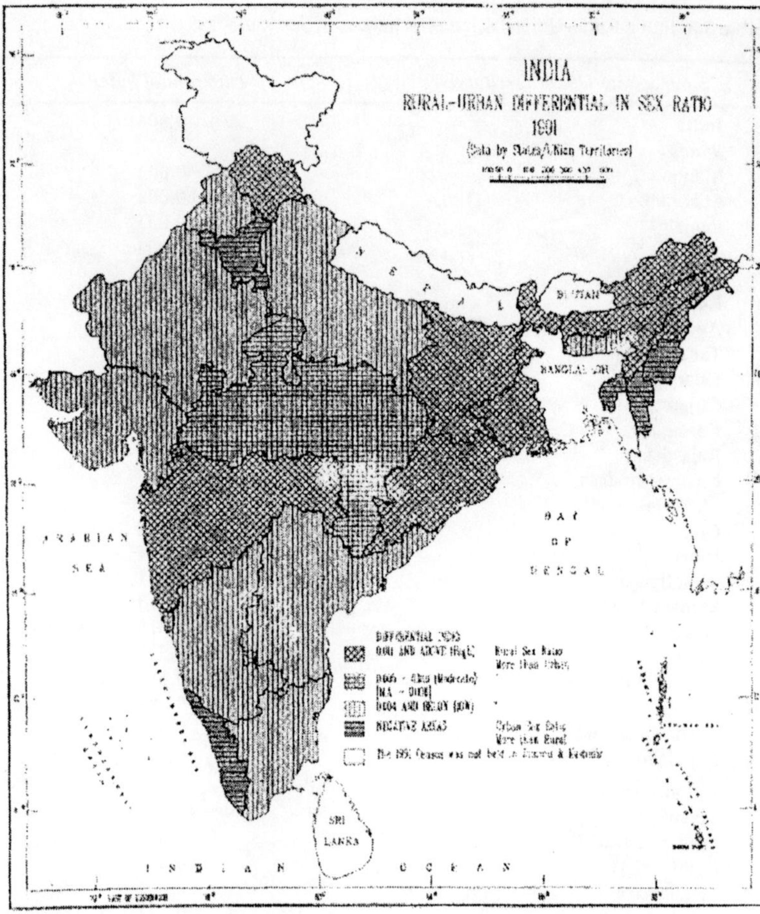


**Map 3.2:** India: Rural-Urban Differential in Sex Ratio, 1991 (Data by States / Union Territories)

**Table 3.9:** India: Coefficients of Correlation of Rural-Urban Differential in Sex Ratio, 1991

| *Indicator* | *Coefficient of Correlation* |
|---|---|
| Rural female mortality rate | –0.3513 |
| Road density | –0.2517 |
| Urban female mortality rate | +0.2158 |
| Rural female literacy rate | +0.2416 |
| Rural male mortality rate | +0.4398 |

*Source:* Computed from, Publications made by Census of India (1991) and Economic Intelligence Service (1991, 1993, 1994, 1997).

towns, offer some employment to the females. The rural urban differential in sex ratio is the lowest in south India (Gosal, 1961).

These regional disparities in differential index of sex ratio become more revealing and meaningful when examined at district level. The map of India (Map 3.3) reveals that a large part (one-third of India) is covered by districts where the differential index comes out to be low (0.004 and below), about one-fourth of the total districts have very high

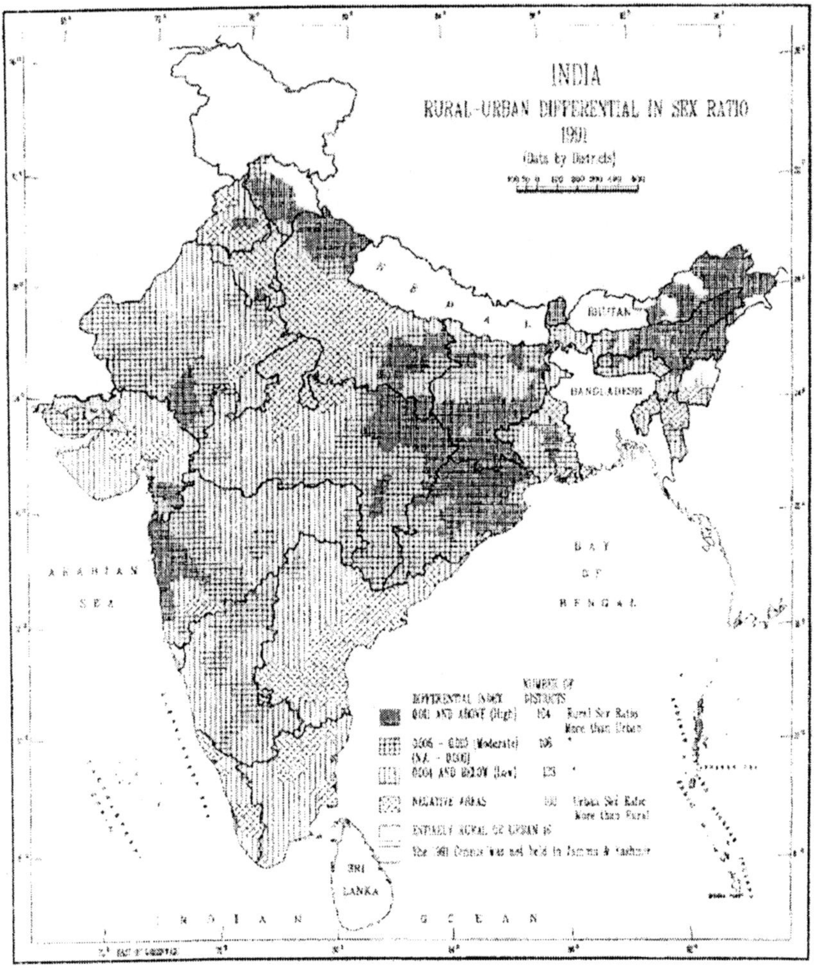


**Map 3.3**: India : Trend of Rural-Urban Differential in Sex Ratio: 1991 (Data by Districts)

index (0.011 and above) of rural-urban differentials. These areas of high differential index are surrounded by one-fifth districts with moderate differential index (0.005-0.010). 22.8 per cent districts are having higher urban sex ratio than the rural. These areas can be seen on eastern coast, upper Ganga plain, Punjab, Haryana and in a few regions scattered here and there all over India. For an understanding of differentials in sex ratio by residence, all the districts are divided into 2 major categories:

1. Areas with Rural Sex Ratio higher than Urban with:
   (a) Areas of high rural-urban differential index (0.011 and above).
   (b) Areas of moderate rural-urban differential index (0.005 to 0.010).
   (c) Areas of low rural-urban differential index (0.004 and below).
2 Areas with Urban Sex Ratio Higher than Rural.

*1. Areas with Rural Sex Ratio Higher than Urban*

Keeping in view the national average (–0.006) of rural-urban differential index, the districts with rural sex ratio higher than urban are divided into 3 sub-categories:

*(a) High Rural-Urban Differential Index (0.011 and above)*

The total number of districts belonging to this category are 104. Among these districts, the maximum differential is found in the north-western Himalayan districts. The Tehri Garhwal district has the highest rural-urban differential index value (0.103) and is followed by Chamoli (0.076), Almora (0.052), Uttar Kashi (0.046) and Pithoragarh (0.032) in Uttar Pradesh. In the district of Tehri Garhwal, urban sex ratio (563) is nearly half of the rural sex ratio (1098). This is the main reason for maximum rural-urban differential index value. In rest of the districts of Uttar Pradesh and districts of high differential index in north India, the rural sex ratios are comparatively high and urban sex ratios are very low, because north India is characterised by patriarchal society. These areas experience male-selective out-migration, particularly to armed forces and paramilitary personnel. There is lot of migration of men who work as men-servant. The differential is high in north-eastern hilly districts also. In the districts of Assam, Arunachal Pradesh, Nagaland,

Sikkim and Meghalaya, the male-selectivity among migrants is the root cause of high differential index. Moreover, these states are relatively less densely populated, where even small number of immigrants affected the sex ratio considerably. Another reason of male-selectivity in migration is the high cost of living and lack of housing facilities in urban areas. Lack of medical facilities and high female mortality rate in all age groups is typical of hilly areas.

In middle and lower Ganga plain and in Orissa Highland region and Chhota Nagpur region also, the rural-urban differential index is high. The districts of Howrah (0.017), Hugli (0.012) and Barddhaman (0.014) in West Bengal; Sonbhadra (0.022), Azamgarh (0.012), Jaunpur (0.012), Gorakhpur (0.012), Deoria (0.012), Sultanpur (0.013), Faizabad (0.011), Pratapgarh (0.014) and Allahabad (0.011) in Uttar Pradesh; and Saran (0.015), Siwan (0.016), Muzaffarpur (0.011), Saharsa (0.012), Madhepura (0.014), Katihar (0.011), Godda (0.012), Dumka (0.014), Deoghar (0.013), Dhanbad (0.018), Giridih (0.018), Hazaribagh (0.023), Palamau (0.013), Gumla (0.012), Ranchi (0.013), Purbi Singhbhum (0.013), Paschimi Singhbhum (0.016) and Kishanganj (0.011) in Bihar also have high differential index values. Most of these districts are industrially and agriculturally rich. Besides, Bihar is one among the BIMARU states of India. It lacks medical and health facilities. Female mortality rate is high, incidence of masculinity at birth is high, level of status of women is very low and they are a neglected part of the society. Male-selectivity in rural-urban migration is common.

### *(b) Moderate Rural-Urban Differential Index (0.005-0.010)*

Almost all the areas of high differential are surrounded by areas of moderate differential. There are 106 districts which fall in this category. More than half of the districts falling in this category are found in eastern half of India. This region includes the districts falling in middle and lower Ganga plain, southern part of Orissa Highland region, Chhatisgarh region and a few districts in Meghalaya-Mikir region. These are the districts of Kokrajhar (0.007) and Nagaon (0.007) in Assam; Chandel (0.007) in Manipur; East Khasi Hills (0.008) and West Garo Hills (0.008) in Meghalaya; Lunglei (0.006) in Mizoram; Jehanabad (0.009), Gaya (0.009), Gopalganj (0.009), Sahibganj (0.010) and Araria (0.009) in Bihar; Kachchh (0.009) in Gujarat; Una (0.010) in Himachal Pradesh; Tumkur (0.010) in Karnataka; Chandrapur (0.009) and Gadchiroli (0.009) in Maharashtra; Dhar (0.009) and Betul (0.010) in Madhya

Pradesh; Baleshwar (0.010), Bolangir (0.009) and Kalahandi (0.009) in Orissa; Alwar (0.009), Jaisalmer (0.010), Jodhpur (0.009), Pali (0.009), Jalaur (0.009) and Sirohi (0.010) in Rajasthan; Basti (0.009) and Ghazipur (0.009) in Uttar Pradesh; Darjeeling (0.009) in West Bengal have the maximum differential index values of this category. In the districts of north-eastern region of India, the gap between rural and urban sex ratio squeezed because of male-selective migration and high female mortality in rural areas during reproductive years. In these districts (regions), birth rates as well as death rates are above national average. Level of status of women is also very low.

A few patches are also found in the Thar Desert, Punjab and Haryana plain and Himachal region. The main cause of differential is sex-selectivity in migration and trend of male-recruitment in military and paramilitary forces.

A few districts of Konkan coast and Malabar coast also fall within the premises of this moderate differential index. These areas, since long, have been suffering from male-selective out-migration particularly in Bombay-Pune industrial belt, but now these seem to have entered the stage of family out-migration. Here, high female mortality in reproductive period is another cause (Bhutani, 1995).

In Punjab-Haryana plain and in many districts of Rajasthan, moderate differential is the result of small gap between sex ratio of rural and urban areas because most of the towns in north-western India are simply overgrown villages sharing many of the rural attributes and partly because migration to large towns of these areas was generally in families.

The preponderance of family migration to large towns and rural character of small towns in India are the main factors for moderate differential index.

*(c) Low Rural-Urban Differential Index (0.004 and below)*

A total of 123 districts fall in this category. More than half of western India falls in this category. These constitute one broad belt running through the sub-continent from Punjab and Haryana plain, northern part of Rajasthan plain, most of the Gujarat region, western half of central India, Malwa region, Maharashtra region, northern part of Karnataka plateau and Andhra plateau, Tamil Nadu upland, south Sahyadri, a few districts of middle and lower Ganga plain and a few districts of Meghalaya-Mikir region.

The maximum differential of this category *i.e.* 0.004 is found in the districts of Mahbubnagar, Rangareddi, Adilabad, Karimnagar and Nalgonda in Andhra Pradesh; Karimganj in Assam; Aurangabad and Munger in Bihar; Jamnagar, Amreli, Sabar Kantha, Mehsana and Ahmedabad in Gujarat; Sirmaur in Himachal Pradesh; Mandya, Raichur and Shimoga in Karnataka; Sangli, Jalna and Yavatmal in Maharashtra; Dewar ar ! Raisen in Madhya Pradesh; Ganganagar, Jaipur and Sikar in Rajasthan; Chengalpattu-MGR in Tamil Nadu; and Maharajganj in Uttar Pradesh.

In 1991, the gap between rural and urban sex ratio became negligible in these districts. This is related to rapid fall in rural female mortality rates due to better socio-economic conditions, increased nutrition and economic conditions better for females, which caused improved fertility and mortality rates and family migration to urban areas. Perhaps the highly industrialized and urbanized cities of India are in the process of feminization (United Nations, 1980).

The districts in Kerala and Tamil Nadu are experiencing emigration and out-migration on a large scale. Largely this migration is male-selective. Not only this, Kerala is the only state in the country which has experienced net out-migration to the Gulf even from its towns (National Institute of Urban Affairs, 1988). The out-migration, in general, was the result of acute population pressure upon the limited resources of the state. Besides, improvement in levels of female emancipation as found in literacy levels, the sex ratio in Kerala is in line with developed countries, because matrilineal society is typical of this region.

In the northern half of Karnataka, eastern parts of Maharashtra alongwith adjacent districts of Andhra Pradesh also have low differential index. In this area, there is male-selective out-migration from both rural and urban areas. The migration here is generated by the push of the area under the increasing stress of population upon the resources of the concerned districts. A large part of this area falls in the rain-shadow zone of the western Ghats and recorded low to moderate growth of population.

Other districts belonging to this category fall in the tribal areas of Gujarat and adjacent districts of Madhya Pradesh which too recorded low rural-urban differential index. This region has been experiencing some out-migration, particularly of males, due to unfavourable population-resource relationship and limited development activity in the region. It is worth mentioning, here, that 40 to 60 per cent of the population in some of the districts belongs to the scheduled tribes. Parts of Rajasthan, south and western Haryana and north, north-western and southern Punjab, which fall in this belt of low rural-urban differential index are recording increase in sex ratio. In most of these districts, growth rate is relatively high in urban areas. Migration to urban areas is in the form of family-migration for the purpose of employment and education.

Thus, the shift in the form of migration, availability of health and medical facilities, improvement in drinking water and sanitation have reduced the rural-urban differential to a great extent.

*2. Areas with Urban Sex Ratio Higher than Rural*

A total of 103 districts have the urban sex ratio higher than the rural. These districts are found in east coastal plains, a few southern districts of Kerala, Gujarat, Tripura, Mizoram, Punjab and Haryana Plain, Upper Ganga plain, and Bundelkhand region. The highest differential index in this category is found in the union territory of Chandigarh (–0.042), where rural sex ratio is 632 and urban sex ratio is 810. In the districts belonging to this category, the feminisation of rural-urban migration streams is most important. In the districts of east coastal region, birth rates are low, but rest of the districts in this category are having average to high birth rates. The fall in female mortality rates in urban areas owing to better economic, health and sanitary conditions is another cause. Similarly, the death rates are below national average in east coastal region, but in all the other areas of this category it is similar to or above the national average. Infant mortality rates are above national average in all the regions except a few districts of Punjab and Tamil Nadu.

With expansion of transport and communication network, raised level of literacy, improved health and medical facilities, general awareness, improvement in level of status of women with feminization in migration streams have made the sex ratio of urban areas higher, even to cross the rural sex ratio. All these facilities have also reduced the gap between rural and urban sex ratio and this gap is continuously decreasing and the rural-urban differential is also becoming minimal.

## CONCLUDING REMARKS

1. Right from the beginning of the census operations, the sex ratio in India has been adverse to women not only in rural areas but also in urban counterparts. However, urban areas were characterised with excessive deficiency of women resulting into more rural-urban

differentials. These rural-urban differentials in sex ratio in India were largely the product of male-selectivity in rural-urban migration which, in turn, was the result of high cost of living and problem of housing for families in urban centres.

2. The rural-urban differential in sex ratio is declining continuously especially after 1961 mainly because of increasing urban sex ratio and decreasing rural sex ratio. The decrease in rural sex ratio from 963 in 1961 to 939 in 1991 can be explained in terms of faster fall in male mortality rate than female mortality rate, family out-migration and commuting from the surrounding rural areas because of the rapid development of transport and communication. The increase in urban sex ratio from 845 in 1961 to 894 in 1991 is a result of improvement in level of status of woman, feminization of migration streams, and better health and medical facilities bringing down the female mortally rates in urban areas.
3. It can be inferred from trends that male-selective migration now-a-days does not remain crucial in the circumstances. Besides, the factors of feminization of cities, commuting and family migration are playing an important role in reducing rural-urban differentials in sex ratio.
4. Spatially speaking, there are wide regional variations in rural–urban differentials and the maximum differential is found in Nagaland (.028), whereas it is minimum in Haryana (0.001). However, these regional disparities in differential index of sex ratio become more revealing and meaningful when examined at district level. About 77 per cent districts are characterized by higher rural sex ratio than the urban, whereas the remaining 23 per cent districts have higher urban sex ratio than the rural. The rural sex ratio higher than urban is the characteristic of north-western Himalayan districts, north-eastern hilly districts and the districts falling in middle and lower Ganga plain, Orissa Highland region, Chhota Nagpur region, Chhattisgarh region and Punjab-Haryana plain. The higher rural sex ratio than the urban in these areas is mainly because of male-selectivity in rural-urban migration, high female mortality rate, low level of status of women and dominance of males in a patriarchal society.

   By contrast, a higher urban sex-ratio than rural is typical of eastern half of Andhra Pradesh, upper Ganga plain, major parts of Haryana and adjoining districts of Punjab and a few districts scattered in Gujarat, Kerala, Maharashtra, Tamil Nadu and in southern parts of eastern hill states. Feminisation of rural-urban migration streams, decreasing female mortality rates, greater longevity of urban females and better medical facilities in urban areas are some of the reasons.

5. The resultant high rural-urban differential because of higher rural sex ratio than the urban is the characteristic of those areas which are dominated by patriarchal society, experience male-selective out-migration, high female mortality rate, high incidence of masculinity at birth and attributed with very low level of status of women. A total number of 104 districts experience high rural-urban differential index (0.011 and above). In the Himalayan region of Uttar Pradesh, the district of Tehri Garhwal has the highest rural-urban differential index value (0.103) and is followed by Chamoli (0.076), Almora (0.052), Uttar Kashi (0.046), and Pithoragarh (0.032). The other notable districts attributed with high rural-urban differential index are Sonbhadra (0.022), Pratapgarh (0.014) and Azamgarh (0.012) in Uttar Pradesh; Hazaribagh (0.023), Dhanbad (0.018), Giridih (0.018) and Paschimi Singhbhum (0.016) in Bihar; Howrah (0.017), Barddhaman (0.014) and Hugli (0.012) in West Bengal and the north-eastern hilly districts of Assam, Arunachal Pradesh, Nagaland, Sikkim and Meghalaya.

   On the contrary, a total of 123 districts are characterized with low rural-urban differential in sex ratio (0.004 and below). These constitute one broad belt running through the sub-continent from north of Rajasthan plain, most of Gujarat region, western half of central India, Malwa region, Maharashtra, northern part of Karnataka plateau, north-western Andhra plateau, Tamil Nadu upland, south Sahyadri, a few scattered districts of middle and lower Ganga plain, and Meghalaya-Mikir region. The notable districts with maximum rural-urban differential (0.004) are Mahbubnagar, Rangareddi, Adilabad, Karimnagar and Nalgonda in Andhra Pradesh; Karimganj in Assam; Aurangabad and Munger in Bihar; Jamnagar, Amreli, Sabar Kantha, Mehsana and Ahmedabad in Gujarat; Sirmaur in Himachal Pradesh; Mandya, Raichur and Shimoga in Karnataka; Sangli, Jalna and Yavatmal in Maharashtra; Dewas and Raisen in Madhya Pradesh; Ganganagar, Jaipur and Sikar in Rajasthan; and Chengalpattu-MGR in Tamil Nadu; and Maharajganj in Uttar Pradesh.

   The low rural-urban differential in sex ratio is mainly because of rapid fall in rural female mortality rates due to better socio-economic conditions and improved health and medical facilities, family migration to urban areas, male-selective emigration and out-migration on a large scale and prevalence of matrilineal society.

6. The rural-urban differential in sex-ratio correlated negatively with rural female mortality rates, road density and positively with urban female mortality, rural male mortality and rural female literacy rate. Thus, improvement in health care delivery system and thrust on female education including improvement in their status shall go a long way in reducing rural-urban differential in sex ratio.
7. One redeeming feature of sex-composition of India's population is that the regional disparity has got squeezed over time. In 1901, the urban sex-ratio's coefficient of variability (65.37) was much higher than rural (31.46) implying that urban sex ratio had a greater variation and inconsistency. However, in 1991 not only both the areas displayed a decline in disparity, coefficient of variability being 7.81 in rural and 8.70 in the urban areas, but a tremendous decline in disparity within urban areas was noticeable.
8. In fine, family migration as a result of increased social approval for out-of-home female mobility, large number of avenues for females towards nuclear families, improved mortality rates, feminization of cities, commuting, index of relative advancement of society in terms of housing facilities, finance and culture in urban areas indicate a healthy trend of minimizing the rural-urban differential in sex ratio in the country.

# 4

# LITERACY

Literacy greatly expands the range of human potentialities and is a worthwhile goal in its own right. Literacy is also an important driving force behind economic and social development, and it is a powerful influence that tends to reduce fertility and, therefore, helps to ameliorate India's pressing population problem (Sharma & Retherford, 1993).

Literacy and education are reasonably good indicators of development in a society. Spread and diffusion of literacy is generally associated with essential traits of today's civilization such as modernization, urbanization, industrialization, communication and commerce. It forms an important input in the overall development of individuals enabling them to comprehend their social, political and cultural environment better and respond to it appropriately. Higher levels of education and literacy lead to a greater awareness and also contributes in improvement of economic conditions. It acts as a catalyst for social upliftment enhancing the returns on investments made in almost every aspect of development effort, be it population control, health, hygiene, environmental degradation control, empowerment of women and weaker sections of the society. Improved levels of literacy also are pre-requisites for acquiring various skills (Banthia, 2001).

Literacy is essential for eradicating poverty and mental isolation, for cultivating peaceful and friendly international relations and for permitting the free play of democratic processes. Illiteracy, on the other hand, takes away from man his dignity, perpetuates ignorance, poverty and mental isolation, deters peaceful and friendly international relations and free democratic processes and hampers social advancement, economic growth and political maturity. Above all, literacy influences other such attributes of population as fertility, mortality, sex ratio, mobility and occupation, etc. Trends of literacy are considered an index of the pace at which the socio-economic transformation of a society is taking place.

Thus, a study of rural-urban differential in literacy in a region provides an insight into occupational structure, economy, stage of technological advancement, urbanization, modernization and policies of the government.

The Third World countries are still characterized by mass illiteracy, while the Developed Nations have reached the final stage of the literacy transition with almost universal literacy. The Developing countries of the world, of which India is a part, are characterized not only by low literacy rates but also by a great disparity in the literacy between urban and rural populations, between males and females and between the young and the aged, a disparity in consonance with differences in necessity, propensity and opportunity to become literate (Krishan and Shyam, 1978). A considerable growth has taken place in literacy during twentieth century, but it has not been satisfactory. It is, however, well known that this progress is mainly concentrated in the urban areas, while the vast rural areas are far behind. This, in turn, gives rise to rural-urban differential in literacy. According to 1981 census, only 36.09 per cent rural population was literate in comparison to 67.34 per cent urban literate population. However, these percentages increased to 44.69 and 73.08 per cent respectively for rural and urban areas in 1991, although there exists a wide gap between the two.

Similarly, the rural-urban differential in the country also vary from one state to another. In 1991, rural-urban differential in literacy rates was 28.47 per cent for the country as a whole. This differential was lowest in Kerala (3.35 per cent) followed by Lakshadweep (5.10 per cent) and Goa (7.79 per cent). On the other hand, the differential was highest in Dadra and Nagar Haveli (41.44 per cent) followed by Meghalaya (40.69 per cent), Rajasthan (34.96 per cent) and Madhya Pradesh (34.94 per cent) among all the states and union territories. These rural-urban differences in literacy rates are usually related to the regional differences in historical background, social composition, degree of urbanization, level of agricultural/industrial development, etc.

Literacy is a powerful instrument of socio-economic advancement of an area. Despite this fact, analysis of literacy has not received adequate attention of the geographers, particularly in the West. Lack of interest of western geographers in this attribute of population may be due to the ubiquitously high literacy rates prevailing in the West (Chandna, 2000).

However, in India a substantial literature on literacy aspects has been developed, but most of the studies have been conducted on patterns and trends in literacy either at national or at regional level. The studies having their focus on the differentials in literacy by sex, residence, and age are only few to count. The notable contributions at regional level are that of Ram (1981), Mathur (1982), Usha Rao (1981), Sharma (1985), and Goel (1994) who have studied the literacy differentials in Punjab, Uttar Pradesh, Karnataka, Assam, and Uttar Pradesh respectively. At national level, only a few scholars, notably Krishan and Shyam (1978), Sopher (1980), Sagar (1990) and Sangwan (1999) have made valuable contributions to find out the rural-urban differentials in literacy particularly at district level for the entire country. The present study has endeavoured, therefore, to describe and interpret the trends and regional aspects of rural-urban differentials in literacy rates.

## India: Rural-Urban Differentials in Literacy, 1991

Rural-urban differentials are essentially a function of the differential rates of change occurring in towns and villages. Literacy, like other innovations, originates in urban places and diffuses subsequently into the countryside; the process of literacy begins in the town and trickles down to the village. The degree of urban influence and the intensity of rural-urban interaction are evidently the two major factors involved in the reduction of disparities between rural and urban literacy rates (Krishan and Shyam, 1978).

In 1991, while 73.08 per cent of urban population in India was literate, the corresponding figure for rural population was only 44.69 per cent, implying wide disparity in rural and urban literacy rates. This rural-urban disparity was sharper among females than among males. The female literacy in rural areas of India was only 30.62 per cent, while in urban areas 64.05 per cent of the females were literate. By comparison, the male literacy rates in rural and urban areas were 57.87 per cent and 81.09 per cent, respectively (Table 4.1).

**Table 4.1:** India*: Literacy Rate and Differential Index by Sex and Rural-Urban Residence, 1991

| *Person/Male/Female/ Differential Index* | *Literacy Rate (Per Cent)* | | | *Rural-Urban Differential Index* |
|---|---|---|---|---|
| | *Total* | *Urban* | *Rural* | |
| Persons | 52.21 | 73.08 | 44.69 | 0.3013 |
| Males | 64.13 | 81.09 | 57.87 | 0.2459 |
| Females | 39.29 | 64.05 | 30.62 | 0.4160 |
| Male-Female Differential Index | 0.2857 | 0.1606 | 0.3526 | |

*Source*: Computed from, Census of India (1991), *Final Population Totals: Brief Analysis of Primary Census Abstract*, Paper 2 of 1992, Series-I, India, Table 6, pp. 210-211.

* Excludes Jammu & Kashmir where census was not held in 1991.

These rural-urban differentials in literacy rates are associated with a number of factors. Firstly, the urban occupations require greater skills and hence, need literate persons. Secondly, urban places are far better equipped with educational facilities. Thirdly, the need to be educated is more in urban areas than in the countryside. Fourthly, urban population is socially more awakened and economically more capable of imparting education to their children. Fifthly, females are not denied the opportunities of education in urban places as is the case in many rural areas. Lastly, many literate rural persons migrate to urban places in search of jobs as a result of which the number of literates in urban areas increases at the cost of rural areas. (Krishan and Chandna, 1974).

The differences in rural-urban literacy were also associated with many histo-political factors—particularly in the pre-Independence period. Britishers were more concerned with the urban areas and had paid little attention for the development of welfare activities in rural areas (Ojha, 1966). In post-Independence period, some progress has been made in propagating literacy even in the countryside. But, in rural areas, the parents were rigid not to send their children to school, when they could be helping hands. In many cases they were too poor to meet the expenses of schooling. As Naik (1978) pointed out that the existing system of full time formal education suites only those who can afford to feed, clothe and send their children to school on a whole-time basis. So, before 1951, literacy was a rare privilege in rural areas. The literacy rates were relatively high in towns and cities, which stood as islands in the ocean of illiteracy in the Indian sub-continent (Gosal, 1967). After Independence, the improvement in standards of living, improvement in technology and means of communication, diversification of economy, constructive policies for the uplift of the down-trodden, increasing degree of rural-urban interaction and increasing social and economic functional value of education in rural areas are responsible for narrowing down the rural-urban disparity index significantly in the country (Sagar, 1990). It is worth mentioning here that about 93 per cent of the rural population in 1978 had the primary school facilities either in their own village or within a distance of one kilometre (Raza and Aggarwal, 1986).

## India: Trend of Rural-Urban Differentials in Literacy, 1951-1991

The analysis of literacy differential by residence has not been possible for the pre-Independence period because of the non-availability of census data for this period. Hence, the data on growth of literacy have been provided for the post-Independence period from 1951 to 1991. It may be noted that state-wise literacy rates for 1951, 1961 and 1971 relate to population aged 5 years and above. In the 1991 census, since the question on literacy was conversed only for population aged seven years and above, therefore, for the present purpose of trends and spatial patterns of literacy, the estimated population of 1981 and census population of 1991, aged seven years and above is taken into account to calculate literacy rates. In view of constraints of data strict comparison with earlier census decades cannot be made.

It can be observed that literacy rate improved from 18.33 per cent in 1951 to 34.45 per cent in 1971 and rose further to 52.21 per cent in 1991. Similarly, the literacy rate for urban areas which was 39.70 per cent in 1951 rose to 52.44 per cent in 1971 and then increased further to 73.08 per cent in 1991. In rural areas, the literacy rate which was only 14.01 per cent in 1951 increased to 23.74 per cent in 1971 and further improved to 44.69 per cent in 1991 (Table 4.2 and Fig. 4.1).

**Table 4.2:** India: Literacy Rate, Differential Index and Disparity Ratio by Rural-Urban Residence, 1951-91

| *Census Year* | *Literacy Rate (Per cent)* | | | *Rural-Urban Differential Index* | *Rural-Urban Disparity Ratio* |
|---|---|---|---|---|---|
| | *Total* | *Urban* | *Rural* | | |
| 1951 | 18.33 | 39.70 | 14.01 | 0.5169 | 1:2.83 |
| 1961 | 28.31 | 46.94 | 19.00 | 0.4656 | 1:2.47 |
| 1971 | 34.45 | 52.44 | 23.74 | 0.4214 | 1:2.21 |
| 1981 | 43.67 | 57.40 | 29.65 | 0.3641 | 1:1.94 |
| 1991 | 52.21 | 73.08 | 44.69 | 0.3013 | 1:1.64 |

*Sources*: Computed from,

(i) UNESCO (1982), *Population of India*, ESCAP, Country Monograph, Series No. 10, Table 220, p. 322.

(ii) Census of India (1991), *Final Population Totals: Brief Analysis of Primary Census Abstract*, Paper 2 of 1992, Series-I, India, Statement 14, p. 51.

(iii) Jolly, K.G. (1991), "Strategies to Attain Universal Literacy in India by 2001", *Demography India*, Vol. 20, No. 1, Table 3, p. 144.

The rural-urban differential index is decreasing continuously over the time since 1951, when it was sharper (0.5169), as there was only one rural literate for nearly every three urban literates (1:2.83). This disparity ratio declined from 2.83 in 1951 to 1.64 in 1991. The rural literacy had, nonetheless, registered a gradual increase from 14.01 per cent in 1951 to 44.69 per cent in 1991 and the differential index narrowed down gradually from 0.5169 in 1951 to 0.3013 in 1991.

The narrowing down of the rural-urban differential index as well as disparity ratio was associated with increasing degree of rural-urban interaction, increasing socio-economic functional value of education in the countryside, improving standards of living, and increasing facilities for schooling in the countryside (Sagar, 1990).

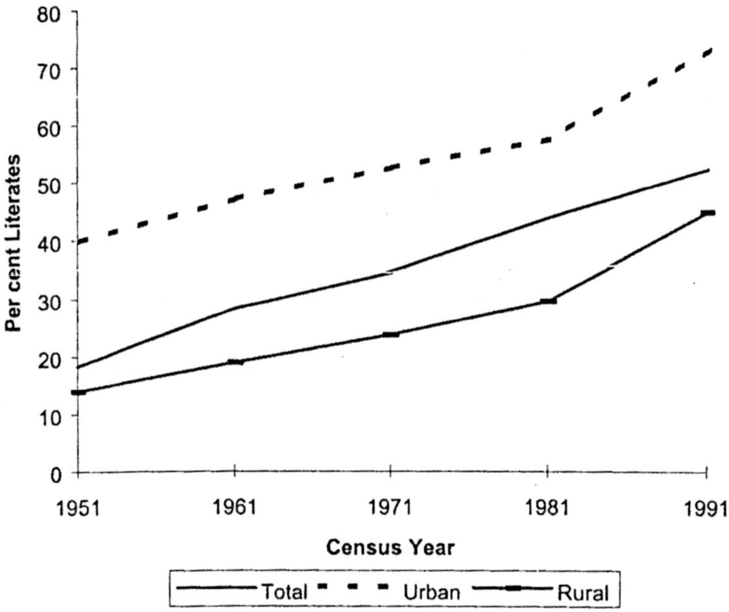


**Fig. 4.1:** India: Literacy Rate by Rural-Urban Residence, 1951-91

Despite an appreciable increase in the proportionate share of literate population both in rural and urban areas, the illiterate population in absolute numbers continues to register an increasing trend. The number of illiterates increased from 302 million in 1981 to 320 million in 1991. Whereas in urban areas they have grown from 42.5 million to about 48 million, in rural areas, the increase is by 12 million from 260 million to 272 million (Table 4.3).

### India: Trend of Rural-Urban Differentials in Literacy by States, 1981-91

The literacy rates in both the rural and urban areas have increased

**Table 4.3**: India: Distribution of Literates and Illiterates among Population Aged 7 Years and Above by Sex and Area, 1981 and 1991.

*(Number in million persons)*

| *Year/Area* | *Literate* | | | *Illiterate* | | |
|---|---|---|---|---|---|---|
| | *Persons* | *Males* | *Females* | *Persons* | *Males* | *Females* |
| 1981* | | | | | | |
| All Areas | 234.15 | 157.08 | 77.07 | 302.06 | 120.96 | 181.10 |
| | (43.6) | (56.5) | (29.8) | (56.4) | (43.5) | (70.2) |
| Rural Areas | 146.60 | 103.51 | 43.09 | 259.59 | 104.80 | 154.79 |
| | (36.1) | (49.7) | (21.8) | (63.6) | (50.3) | (78.2) |
| Urban Areas | 87.55 | 53.57 | 33.98 | 42.47 | 16.16 | 26.31 |
| | (67.3) | (76.8) | (56.4) | (32.7) | (23.2) | (43.6) |
| 1991** | | | | | | |
| All Areas | 349.76 | 223.70 | 126.06 | 320.41 | 124.77 | 195.64 |
| | (52.2) | (64.2) | (39.2) | (47.8) | (35.8) | (60.8) |
| Rural Areas | 218.32 | 146.38 | 71.94 | 271.81 | 106.69 | 165.12 |
| | (44.5) | (57.8) | (30.3) | (55.5) | (42.2) | (69.7) |
| Urban Areas | 131.44 | 77.32 | 54.12 | 48.60 | 18.08 | 30.52 |
| | (73.1) | (81.0) | (63.9) | (26.9) | (19.0) | (36.1) |

*Source*: Census of India (1991), *Final Population Totals: Brief Analysis of Primary Census Abstract*, Paper 2 of 1992, Series-I, India, Statement 14, p. 51.

* Excludes Assam where census was not held in 1981.

** Excludes Jammu & Kashmir where census was not held in 1991.

*Note*: Figures in parentheses indicate percentage to the corresponding total population (literates plus illiterates).

continuously since Independence resulting in decline of rural-urban differentials in whole of the country except in the state of Mizoram and union territory of Dadra and Nagar Haveli.

The decline is, however, not uniform every where (Map 4.1 and Table 4.4) and for the purposes of explanation of this trend between 1981-1991, the states have been divided in four categories.

1. Areas of high decline of rural-urban differential.
2. Areas of moderate decline of rural-urban differential.
3. Areas of low decline of rural-urban differential.
4. Areas of increased rural-urban differential in 1991.

*1. Areas of High Decline of Rural-Urban Differential*

The maximum decrease in rural-urban differential is in the state of Tripura (–10.57 per cent). Here, the rural literacy was 45.78 per cent in 1981 and increased to 56.08 per cent in 1991 but the urban literacy rate

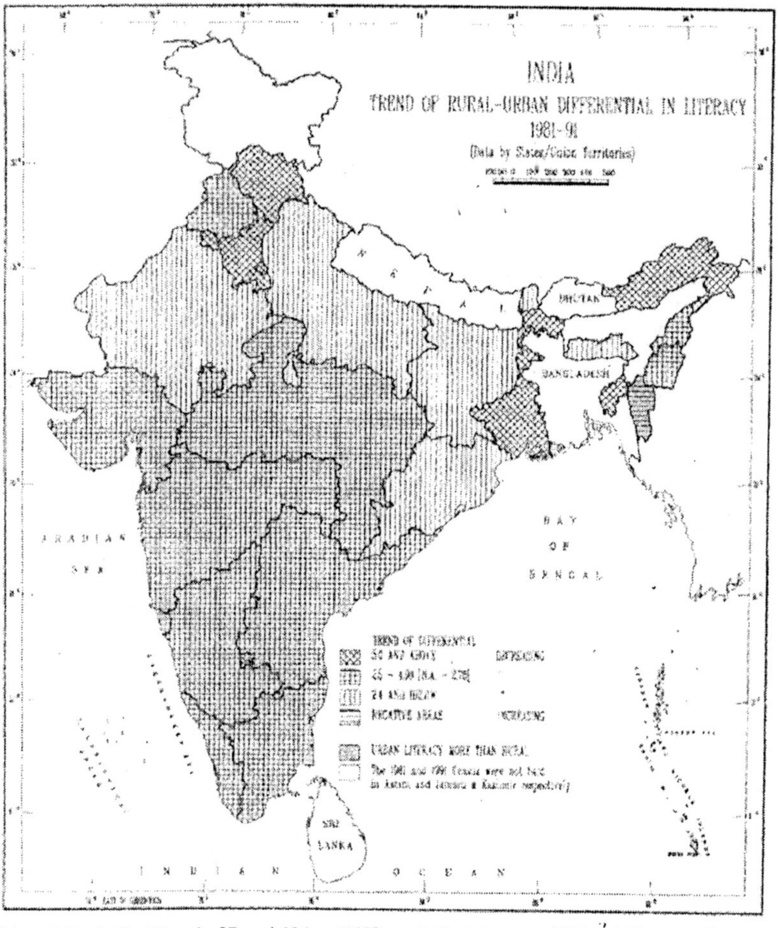


**Map 4.1:** India: Trend of Rural-Urban Differential in Literacy, 1981-91 (Data by States / Union Territories)

decreased from 83.36 in 1981 to 83.09 in 1991. The other states and union territories which fall in this category are Andaman and Nicobar Islands (–6.63 per cent), Arunachal Pradesh (–6.37 per cent), Delhi (–5.90 per cent), Haryana (–5.76 per cent), West Bengal (–5.73 per cent) and Himachal Pradesh (–5.60 per cent). In all these states and union territories, the growth of rural literacy rates was much more than the urban. In rural areas also, female literacy rates increased steadily. The prejudice against female education and their employment outside the home (Davis, 1951), however, are disappearing rather rapidly in recent years.

**Table 4.4**: India: Trend of Rural-Urban Differentials in Literacy Rates, 1981-91

| *Country/State/ Union Territory* | *Literacy Rate (Per cent), 1991* | | | *Rural-Urban Differential* | | *Trend of Differential (1981 – 91)* |
|---|---|---|---|---|---|---|
| | *Total* | *Rural* | *Urban* | *1991* | *1981* | |
| **INDIA*** | **52.19** | **44.54** | **73.01** | **28.47** | **31.25** | **–2.78** |
| *States* | | | | | | |
| Tripura | 60.44 | 56.08 | 83.09 | 27.01 | 37.58 | –10.57 |
| Arunachal Pradesh | 41.59 | 37.02 | 71.59 | 34.57 | 40.94 | –6.37 |
| Haryana | 55.85 | 49.85 | 73.66 | 23.81 | 29.57 | –5.76 |
| West Bengal | 57.70 | 50.50 | 75.27 | 24.77 | 30.50 | –5.73 |
| Himachal Pradesh | 63.86 | 61.86 | 84.17 | 23.31 | 28.91 | –5.60 |
| Maharashtra | 64.87 | 55.52 | 79.20 | 23.68 | 28.64 | –4.96 |
| Goa | 75.51 | 72.31 | 80.10 | 7.29 | 12.70 | –4.91 |
| Tamil Nadu | 62.66 | 54.59 | 77.99 | 23.40 | 28.25 | –4.85 |
| Nagaland | 61.65 | 57.23 | 83.10 | 25.87 | 30.51 | –4.64 |
| Gujarat | 61.29 | 53.09 | 76.54 | 23.45 | 27.43 | –3.98 |
| Punjab | 58.51 | 52.77 | 72.08 | 19.31 | 23.23 | –3.92 |
| Madhya Pradesh | 44.20 | 35.87 | 70.81 | 34.94 | 38.25 | –3.31 |
| Kerala | 89.81 | 88.92 | 92.25 | 3.35 | 6.60 | –3.25 |
| Manipur | 59.89 | 55.79 | 70.53 | 14.74 | 17.58 | –2.84 |
| Karnataka | 56.04 | 47.69 | 74.20 | 26.51 | 29.28 | –2.77 |
| Andhra Pradesh | 44.09 | 35.74 | 66.35 | 30.61 | 33.15 | –2.54 |
| Uttar Pradesh | 41.60 | 36.66 | 61.00 | 24.34 | 26.34 | –2.00 |
| Sikkim | 56.94 | 54.38 | 80.89 | 26.51 | 27.99 | –1.48 |
| Rajasthan | 38.55 | 30.37 | 65.33 | 34.96 | 33.58 | –0.62 |
| Orissa | 49.09 | 45.46 | 71.99 | 26.53 | 27.04 | –0.51 |
| Bihar | 38.48 | 33.83 | 67.89 | 34.06 | 34.07 | –0.01 |
| Meghalaya | 49.10 | 41.05 | 81.74 | 40.69 | 40.70 | –0.01 |
| Mizoram | 82.27 | 72.47 | 93.45 | 20.98 | 20.29 | +0.69 |
| *Union Territories* | | | | | | |
| Andaman and Nicobar Islands | 73.02 | 69.63 | 81.69 | 11.96 | 18.59 | –6.63 |
| Delhi | 75.29 | 66.90 | 76.18 | 9.28 | 15.18 | –5.90 |
| Daman & Diu | 71.20 | 61.55 | 81.61 | 20.06 | 24.87 | –4.81 |
| Pondicherry | 74.74 | 65.36 | 79.88 | 14.52 | 17.08 | –2.56 |
| Chandigarh | 77.81 | 59.12 | 79.87 | 20.75 | 22.97 | –2.22 |
| Lakshadweep | 81.78 | 78.89 | 83.99 | 5.10 | 6.29 | –1.19 |
| Dadra & Nagar Haveli | 40.71 | 37.00 | 78.44 | 41.44 | 35.41 | +6.03 |

*Source*: Computed from, Census of India (1991), *Final Population Totals: Brief Analysis of Primary Census Abstract*, Paper 2 of 1992, Statement 20, p. 67, Office of the Registrar General and Census Commissioner, India, New Delhi.

* Excludes Jammu & Kashmir and Assam.

*Note*: States and union territories are arranged in descending order of trend of differential (1981 – 91).

The male-female differential has been narrowing consistently due to faster increase in female literacy than that of males in recent decades. Furthermore, with increasing socio-economic awareness, the literacy among females is increasingly becoming a matrimonial necessity which increases literacy rates among females in rural as well as urban areas. The availability of educational institutions equally for males and females in rural areas is another factor to reduce the rural-urban differential.

*2. Areas of Moderate Decline of Rural-Urban Differential*

This category covers more than half of India, which includes whole of central, south and south-western India. The maximum decline in differential was in the state of Maharashtra (–4.96 per cent). The states which have a decrease in differential above national average (–2.78 per cent) of decline are Goa (–4.91 per cent), Tamil Nadu (–4.85 per cent), Nagaland (–4.64 per cent), Gujarat (–3.98 per cent), Punjab (–3.92 per cent), Madhya Pradesh (–3.31 per cent), Kerala (–3.25 per cent), Manipur (–2.84 per cent) and union territory of Daman and Diu (–4.81 per cent). Karnataka (–2.77 per cent), Andhra Pradesh (–2.54 per cent) and union territory of Pondicherry (–2.56 per cent) display a differential decrease below national average in this category. In Goa, Tamil Nadu, Nagaland and Gujarat, the rural literacy increase is more than double of what it is in urban areas. In rest of the states and union territories also, the growth of literacy is more in rural than in urban areas. In most of the southern states, high literacy rates are prevalent in both rural and urban areas due to colonial impact and existence of Christian missionaries. A higher status is accorded to women in southern states. The female literacy rates are high in south India, because females are free to get educated and get a job for self dependence. The means of communication and transportation are also developed, which made the education facilities accessible for females as well as to rural people. In rural areas of Madhya Pradesh, the literacy rate is very low but it increased a little in 1991 both in rural and urban areas. There exists a wide rural-urban differential in Madhya Pradesh but it decreased moderately. In Gujarat, Nagaland and Punjab, opening of new schools in rural areas has made more and more people educated.

*3. Areas of Low Decline of Rural-Urban Differential*

The areas included in this category are the Upper and Middle Ganga plain, Assam Valley, Meghalaya-Mikir region, Orissa Highland region and Dandakaranya region, Rajasthan plain and Udaipur-Gwalior region. The maximum decrease of differential in this category is in the union territory of Chandigarh, where the rural-urban differential decreased to –2.22 per cent between 1981-91. The rural-urban differential was 22.97 per cent in 1981 and 20.75 per cent in 1991. The other states and union territories which come in this category are Uttar Pradesh (–2.00 per cent), Sikkim (–1.48 per cent), Lakshadweep (–1.19 per cent), Rajasthan (–0.62 per cent), Orissa (–0.51 per cent), Bihar (–0.01 per cent), and Meghalaya (–0.01 per cent). In all these states and union territories, the rural as well as urban literacy rates increased at somewhat similar rate. In this category, three states of Uttar Pradesh, Rajasthan and Bihar belong to *BIMARU* states. These states have a large proportion of the country's population. Resources are not equal to the demand of people. There is lack of educational facilities in all these states and union territories because of backwardness and weak economic base. Female literacy is far less than that of males and rural literacy is low than the urban. Most of the population is engaged in primary activities so they take their family members as economic assets. They do not send their children to schools as they are utilized as a contributory labour for their parents in their productive activities.

*4. Areas of Increased Rural-Urban Differential in 1991*

Only two states/union territories *viz.* Mizoram with an increase of +0.69 per cent and Dadra and Nagar Haveli with an increase of +6.03 per cent points fall in this category. In Mizoram, the rural-urban differential in literacy increased from 20.29 per cent in 1981 to 20.98 per cent in 1991, because the rate of literacy increase was more in urban (3.99 per cent) than in rural (3.30 per cent) areas, which was true for urban areas in the past. Similarly, in Dadra and Nagar Haveli, the impact of Christian missionaries can be seen more in urban than in the rural areas. The rural-urban differential in 1981 was 35.41 per cent and is 41.44 per cent in 1991, because the increase in literacy rate is 6.71 per cent in rural areas and is just double *i.e.* 12.74 per cent in urban areas. The literacy rates for females are also high in urban as compared to the rural areas.

Thus, rural-urban differential in literacy emanates from the differences in the type of economy, degree of concentration of educational institutions, status granted to the females, and migratory patterns of the two areas. The rural-urban differentials in literacy have been narrowing down largely due to the opening up of a large number of schools in the countryside and also due to the increasing degree of socio-economic awakening among the rural masses. Attempts to diversify the economy of rural areas in

India with a view to absorbing surplus farm labour in the countryside itself have also stimulated rural males to seek education more willingly.

## India: Spatial Patterns of Rural-Urban Differentials in Literacy, 1991

According to the Census of India (1991), the rural-urban differential index of literacy for the country is 0.3013 (Table 4.5). Rajasthan with subsistence

**Table 4.5**: India: Rural-Urban Differential Indices of Literacy, 1991

| *Country/State/Union Territory* | *Differential Index* |
|---|---|
| **India*** | **0.3013** |
| *States* | |
| Rajasthan | 0.4329 |
| Meghalaya | 0.4276 |
| Bihar | 0.4021 |
| Madhya Pradesh | 0.3993 |
| Arunachal Pradesh | 0.3899 |
| Andhra Pradesh | 0.3583 |
| Assam | 0.3034 |
| Uttar Pradesh | 0.2912 |
| Orissa | 0.2814 |
| Karnataka | 0.2750 |
| Tripura | 0.2610 |
| Sikkim | 0.2570 |
| West Bengal | 0.2520 |
| Nagaland | 0.2488 |
| Haryana | 0.2446 |
| Gujarat | 0.2344 |
| Maharashtra | 0.2320 |
| Tamil Nadu | 0.2311 |
| Himachal Pradesh | 0.2125 |
| Punjab | 0.1965 |
| Mizoram | 0.1885 |
| Manipur | 0.1486 |
| Goa | 0.0718 |
| Kerala | 0.0292 |
| *Union Territories* | |
| Dadra & Nagar Haveli | 0.4537 |
| Daman & Diu | 0.3943 |
| Lakshadweep | 0.3450 |
| Chandigarh | 0.1998 |
| Pondicherry | 0.1367 |
| Andaman & Nicobar Islands | 0.1106 |
| Delhi | 0.0878 |

*Source*: Computed from, Census of India (1991), *Final Population Totals: Brief Analysis of Primary Census Abstract*, Paper 2 of 1992, Statement 20, p. 67, Office of the Registrar General and Census Commissioner, India, New Delhi

* Excludes Jammu & Kashmir where census was not held in 1991.

*Note*: States and union territories are arranged in descending order of differential index, 1991.

nature of agricultural economy, low degree of urbanization, strong prejudices against female education and their mobility outside home and the last but not the least the high ratio of the socially and economically backward sections of scheduled castes and non-Christian tribes displayed highest rural-urban differential index (0.4329). On the other hand, the minimum rural-urban differential index in Kerala (0.0292) is due to early start of education, highly diversified nature of rural economy, high percentage of Christian population and high proportion of non-agricultural workers. Not only this, the role played by the Christian missionaries and high degree of exposure to West European countries is also important. This exposure to West European countries had contributed positively to the propagation of education among the rural masses.

Among the union territories, the highest rural-urban differential index of 0.4537 is in Dadra and Nagar Haveli, because most of the population in rural areas is engaged in agricultural activities. The female literacy of 23.30 per cent in rural areas is also below national average (30.62 per cent), while the urban female literacy rate (68.42 per cent) is well above national average (64.05 per cent). The minimum rural-urban differential in Delhi is explained by more than two-fifth of population in rural areas engaged in non-agricultural activities, availability of schooling facility and a dense network of transport lines.

When rural-urban differential index was correlated with some indicators for states and union territories of India (Table 4.6), it was observed that the

**Table 4.6**: India: Coefficients of Correlation of Rural-Urban Differentials in Literacy, 1991

| *Indicator* | *Coefficient of Correlation* |
|---|---|
| Rural literacy rate | –0.7605 |
| Rural female literacy rate | –0.7228 |
| Proportion of rural population in other services | –0.5512 |
| Proportion of non-agricultural workers in rural areas | –0.5077 |
| Level of urbanization | –0.4992 |
| Per capita income | –0.4611 |
| Rural Christian population | –0.2271 |
| Rural Muslim population | +0.0206 |
| Percentage of scheduled castes and scheduled tribes population to urban population | +0.3391 |
| Proportion of scheduled castes and scheduled tribes population to total population | +0.4626 |

*Source*: Computed from, Publications made by Census of India (1991) and Economic Intelligence Service (1991, 1993, 1994, 1997).

rural-urban literacy differential finds a strong negative correlation with rural literacy rate, rural female literacy rate, proportion of rural population in other services, proportion of non-agricultural workers in rural areas, level of urbanization, per capita income and rural Christian population.

It is observed that the differential index is low in all those areas that have high literacy rates and high female literacy rates in rural areas and the female literacy rates are high in areas where the females enjoy high social status. Similarly, it is also low in areas where the percentage of rural population in other services is more than in agricultural activities. Percentage of non-agricultural workers to total workers in rural areas also affect the rural-urban differential. As this percentage in rural areas increases, the rural-urban differential decreases. These apart, the rural-urban differential is also low in areas having higher concentration of urban population to total population and rural Christian population.

On the other hand, the rural-urban differential is positively correlated (Table 4.6) with the rural Muslim population and percentage of scheduled caste and scheduled tribe population to urban population as well as total population. As Muslim population in rural areas and scheduled caste and scheduled tribe population in urban areas increases, the rural-urban differential also increases. Apart from these, there are a few other factors which influence the differential (but the rural and urban data separately for these indicators are not available). These are per capita income, road density, number of schools and the level of socio-economic development. As the intensity of these factors in rural areas increases, the rural-urban differential decreases.

The rural-urban differentials become more pronounced when examined at district level. In 436 districts, where both the rural and urban populations exist, it can be observed that the urban literacy rates are higher (except in two districts of Kerala *i.e.* Alappuzha and Kollam where rural literacy rates are higher than the urban) than literacy rates in rural areas. In these 436 districts, the rural-urban differential index ranges between 0.0020 (lowest) in Kottayam district of Kerala to 0.8632 (highest) in Jhabua district of Madhya Pradesh.

The spatial patterns of rural-urban differentials in literacy rates are not uniform throughout the country (Map 4.2). Keeping in view the national average (0.3013) of rural-urban differential index and to obtain a comprehensive regional picture of the rural-urban differentials in literacy rates in 1991, all the districts of India are grouped into the following categories:

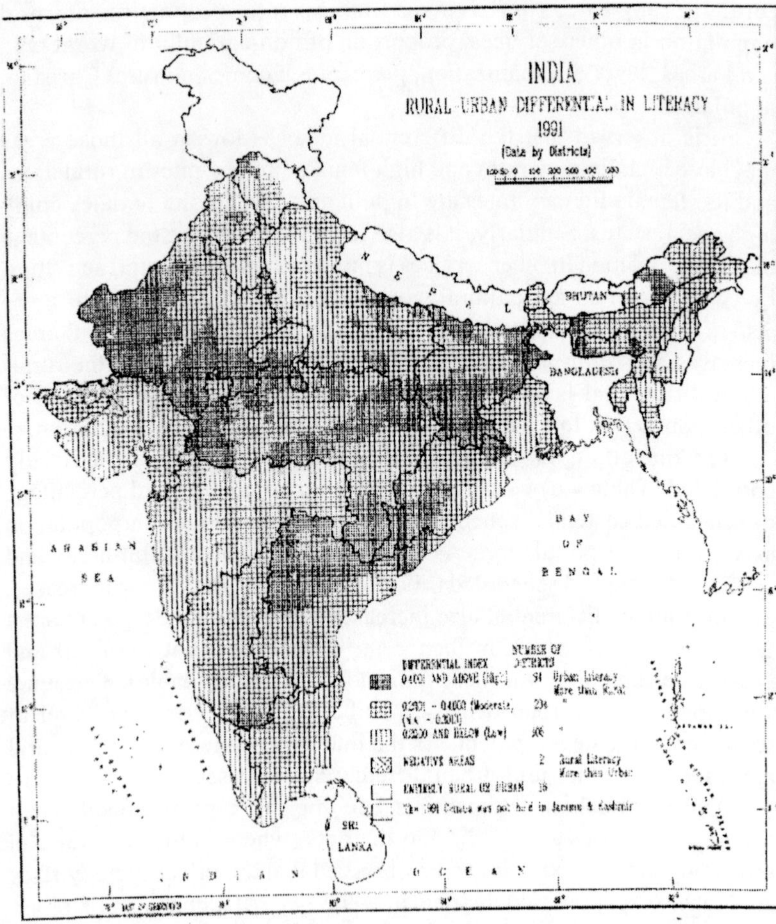


**Map 4.2**: India: Rural-Urban Differential in Literacy, 1991 (Data by Districts)

1. Areas of high rural-urban differential in literacy (0.4001 and above).
2. Areas of moderate rural-urban differential in literacy (0.2001-0.4000).
3. Areas of low rural-urban differential in literacy (0.2000 and below).
4. Areas where the rural literacy rates are more than urban with very low rural-urban differential.

*1. Areas of High Rural-Urban Differential in Literacy (0.4001 and above).*

There are 94 districts where the disparity index values are 0.4000 and above. Out of these 94 districts, 27 districts have very high rural-urban differential index which is more than 0.5000. There are six districts where the rural-urban differential is more than double the national average (0.3013). The areas of high rural-urban differential index are Rajasthan plain, Udaipur-Gwalior region, central part of Maharashtra region, Chhatisgarh region, Chhota Nagpur region, northern part of Lower Ganga plain, Dandakaranya, Andhra Plateau and a few other areas scattered here and there mostly northern half of India. In south India, the district of Mysore in the extreme south of Karnataka Plateau is the only district which is characterized with high rural-urban differential index (0.4227). Most of these areas are Hindi speaking areas of north India. The reasons for high literacy differentials are, low level of urbanization, high concentration of socio-economically backward sections of society, primarily traditional agricultural economy, low incidence of rural-urban interaction, high percentage of child labour in agricultural operations and inadequate educational infrastructure and late start of education in rural areas.

The Jhabua district of Madhya Pradesh has the highest rural-urban differential index value (0.8632) with the lowest rural literacy rate (13.74 per cent) in India. The rural female literacy is very low (6.83 per cent) in this district. In the central parts of this belt, the high disparity in urban and rural literacy is attributable to widespread poverty, low degree of urban-rural interaction, inadequacy of schooling facilities in rural areas and in hilly regions, extremely low level of urbanization, high incidence of unemployment and under-employment, poor health, rapid population growth, high degree of dependency ratio, subsistence level of farming, under-utilisation of resources, meagre industrialization, and high percentage of socially and economically backward sections of society (scheduled castes and non-Christian tribes/Muslims). In the Lower Himalayan Tract or the Terai region, appalling poverty of rural masses, long history of administrative neglect of education in rural areas, backward and subsistence level of farming, huge backlog of rural illiteracy, acute pressure of population on the farm land, low degree of urbanization, the result of which is low level of development of industries and commerce, poor resource base, etc., low functional value of education for rural population, highly restricted female mobility in rural areas, poor administration and high proportion of Muslim and scheduled caste population have produced high literacy differentials. In the Thar desert area of Rajasthan, high rural-urban differential is the outcome of general low level of living, prevalence of feudalistic system, lack of educational institutions particularly in rural areas, relatively low level of rural-urban interaction, low level of social status of women (especially rural) and large scale immigration of illiterate scheduled caste population to work as agricultural labourers (Chandna, 1989). In the highlands of Orissa and adjoining districts of Madhya Pradesh, high literacy differential was associated with abject poverty of the rural population, predominance of primitive cultural values, low degree of social acceptability of modern education, lack of educational institutions in rural areas, scarcity of female teachers in tribal areas, lack of urbanization, long history of administrative neglect and of inaccessibility, and high percentage of non-Christian tribal population.

In peninsular India, high rural-urban literacy differential was recorded in Dandakaranya and Andhra Plateau region. It comprises the districts of Vizianagaram, Visakhapatanam, Mahbubnagar, Rangareddi, Medak, Nizamabad, Adilabad, Warangal, Khammam, Nalgonda of Andhra Pradesh and the adjoining district of Gulbarga of Karnataka. Most of the districts of Andhra Pradesh displayed very high disparity index of over 0.4500. The rural literacy rates were relatively low (less than 30 per cent). In most of these districts, the poor agricultural economy of these districts that demanded the participation of every member of the family in the economic struggle, accounted for high rate of drop-outs in rural areas. The low level of urbanization coupled with the inadequate means of transportation and communication had restricted the rural-urban mobility. Above all, high rate of illiteracy among Muslims and scheduled castes, who had a sizable proportion of population in the countryside, was also responsible for the wide rural-urban disparity in literacy in the region (Sagar, 1990).

Similarly, the high rural-urban literacy differential index was found in the mountainous ranges of western Himalayas. It covered the districts of lower Subansiri (0.4477) and Tirap (0.6837) of Arunachal Pradesh, Dhubri (0.4206) and Kokrajhar (0.4290) of Assam, Mon (0.4384) of Nagaland, Jaintia Hills (0.5837) and West Garo Hills (0.4918) of Meghalaya in eastern Himalayas and Chamba (0.4355) of Himachal Pradesh in western Himalayas. The rural literacy rates ranged from 26.75 per cent in Tirap to 41.39 per cent in Chamba. The literacy rates ranged from 69.36 per cent in Dhubri to 85.43 per cent in Tirap. In all these districts, the urban literacy rates are more than double to that of the rural. In a few districts, it is near to three times more than rural literacy rates. In eastern Himalayas, high literacy differential was the result of late start of education in rural areas, high degree of inaccessibility of educational institutions, small proportion of urban population, low incidence of rural-urban interaction, poor base of agricultural economy, and high percentage of non-Christian tribal population. In the western Himalayas, the district of Chamba also shows high rural-urban literacy differential. Here, the backward agricultural economy, limited rural-urban population, high concentration of scheduled tribe population, more widely scattered population distribution and consequent high cost of running educational institutions (Krishan & Shyam, 1977) and extremely small proportion of urban population (constituting generally literate immigrants) produced high rural-urban disparity in literacy. Similarly, a few districts of Uttar Pradesh, Bihar and West Bengal in the Tarai region also fall in this category. These are Kheri (0.4105), Bahraich (0.4576), Gonda (0.4867), Faizabad (0.4638), Maharajganj (0.4120) and Lucknow (0.4035) of Uttar Pradesh, Pashchmi Champaran (0.4374), Purbi Champaran (0.4560), Sitamarhi (0.4107), Muzaffarpur (0.4586), Darbhanga (0.4200), Araria (0.4622), Purnia (0.5181), Katihar (0.5523) of Bihar and West Dinajpur (0.4963) and Maldah (0.4716) of West Bengal. The high differential index was also understandable in these widely scattered districts.

Thus, the maximum rural-urban differential in literacy rates is found in the areas, where feudal landlords are entrenched economically and socially and where landless labour classes constitute a high percentage of the total population, inaccessible areas having widespread poverty, subsistence nature of economy, rural-urban interaction is low, low level of urbanization, scheduled caste population forms a sizable section of the total population, low proportion of population engaged in tertiary activities, non-Christian scheduled tribes predominate, and where there is high concentration of Muslim population. The great rural-urban differential in literacy suggests that India's modernization is still only skin deep (Gosal, 1979).

### *2. Areas of Moderate Rural-Urban Differential in Literacy (0.2001-0.4000)*

Almost half of India consisting of 234 districts falls in this category of moderate rural-urban differential. These districts are scattered widely in all parts of the country. It covers the transitional zones between the areas of high and low differentials. This category includes southern half and western bordering areas of Punjab, northern half of Haryana, upper half of Marwar and Mewar, southern half of Himachal Pradesh, Tehri Garhwal and Kumaon region, Rohilkhand and other scattered districts of Uttar Pradesh, Magadh region of Bihar, central part of West Bengal, whole of Sikkim, central part of Assam Valley, central part of Meghalaya, eastern-most Arunachal Pradesh and a few districts in Nagaland, Manipur and Mizoram, Orissa Highlands, Chhatisgarh and some central districts of Madhya Pradesh, Kachchh and north-eastern Gujarat, southern half of Vidarbha, a few coastal districts of Maharashtra, Orissa, Andhra Pradesh and Tamil Nadu, almost whole of Karnataka, southern and north-eastern Andhra Pradesh and central and northern parts of Tamil Nadu. In these areas, rural literacy ranged between 19.17 per cent in Rampur district of Uttar Pradesh to 67.49 per cent in Lunglei district of Mizoram among the states.

Diu with 45.04 per cent literacy rate is one of the two districts of the union territory of Daman & Diu which bears moderate rural-urban differential in literacy. In the districts of Gujarat, Maharashtra, West Bengal, Andhra Pradesh, Karnataka and Tamil Nadu, the moderate literacy differential was due to the closeness of these areas to that of high general literacy areas, speedy increase in the level of urbanization, increasing degree of rural-urban interaction, increasing awareness about literacy among rural people and the inland extension of educational facilities from coastal areas. The means of transportation also made educational institutions accessible to rural people to some extent. The rural-urban differential in literacy would have been still lower but for late start in education, in urban-industrial growth and in rural mobility and inheritance of rural mass illiteracy. The northern districts of Bihar and majority of districts in Uttar Pradesh are also having moderate literacy differential because of moderate rural (25 to 50 per cent) and urban (40 to 80 per cent) literacy rates. The presence of age old national link route (Calcutta-Delhi-Amritsar) that brought a lot of socio-economic awakening about the educational value and outside employment, continuous sub-division of districts that had accelerated the rural-urban interaction, construction of new link roads that had increased the rural mobility and the expansion of schooling facilities in rural areas, were the factors responsible for moderate literacy differential (Sagar, 1990).

In the western Himalayan region, Garhwal and Kumaon are the areas of moderate literacy differential. Despite the general socio-economic backwardness, the above-average literacy rates of these areas are associated with massive recruitment of the natives to the armed forces. As a result, not only the personnel of armed forces learn reading and writing but also they appreciate the necessity of sending their children to school (Gosal, 1967). The constant in-migration of retired officials, educationists and various other elite who had contributed a good deal in the establishment of a number of missions, higher educational centres and other government agencies (Siddiqui, 1977) had played a vital role in arresting the rural-urban disparity in literacy.

Similarly, in Punjab plain, which has been an important source of recruitment to armed forces and considerable out-migration and where several private organizations have played an important role in educational expansion, literacy rates are fairly high among both males and females. Moreover, the extension of manufacturing industries and commerce to the rural areas has stimulated the progress of literacy (Gosal, 1967). In the districts of Himachal Pradesh, relatively high per capita income (due to commercialization of horticulture), promotion of tourism, expanding non-agricultural sector, constantly increasing rural mobility, intensive package programme in agricultural sector under India-German collaboration (Bala, 1986), long history of exposure to modern education (Shimla and Solan) and the concerted efforts of the state government for the propagation of education had minimized the rural-urban differential in literacy.

The impact of the capital city of Chandigarh can be visualized on the adjoining districts of Ambala and Patiala, where literacy differentials are moderate and the schooling facilities are expanded to almost all the rural areas. These apart, moderate literacy differential was also typical of areas which had relatively prosperous agricultural economy (Mathura, Agra in Uttar Pradesh, Krishna and East Godavari in Andhra Pradesh), that had rapidly growing urbanization (Karnal of Haryana, Ganjam of Orissa and Darjeeling of West Bengal), and that were relatively more industrialized (Durg in Madhya Pradesh and Dhanbad in Bihar).

Hence, the moderate rural-urban differential in literacy was found in those areas where there are moderate literacy rates of general population. The rural-urban interaction is increasing with the help of improvement in transportation system which increased accessibility between rural and urban areas. The differential is moderate in areas of rapidly growing urbanization and where the rural economy is more diversified. The areas where rural population is socio-economically more aware about benefits of literacy, are also having moderate differential.

*3. Areas of Low Rural-Urban Differential in Literacy (0.2000 and below)*

This category covers 106 districts of India. The major part of this low rural-urban differential exists on the Western Coast of India. It includes south and south-west Maharashtra, Goa, western part of Karnataka, whole of Kerala and southern-most districts of Tamil Nadu. Thanjavur district on east coast and North Arcot-Ambedkar district in the extreme north of Tamil Nadu also fall in this category. The northern districts of Maharashtra, Saurashtra and a few other districts in central part of Gujarat region, eastern parts of Orissa (near Chilka Lake and Mahanadi Delta), a few districts in Upper Ganga plain, southern half of Haryana and adjoining districts of Uttar Pradesh and Rajasthan, a few districts of north Punjab plain and adjoining districts of Himachal Pradesh and a few districts in eastern-most states (*i.e.* Nagaland, Eastern Assam, Manipur and Mizoram) are characterised by low literacy differential. The union territory of Andaman and Nicobar Islands, Delhi, Chandigarh and Lakshadweep also fall in this category. In all these areas, both the rural and the female literacy rates were relatively high. Broadly speaking, the rural-urban literacy differential was low along the coastal, peripheral, agriculturally and industrially prosperous and metropolitan areas.

On the Western Coast region, the reasons of low literacy differential are that the entire area has for long been exposed to European countries. Since long, it has high degree of diversification of rural (cotton, dairy-farming, tobacco, banana, tea and coffee) as well as urban economy (textiles, chemicals, rayon, food processing, oil refining and port facilities) (Dikshit, 1970). This has resulted in high proportion of non-agricultural workers even in the countryside, high percentage of urban population, relatively better standards of living and higher incidence of rural-urban interaction. By and large, the entire area is an area with a long history of educational efforts on the part of enlightened rulers and missionaries (in some parts of the belt). The local communities like Nairs and Ezhawas in Kerala, Nadirs in Tamil Nadu, Lingayats in Karnataka and Parsees, Jains, Marwaris and Mehtas in Gujarat and Maharashtra have made commendable contribution in the propagation of modern education (Sagar, 1990). These apart, high proportion of Christian population, high degree of exposure to Christian culture free of socio-cultural taboos and inhibitions about education in the countryside, especially of females, long history of liberal tradition of education, high per capita expenditure on education by the state government, more progressive nature of the administration, long history of political stability, and satisfactory conditions of law and order, are some other factors responsible for low rural-urban differential. The rural-urban differential would be still lower if the literate rural population won't migrate to urban areas thereby increasing the urban literacy rate and decreasing the rural one.

Similarly, the North-Eastern region also experiences low rural-urban differential in literacy. It includes the districts of Aizawl (0.1137) in Mizoram; Kohima (0.1989), Phek (0.1969), Wokha (0.1553) and Mokokchung (0.1041) of Nagaland; Chandel (0.0226), Toubal (0.1193), Bishnupur (0.1180) and Imphal (0.0912) in Manipur; Lakhimpur (0.1740), Jorhat (0.1631) and Sibsagar (0.1913) in Assam. Of these eastern hilly districts, the lowest rural-urban differential index value (0.0226) is found in Chandel district. All these districts have high rural literacy rates *i.e.* more than 55 per cent. In terms of general literacy as well as rural literacy, this area comes next to the west-coastal region. This area has a large proportion of Christian population even in the rural areas. The impact of Christian missionaries who are responsible for propagation of education even in the poorest tribal areas of this hilly region can clearly be seen. Besides, state governments had also contributed a lot by providing funds liberally for the propagation of education (Tilak, 1981).

Another area of low rural-urban differential in literacy comprises the southern districts of West Bengal and the adjoining districts of Orissa. The districts of Baleshwar, Cuttack, and Puri of Orissa and Howrah, Hugli, Medinipur, and Barddhaman of West Bengal constitute this pocket. In these districts, the rural literacy rates were high and ranged between 55 and 70 per cent. The rural female literacy rates also ranged between 40 to 55 per cent. In West Bengal, low rural-urban literacy differential was the result of high degree of urban-industrial development (Dutta, 1982). Urbanization and industrialization have provided new avenues of employment for rural literates which stimulated the expansion of educational facilities in the region. Kolkata, being a metropolitan city, international port and erstwhile capital of the country, had its impact on the surrounding rural areas. Its most important contribution was in enhancing the socio-economic and functional value of education in the countryside. In Orissa, the early start of education, contribution of Christian missionaries (Gosal, 1967), increasing urbanization, continuous exposure to external influences (Krishan & Shyam, 1978), comparatively better economic condition of rural population, were the factors responsible for narrowing down the differences in rural and urban literacy rates. The developmental activities *i.e.* expansion of mining activities, irrigation facilities (Hirakud Project), education facilities in rural areas and tribal development programmes (Sagar, 1990) helped in minimizing the rural-urban gap in terms of literacy.

Similarly, the area of low rural-urban differential in literacy includes the districts of Gurdaspur, Jalandhar, Kapurthala, Hoshiarpur and Rupnagar of Punjab and adjoining districts of Himachal Pradesh, *i.e.* Kangra, Hamirpur, Una, Bilaspur. The union territory of Chandigarh also comes in this category. In Punjab, the literacy rates increased significantly from 12.42 per cent in 1951 to 58.51 per cent in 1991. The commercialization of agriculture in Punjab and horticulture in Himachal Pradesh brought economic prosperity in rural areas where the rural population started appreciating the value of education. The long tradition of military service and emigration and positive use of remittances for educational purposes (Gosal, 1979) had made a significant contribution to the propagation of education in the countryside. An early exposure to outside world (since the times of Alexander) coupled with social, political and economic awareness, had created a socio-cultural set-up conducive to the promotion of education. Besides, the increasing incidence of rural-urban interaction, expanding infrastructural facilities in the countryside, gradually increasing availability of female teachers to work in rural areas and growing functional value of education in the countryside had strengthened the base of rural literacy in the region. The growth of road transport and link roads had contributed a lot to the diversification of economy that stimulated rural-urban interaction and also significantly improved the per capita income of the people. The differential index was negatively associated with these. It is worth mentioning here that the per capita expenditure on education is maximum in Chandigarh.

In the interior part of the country, low literacy differential is also found around Delhi and the adjoining districts of Ganga-Yamuna Doab. This belt constitutes Sonipat, Rohtak, Rewari, Mahendragarh and Bhiwani districts of Haryana, adjoining districts of Jhunjhunu and Sikar in Rajasthan and Garhwal, Nainital, Bijnor, Muzaffarnagar, Meerut, Ghaziabad, Bulandshahr, Aligarh, Firozabad, Mainpuri, Farrukhabad, Etawah, Kanpur Dehat, Jalaun in Uttar Pradesh. In both the districts of Rajasthan, the rural female as well as overall rural literacy rates along with rural-urban differential are low. In Uttar Pradesh, the districts of Bijnor, Muzaffarnagar, Meerut, Ghaziabad, Bulandshahr, Aligarh and Mainpuri show the low rural literacy as well as low differential index. The rural female literacy is also very low (below 25 per cent) in all these districts. In the districts, which are near to the National capital, the differential index was low due to urban industrial development of the National Capital Region (Bala, 1986), highly diversified economy, high degree of rural mobility, better avenues of employment and business promotion (Krishan & Chandna, 1973), relatively high proportion of non-agricultural workers, and relatively high functional value of education among ruralites. In the Ganga-Yamuna Doab region of Uttar Pradesh, the rural literacy rates are more due to semi-commercial nature of the agricultural economy, frequency of denominational schools associated with various castes, such as Jats, Brahmins, Vaishyas, Rajputs and Ahirs (Rudolph and Rudolph, 1972), the high degree of rural-urban interaction, age old impact of Delhi-Kolkata (G.T. Road) rail-road link and the long duration of active political participation in the functioning of government (Siddiqui, 1977). In the border district of Nainital, the differential index is low due to the district's agricultural prosperity and high degree of urbanization (Bala, 1986).

Another area of low rural-urban differential in literacy is northern Maharashtra including Vidarbha region. It comprised the districts of Jalgaon, Buldana, Akola, Amravati, Wardha, Nagpur and Bhandara. Of these districts, Akola (0.1513) and Amravati (0.1446) have the differential index, which is about half that of the national average (0.3013). All these districts have high rural literacy rates (above 58 per cent). The agricultural economy in these districts is relatively prosperous, the level of urbanization is increasing (similar to national average), the degree of rural-urban mobility is high, the traditional culture of rural areas had for long been exposed to outside world (Bombay-Nagpur-Kolkata route), and socio-political and economic awareness was age old (Sagar, 1990). All these resulted in low rural-urban differential in literacy.

Finally, low differential in literacy has also been observed in a few scattered districts such as, Thanjavur, North Arcot-Ambedkar (Tamil Nadu), West Godavari (Andhra Pradesh), Bhind and Jehanabad (Bihar) and in the union territories, the districts of Andaman and Nicobar (Andaman & Nicobar Islands), Lakshadweep (Lakshadweep), Pondicherry, Karaikal (Pondicherry) and Daman (Daman & Diu). In the districts of Tamil Nadu and Andhra Pradesh, the low differential index value is due to relatively high degree of urbanization. In Lakshadweep, Andamans and Pondicherry, the literacy differential is low due to liberal financial assistance from the Central Government for their development (Kothari, 1970). In Jehanabad, both the rural and urban literacy rates are low and are close to each other, so the resultant rural-urban differential is low. In Bhind, the impact of adjoining districts of Uttar Pradesh with low rural-urban differential index is visible. The literacy rates by rural-urban residence are also low.

Thus, the low rural-urban differential in literacy is found in both the less developed areas and rapidly developing areas. In the former case, both rural and urban literacy rates are low and resultant differential is low. In the latter case, both the rural and urban literacy rates are high and the resultant differential is also low. In the areas of high literacy (both rural and urban), coastal location, early start of education, diversification of rural economy and relatively high degree of urbanization, Christian missionaries, and overseas relations have their strong impact. In rural areas, commercialization of agriculture, opening of more schools and high proportion of Christian population have played a vital role in the increase of literacy rates, thereby decreasing rural-urban gap.

*4. Areas where the Rural Literacy Rates are More than Urban with Very Low Rural-Urban Differential*

There are only two districts in India which fall in this category. These districts both in Kerala recording negative index values are Alappuzha (–0.0056) and Kollam (–0.004). In these districts the rural literacy rates are higher than the urban or we can say that the rural literacy outmatched the urban literacy. In both these districts, rural literacy rates are 94.06 per cent and 90.48 per cent respectively, while the urban literacy rates are 93.42 per cent and 90.44 per cent respectively. Both the rural and urban literacy rates are high and the marginal difference between the two doesn't warrant any special explanation. However, the out-migration of literate urban population from these districts to their rural counterparts in search of employment is considered as an effective reason (Gill and Singh, 1986).

## CONCLUDING REMARKS

1. Independence in 1947 provided the real impetus to literacy in the country because of the more attention of administration to social advancement, opening up of large number of schools in rural areas, apart from upgrading the existing ones and multiplication of institutions of higher education. Since then, continuous increase in

literacy rates for persons, males and females have been recorded. The literacy rate for the country as a whole in 2001, works out to 65.38 per cent for the population aged seven years and above, which increased from 18.33 per cent for the population aged five years and above in 1951. The corresponding figures for males and females are 75.85 and 54.16 per cent respectively, which increased from 27.16 per cent for males and 8.86 per cent for females in 1951. Thus, three-fourth of the male and more than half of the female population aged seven years and above is literate in the country today.

2. Regionally, Kerala with 90.92 per cent of its population as literate has the distinction of having highest literacy in the country not only in case of persons, but also in male literacy (94.20 per cent) and female literacy (87.86 per cent). The highest rates of literacy in Kerala may be attributable to the state's long tradition of education due to enlightened administration, and high proportion of non-agricultural workers, besides the efforts of the Christian missionaries in the field of education.

   By contrast, Bihar with 47.53 per cent of its population as literate is at the other end of the scale, not only in case of total literacy but also for male literacy (60.32 per cent) and female literacy (33.57 per cent). This is the state which is characterized with subsistence type of backward agricultural economy and a sizeable population of scheduled castes and the Muslims.

3. At the district level, Aizawal district in Mizoram recording 96.44 per cent of its population as literate has the distinction of being the most literate district of the country. By contrast, Dantewada district in Chhatisgarh with 30.01 per cent of its population as literate is the least literate district in the country. The ratio of 1:3 between the least and the most literate districts speaks volumes of the contrasting socio-economic conditions prevailing in the country.

4. Broadly speaking, south India is most literate than north India. Within south India, the coastal areas are more literate than the interiors and between the coastal areas, the western coast is more literate than the eastern coast. Within north India, parts of Punjab plain in the north-west and hill states like Mizoram, Tripura, Manipur, Nagaland and Meghalaya in the north-east constitute the two nodes of higher literacy than the rest of north India. Thus, high literacy is characteristic of areas that have coastal location, high percentage of non-agricultural workers, high degree of

urbanization, more diversified economy, a sizeable proportion of Christian population, a well-developed network of infrastructural facilities, an early start of modern education, high per capita income, and high percentage of state expenditure on education because of enlightened and efficient administration.

5. The most notable feature of Indian literacy is that the females always lagged for behind the males in terms of literacy rates. The gap in male-female literacy rates, which was 18.30 percentage points in 1951, increased to 26.62 in 1981. Low status of women in Indian society, prevalence of early marriage especially among the rural girls resulting in a very high incidence of drop-outs, and the prejudices against females' mobility, education and employment are the important factors responsible for such wide male-female literacy differentials in India. However, with increasing socio-economic awareness and with literacy among females increasingly becoming a matrimonial necessity, the male-female literacy differentials, in India, are narrowing down, though only steadily. The highest ever male-female differential, which was 26.62 percentage points in 1981, was marginally reduced to 24.84 per cent in 1991 and in 2001, it has further gone down to 21.70 percentage points.
6. While two-fold increase was observed in literacy rate for urban areas (from 39.70 per cent in 1951 to 73.08 per cent in 1991), the increase in literacy rate for rural areas was more than three-fold (from 14.01 per cent in 1951 to 44.69 per cent in 1991). It shows that the proportionate share of literate population both in rural and urban areas continue to register an increasing trend over the decades.
7. The increase in literacy rate being sharper in rural areas has resulted in decline of rural-urban differential index as well as disparity ratio. The values of rural-urban differential index and disparity ratio are decreasing continuously over the time since 1951. The differential index (0.5169) was sharper in 1951, as there was only one rural literate for nearly every three urban literates (1: 2.83). But it came down to 0.3013 in 1991, when disparity ratio by residence was only 1:1.64. The narrowing down of the rural-urban differential index as well as disparity ratio was associated with increasing degree of rural-urban interaction, increasing socio-economic functional value of education in the countryside, improving standards of living, and increasing facilities for schooling in the countryside.
8. The trend of rural-urban differentials in literacy rates indicates that

the whole of country has experienced decline in literacy differentials between 1981-91, except in the states of Mizoram and the union territory of Dadra and Nagar Haweli, because both of them recorded higher rate of increase in urban literacy as compared to rural literacy. Amongst other states and union territories, Tripura stands at the top in terms of maximum decline (–10.57 per cent) in rural-urban differentials in literacy and is followed by Andaman & Nicobar Islands (–6.63 per cent), Arunachal Pradesh (–6.37 per cent), Delhi (–5.90 per cent), Haryana (–5.60 per cent), West Bengal (–5.73 per cent), and Himachal Pradesh (–5.60 per cent). The factors attributable to such a high decrease in literacy differentials are mainly that of higher rate of increase in rural literacy than the urban because of the availability of educational facilities in rural areas, more social awareness, and the waning prejudices against females' mobility, education and employment.

By contrast, the minimum decline in rural-urban differentials in literacy is experienced by the states of Meghalaya (–0.01 per cent) and Bihar (–0.01 per cent), followed by Orissa (–0.51 per cent) and Rajasthan (–0.62 per cent), all characterized by literacy differentials below one per cent. In these states, the rate of increase in urban literacy is relatively low because of the low degree of urbanization resulting into an increase somewhat equal to that of rural literacy.

9. The rural-urban differential in literacy is negatively correlated with rural literacy, rural female literacy, percentage of rural population in other services, percentage of non-agricultural workers to total workers in rural areas, percentage of urban population and rural Christian population. Thus, low rural-urban differentials are typical of areas which are developed with de-agriculturisation of rural economy, low prejudices against female education and presence of Christian population. By contrast, it is positively correlated with rural Muslim population and percentage of scheduled caste and scheduled tribe population to urban population as well as total population.
10. Spatially speaking, there are marked regional variations in rural-urban literacy differentials in the country. Low differential is found in coastal, near coastal, peripheral and in and around the highly urbanized, industrialized, commercialized areas and in metropolitan cities or areas. The high literacy differential is found in interior areas, particularly those previously ruled by princely states and

mountainous districts of Himalayas. Elsewhere, it is moderate and in two coastal districts of Kerala, it is negative. The low rural-urban differential is characteristic of those areas where there is a relatively high degree of urbanization, commercialization of agriculture, dense road network or transportation network, exposure to external influences through coastal location and emigration, school facilities are more in rural areas, status of females is high and prejudice against female education in rural areas is less. The differential is also low in many of the less urbanized areas, provided that their rural literacy is stimulated by missionary efforts, diversification of the rural economy and efficient administration. By contrast, high rural-urban differential index is found generally in non-Christian tribal tracts, in areas of predominantly subsistence agriculture, in former princely states, areas of low level of urbanization, areas of less developed transportation and communication network, in areas of low status of women and where prejudice against female mobility exists, lack of general awareness and awareness about benefits of literacy, inadequate educational facilities and high proportion of Muslim, scheduled caste and scheduled tribe population which are socially and economically less developed groups of population. Literacy in India, thus, has uneven development with urban bias.

# 5

# VITAL RATES

Vital rates include mainly fertility and mortality of a group of population. Fertility is the occurrence of live births. It is one of the major aspects of population study. It usually exceeds mortality and migration, and is therefore, the main determinant population growth. Fertility is far less constant and predictable. It can be more controlled and may be more influenced by many social, economic, political and psychological factors. Moreover, unlike death, which may occur at any age, human beings give birth to children only during a comparatively short period of their lives.

Mortality, on the other hand, is the occurrence of death. Mortality is essentially individual, inevitable and involuntary. It can occur at any age. The increase in population as a result of the difference between birth rate and death rate is the natural growth.

The study of fertility and mortality is very important, but the vital statistics are often widely inaccurate and lead to very crude guesses about them. In the present case, we will have to satisfy ourselves by the published data available with the Census of India, Vital Statistics division which provides state-wise data on vital rates.

## The Status of Vital Rates

In India, birth rate, which is the most common index of fertility declined to 29.1 per thousand in 1991-93 from 36.3 in 1971-73. This shows a fall of 7.2 points. Meanwhile, death rate dropped to 9.7 from 15.9, with a fall by 6.2 points. As a result, the natural growth rate fell by one point. The Indian performance in controlling death was much better than that in checking birth.

Table 5.1 reveals that the western specifications of the demographic transition model, with threshold points of 35 and 15 for birth rate and death rate respectively was not applicable to the Indian situation. India's birth rate was around 45 and death rate around 35 when it transited from Stage 1 to Stage 2 and its birth rate dropped only marginally to

**Table 5.1:** India: Estimated Birth and Death Rates, 1901-91

| *Census Decade* | *Birth Rate (Per '000)* | *Death Rate (Per '000)* |
|---|---|---|
| 1901-11 | 49 | 43 |
| 1911-21 | 48 | 47 |
| 1921-31 | 46 | 36 |
| 1931-41 | 45 | 31 |
| 1941-51 | 40 | 27 |
| 1951-61 | 42 | 23 |
| 1961-71* | 40 | 18 |
| 1971-81 ▰ | 35 | 15 |
| 1981-91+ | 32 | 11 |

*Source*: Chandrasekhar (1971), *Infant Mortality, Population Growth and Family Planning in India*, George Allen & Unwin, London, p. 62.

* Ministry of Information and Broadcasting (1974), *India: 1974*, Government of India, New Delhi, p. 80.

▰ Straight averages for 1975 and 1976 taken as average for 1971-81. See Dyson, T. (1981), "Preliminary Demography of 1981 Census", *Economic and Political Weekly*, pp. 1349-1365.

\+ *Sample Registration Bulletin* (1998), Vol. 32, No. 1, Registrar General, India, New Delhi, p. 5.

around 40 and death rate sharply to around 20 when it attained the explosive sub-stage of demographic transition in 1971 (Krishan & Kant, 1986). In 1991, India entered the late expanding stage of demographic transition in case of birth rates with crude birth rate around 30 and in late stationary stage in case of death rates with crude death rate under 19. As of present, the condition of birth and death rates given in Jone's model of demographic transition (1981) seem to fit in Indian case. The story for states and union territories (Table 5.2 and Map 5.1) is, however, somewhat different.

It is observed that nearly three-fourth of the states and all the union territories (except Dadra and Nagar Haveli) of India are heading towards late stationary stage according to Jone's (1981) model of demographic transition.

The two important aspects of vital rates *viz.*, fertility and mortality have been discussed in sequence.

## India: Rural-Urban Differentials in Fertility

Fertility refers to the number of children a woman has actually borne. The crude birth rate, which is the most common index of fertility, is the ratio of registered live births during one calendar year to the mid-year

**Table 5.2**: India: Birth and Death Rates, 1991-93

*(Based on three-years moving averages)*

| *Country/State/Union Territory* | *Birth Rate (Per '000)* | *Death Rate (Per '000)* |
|---|---|---|
| **India*** | **29.1** | **9.7** |
| *States* | | |
| Goa | 15.4 | 7.2 |
| Kerala | 17.8 | 6.1 |
| Nagaland | 19.2 | 3.9 |
| Manipur | 20.1 | 5.3 |
| Tamil Nadu | 20.3 | 8.5 |
| Sikkim | 22.8 | 6.7 |
| Tripura | 23.6 | 7.1 |
| Andhra Pradesh | 24.9 | 9.2 |
| Maharashtra | 25.5 | 7.8 |
| West Bengal | 25.8 | 8.0 |
| Karnataka | 26.2 | 8.5 |
| Punjab | 27.0 | 8.0 |
| Himachal Pradesh | 27.8 | 8.8 |
| Gujarat | 27.9 | 8.6 |
| Orissa | 27.9 | 12.2 |
| Arunachal Pradesh | 28.5 | 10.5 |
| Meghalaya | 30.2 | 8.0 |
| Assam | 30.4 | 10.7 |
| Bihar | 31.7 | 10.5 |
| Haryana | 31.9 | 8.3 |
| Rajasthan | 34.6 | 9.9 |
| Madhya Pradesh | 34.7 | 13.1 |
| Uttar Pradesh | 36.0 | 11.9 |
| *Union Territories* | | |
| Chandigarh | 16.2 | 3.5 |
| Pondicherry | 17.9 | 6.6 |
| Andaman & Nicobar Islands | 20.5 | 5.5 |
| Delhi | 24.3 | 5.6 |
| Daman & Diu | 25.9 | 8.4 |
| Lakshadweep | 25.9 | 5.7 |
| Dadra & Nagar Haveli | 34.2 | 11.7 |

*Source:* *Sample Registration Bulletin* (1998), 32,1, Registrar General, India, New Delhi, pp. 6, 39-43, 54-56.

* Excludes Jammu and Kashmir where census was not held in 1991.

*Note:* States and union territories are arranged in ascending order of birth rates in 1991-93.

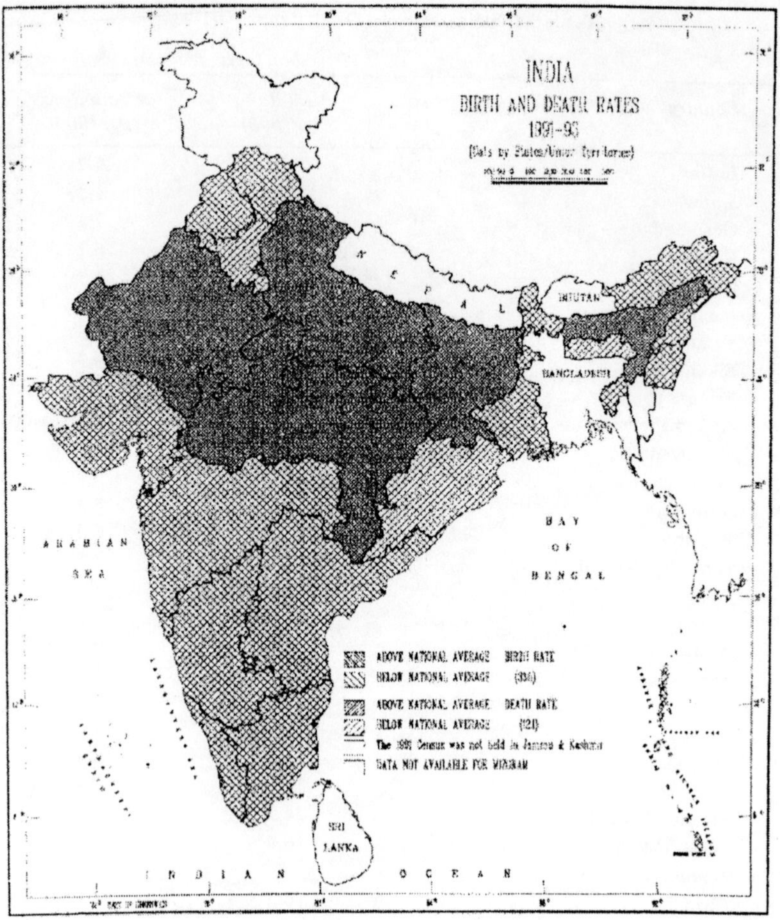


**Map 5.1**: India: Birth and Death Rates, 1991-93 (Data by States / Union Territories)

total population, multiplied by 1000. The formula for calculating crude birth rate (CBR) is:

$$CBR = \frac{\textit{Total number of live births in a year}}{\textit{Total population at mid point of the year}} \times 1000$$

These rates are crude because they relate the number of births to the total population without any regard for the breakdown of this total by age and sex or proportion married. Hence, it is not a highly refined measurement for comparing the birth performances of different countries and regions.

Fertility in India, as in many other developing countries, is very high. Even now when along with the growing population an increasing number of live births are occurring in the country, birth rates continue to maintain a high level. As a result, in an already large population size there is a massive aggregate annual addition of above 20 million people due to births. This characteristic differentiates India from any other country's fertility behaviour having comparable socio-economic development and explains the existence of a number of social and institutional factors in the country which control fertility trends in traditional cultures. A custom of large families, particularly in rural areas (Askhem, 1975), a general desire for having sons, non-popularity of birth control measures (Cassen, 1978) and high mortality of children (Mandelbaum, 1974) accompanied by ignorance, indecision and self interest (Bulatao, 1984) are some of the major causes behind high fertility rates in the country. At the micro level setting in the country, the functioning of these factors have been analyzed by Wyon and Gordon (1971).

## Trend of Rural-Urban Differentials in Fertility

It is a widely observed fact that the urban populations are less fertile than their rural counterparts. But in India, the studies of the census returns and survey data indicate that the rural-urban fertility differentials were not, at least until 1951, a significant factor in India's population growth, because of the narrowness of the differences in fertility rates (Agarwala, 1985).

In 1931, the average number of children per family was 4.2 in rural areas and 4.0 in urban areas. The situation did not materially alter in 1941-51. The corresponding figures for 1951 were 5.01 and 4.07 respectively (Davis, 1951; Paulus, 1966). The National Sample Survey for 1951-52 gave these figures as 5.92 and 5.86 for rural and urban areas respectively. The total fertility rate was 5.8 in rural and 4.3 in urban areas in 1972 and total marital fertility rate was 6.8 in rural areas and 6.0 in urban areas. According to some surveys conducted by various organizations, the average number of children born to women with unbroken marriages during their reproductive span is given in Table 5.3.

It is obvious from the figures of Table 5.3 that rural-urban differentials with regard to the complete family size were minimal.

**Table 5.3:** India: Average Number of Children Born Alive per Woman of Unbroken Marriage during the Reproductive Age

| | | |
|---|---|---|
| 1. | Bengal Survey (1947-1949) | |
| | Ballygunj–Upper middle class urban | 5.7 |
| | Beniatola–Lower middle class, urban | 6.2 |
| | Singur–Rural | 7.3 |
| 2. | Mysore Survey (1952) | |
| | Bangalore city | 6.2 |
| | Rural areas | 6.0 |
| 3. | Poona Survey (1952) | |
| | Poona city | 6.4 |
| | Poona (non-city) | 6.4 |
| 4. | National Sample Survey (1952) | |
| | All India, Urban | 5.86 |
| | All India, Rural | 5.92 |
| 5. | Patna City Survey (1956) | 5.9 |
| | Banaras, rural area (1956) | 6.8 –7.3 |
| 6. | Central India Survey (1958) | |
| | City | 6.6 |
| | Village | 6.3 |

*Source:* Adopted from, B.L. Rainia, *Family Size Norms in Population Problems of India*, p. 49.

Associated with the role played by modernizing elements which cause the transformation from high to low fertility, there has been a traditional existence of rural-urban dimension pertaining to fertility trends in all the societies (United Nations, 1984). On the similar lines in India also, this dimension provides that fertility in the country's rural areas is higher than urban and hence, there is a rural-urban fertility differential (Premi, *et al.*, 1983; Ramu, 1988). The assumption behind this differential is the fact that urban dwellers tend to have fewer children than rural dwellers (Census of India, 1981). Viewed from a broad perspective, it is the function of demand factor for preferring certain number of children that makes the actual difference between the fertility rates of these two areas. In the case of India, the existence of this differential was recognized in the early 1960s by Robinson (1961) and later on by Davis (1968). But these differentials were relatively smaller till 1960's. Besides, various rounds of National Sample Survey (NSS) conducted between 1958 and 1967 have also confirmed the existence of rural-urban fertility differentials at all India level. Table 5.4 shows the crude birth rate (CBR) for rural and urban areas in the country estimated by NSS during this period.

**Table 5.4:** India: Crude Birth Rate by Rural-Urban Residence, 1958-67

| *Period* | *Rural* | *Urban* |
|---|---|---|
| July 1958–June 1959 | 38.3 | DNA |
| July 1959–June 1960 | 38.9 | DNA |
| July 1960–August 1961 | DNA | 33.0 |
| September 1961–August 1962 | 36.0 | 34.0 |
| February 1963–January 1964 | 37.0 | 31.5 |
| July 1964–June 1965 | 37.1 | 31.9 |
| July 1965–June 1966 | 36.3 | 30.3 |
| July 1966–June 1967 | 36.3 | 30.0 |

*Source:* Premi (1982), *Demographic Situation in India*, East-West Population Institute, Honolulu.
DNA = Data not available.

However, it was only with the inception of a more reliable Sample Registration System (SRS) in 1964 that the spatio-temporal trends of this differential came out with a greater degree of reliability. Although the NSS conducted fertility surveys even after 1967, the dual record system of SRS is considered to be a superior method for estimating fertility than time recall system of the NSS. With the introduction of SRS, a whole range of fertility measures have become available which reflect that fertility in urban India is lower as compared to rural areas. The standard measures of fertility, like crude birth rate (CBR), general fertility rate (GFR), total fertility rate (TFR), and gross reproduction rate (GRR) indicate this differential in rural-urban fertility for the period 1970-92 (Table 5.5).

**Table 5.5:** India: Crude, General, To[illegible] ınd Gross Reproduction Rates by Rural-Urban Residence, 1970-92

| *Year* | *Rural* | | | | *Urban* | | | |
|---|---|---|---|---|---|---|---|---|
| | CBR | GFR | TFR | GRR | CBR | GFR | TFR | GRR |
| 1970 | 39.0 | 173.4 | 5.6 | 2.7 | 30.1 | 133.2 | 4.1 | 1.9 |
| 1975 | 36.7 | 158.6 | 5.2 | 2.5 | 28.2 | 118.6 | 3.7 | 1.8 |
| 1981 | 35.6 | 149.4 | 4.8 | 2.3 | 27.0 | 107.2 | 3.3 | 1.6 |
| 1984 | 35.4 | 153.1 | 4.8 | 2.3 | 29.4 | 120.2 | 3.5 | 1.7 |
| 1988 | 33.1 | 139.8 | 4.3 | 2.0 | 26.3 | 103.9 | 3.1 | 1.5 |
| 1992 | 30.9 | 127.6 | 3.9 | 1.8 | 23.1 | 89.1 | 2.6 | 1.2 |

*Source: Sample Registration Systems*, 1970, 1975, 1981, 1984, 1988, 1992.

It is observed that different rates of fertility are continuously declining over time despite the fact that with growing population in the country, increasing number of women are entering the reproductive age group and the aggregate number of live births is continuously increasing. Whereas the CBR, which forms the basis of state level fertility has continuously, though slowly declined, the GFR trends show that fertility measured in terms of the number of children born in a year to 1000 women in reproductive age group has also gone down. However, the sharp difference between rural and urban GFR testifies that besides alteration in marital customs, mainly higher mean age at marriage in urban areas, more urban women are practising family planning than rural women. The magnitude of difference between rural and urban GFR is, to a certain extent, a reflection of fertility trend effected by birth control measures. As Bongaarts has described, if all married women throughout their reproductive span used no contraception, had no induced abortion and experienced no lactation infecundity, they would achieve their maximum fertility level, which he refers to as *natural fertility* (Bongaarts, 1978). Given the Indian circumstances, these observations are more close to reality for rural women and this is one strong reason why rural GFR is higher than urban.

Taking into consideration the declining GFR, it is clear that over time fewer live female births per woman are taking place in the country and urban GRR is lower than rural. This effect, however, seems to have been compensated by the fact that the reduced mortality is ensuring the entry of a larger proportion of women in the reproductive age group and consequently a reproductive women is now being replaced by more woman than a few decades back.

It is observed that about 10 per cent of the population (in the two southern states of Kerala and Tamil Nadu with a total population of 85 million in 1991) has already attained a near or below replacement level of fertility. In another nine states with a total population of 389 million (46 per cent of the total), the total fertility rate (TFR) has declined from 6 or more in the 1950s to between 3.1 and 3.5 (The total fertility rate estimates the average number of children that would be born per woman, if there were no mortality at all during reproductive ages and all women gave birth to children at the rate observed during a particular period). Even in the four large north Indian states with a total population of 336 million (40 per cent of the total), which are regarded as the most backward in terms of demographic transition, the TFR has evidently declined by between 19 to 29 per cent during the past 10 to 20 years.

The latest available SRS data have suggested a TFR of 3.7 during 1990 and 1992. In 1990-92, the rural TFR was estimated at 4.0 and urban TFR at 2.7 (Table 5.6). At the aggregate all-India level, fertility has declined at a rate faster than was expected by all of us. If rural-urban differences in TFR are presumed to be virtually negligible upto about the early 1960s or prior to the recent fertility decline, rural fertility has declined by about one-third and urban fertility by over 50 per cent from a TFR of about 6. These figures suggest considerable progress of the order of 54 per cent in rural areas and 87 per cent in urban areas towards a replacement level of fertility or a TFR of 2.1.

The state-level estimates of TFR in urban areas are often based on a small sample and, therefore, three-year averages are more stable. Such estimates suggest a sharp decline in urban fertility to near or below replacement level in Kerala, Tamil Nadu, Assam, and West Bengal. This decline in urban fertility, with the urban sector including a total population of nearly 230 million by 1995, has considerable significance for the demographic situation in the country as a whole, because continuing interaction between urban and rural populations is likely to generate a fairly strong demonstration effect.

**Table 5.6:** India: Estimated Total Fertility Rates in Major States of India by Rural-Urban Residence according to the SRS, 1990-92

| *Country/State* | *Total* | *Rural* | *Urban* |
|---|---|---|---|
| **India** | **3.7** | **4.0** | **2.7** |
| *States* | | | |
| Andhra Pradesh | 3.0 | 3.1 | 2.5 |
| Assam | 3.4 | 3.6 | 2.1 |
| Gujarat | 3.2 | 3.4 | 2.9 |
| Haryana | 3.9 | 4.2 | 2.9 |
| Himachal Pradesh | 3.1 | 3.2 | 3.1 |
| Karnataka | 3.1 | 3.3 | 2.5 |
| Kerala | 1.8 | 1.8 | 1.7 |
| Madhya Pradesh | 4.6 | 4.9 | 3.3 |
| Maharashtra | 3.0 | 3.4 | 2.5 |
| Orissa | 3.3 | 3.4 | 2.4 |
| Punjab | 3.1 | 3.3 | 2.8 |
| Rajasthan | 4.5 | 4.8 | 3.5 |
| Tamil Nadu | 2.2 | 2.4 | 2.0 |
| Uttar Pradesh | 5.2 | 5.5 | 3.8 |
| Bihar | 4.6 | 4.7 | 3.4 |
| West Bengal | 3.2 | 3.6 | 2.0 |

*Source:* Visaria (1995), *Demography India*, 24, 1, Table 1, p. 6.

The substantial demographic diversity in a country as large as India is not surprising. It also provides a challenging opportunity for analysis of the factors contributing to the observed variations. As reported in a recent paper (Visaria and Visaria, 1994), a multiple regression analysis of the TFR in the 16 more populous states in terms of the conventional indicators of modernization contributing to fertility transition shows neither urbanization nor industrialization to be significant (as is well-known, our progress on both these indices has been rather slow). The female worker-population ratios, adjusted in the light of the generally more dependable NSS data on the level and pattern of employment, also do not explain the inter-state differences in the TFR.

Besides, there is an unfortunate tendency among our analysts to interpret the processes of change in our country in negative terms. The fertility decline in India is branded as poverty-induced, a term that is difficult to substantiate. The average annual rate of growth of per capita income in India was higher during the 1980s (3.0 per cent) than during the preceding three decades (between 0 7 and 1.8 per cent, CMIE, 1993). The proportion of population below the poverty line also appears to have declined from 48-52 per cent during the 1970s to 37 per cent during 1983-84 and 30 per cent during 1987-88. The controversies about the validity of these estimates notwithstanding, the decline in poverty and the direction of the trend are virtually indisputable.

The continuing decline in infant mortality and in crude death rates bears testimony to the improvement in the living standards. Intolerable differences persist and they must be reduced; but the direction of the trends cannot be denied. Besides, couples are understandably concerned about the number of living children and not about births as such. The substantial decline in infant and child mortality is certainly recognized by the people at large and they reduce the gap between wanted fertility and total fertility. The norms of about wanted fertility also seem to be undergoing a change and the desired number of living children per couple seems to be weakening and daughters are being accepted as equals of sons, particularly in urban areas. These tendencies are likely to spread gradually to rural areas as well.

It must be noted that fertility has declined in almost all parts of the country to a greater or lesser extent. Also, the pace of decline is not necessarily the highest in states with the highest per capita income (*i.e.* Punjab or Haryana) or in the poorer states (such as Bihar or Orissa). So, neither a rapid rise in living standards nor poverty seems to have led to a substantial fall in fertility. As suggested above, the gap between aspirations and the achieved level of living and the awareness of the gap might be a more potent force in bringing about a decline in fertility. Continuing on this line of argument, one can propose a hypothesis for exploration and testing that an acceleration of the rate of development, with or even without an accentuation of the inequalities in the level of living or even the recognition of the latter, resulting from the success of a sufficiently large number of enterprising persons in escaping the poverty trap could be an important factor contributing to an accelerated decline in fertility. If this hypothesis holds, the liberalization of the Indian economy during the past four years is likely to generate forces that would accelerate the fertility decline. Admittedly, a democratic polity cannot pursue a policy or a goal of increasing inequalities as a means of accelerating fertility decline but such an outcome seems to be a likely byproduct of the current configuration of various forces.

In Table 5.7 are shown the age-specific fertility rates based on the SRS for the three triennia of 1970-72. 1980-82 and 1990-92, separately by rural-urban residence. There has been a clear shift in the age pattern of childbearing; the peak fertility now occurs in the age group 20-24 instead of in the age group 25-29. More importantly, fertility declines are evident in all age groups, but particularly at ages 30 and above.

**Table 5.7:** India: Age Specific Fertility Rates by Rural-Urban Residence, 1970-92

*(Per '000 population)*

| *Age* | *Total* | | | *Rural* | | | *Urban* | | |
|---|---|---|---|---|---|---|---|---|---|
| *Group* | 1970-72 | 1980-82 | 1990-92 | 1970-72 | 1980-82 | 1990-92 | 1970-72 | 1980-82 | 1990-92 |
| 15-19 | 103 | 89 | 78 | 112 | 96 | 87 | 72 | 62 | 46 |
| 20-24 | 254 | 246 | 235 | 262 | 259 | 248 | 226 | 204 | 196 |
| 25-29 | 259 | 231 | 193 | 267 | 243 | 204 | 228 | 190 | 160 |
| 30-34 | 203 | 165 | 117 | 212 | 179 | 130 | 166 | 117 | 80 |
| 35-39 | 134 | 100 | 68 | 143 | 111 | 78 | 95 | 61 | 38 |
| 40-44 | 63 | 46 | 31 | 68 | 51 | 36 | 37 | 25 | 16 |
| 45-49 | 27 | 21 | 12 | 29 | 23 | 14 | 15 | 12 | 6 |
| TFR | 5.2 | 4.5 | 3.7 | 5.5 | 4.8 | 4.0 | 4.2 | 3.4 | 2.7 |

*Source:* Visaria (1995), *Demography India* 24, 1. Table 2, p. 7.

The trend of rural-urban differentials in birth rates (Table 5.8) reveals that there was a decline of 3 points in 1971-81 in total birth rate and in 1981-91 this decline increased to 4.7 points. In rural areas, the decline in birth rate is showing a similar trend. In urban areas, the decline was 2.3 persons per 1000 in 1971-81 and this rate increased to 4.1 persons per 1000 in 1981-91. Interestingly a very strong positive relationship is seen between rural and urban crude birth rates, the correlation coefficient being .7290 in 1991. This implies that the states having high or low urban crude birth rates are also having high or low rural crude birth rates. Therefore, whereas in low crude birth rate states urban-rural continuum is helping in minimizing these fertility rates in both the areas, in high crude birth rate states, it seems that the dominant presence of values attributed to high rural crude birth rate on the one hand and lack of industrial and occupational structure as well as exposure to many aspects of modernization and development conducive to reduce urban fertility, have contributed in keeping the crude birth rates in both the areas at relatively higher levels.

The low urban fertility is caused by unbalanced sex ratios, high living standards, economic insecurity and unemployment, social capillarity, occupational status, female employment, educational facilities and the availability of clinical aids towards family planning and so on; but there are no simple relationships.

Thus, the different measures of human fertility based on varied standards of reproduction emphasizes that rural-urban differentials are declining over time. It also brings home the point that there has been a clear differential in rural and urban fertility, the former having higher birth rates than the latter. The entire discussion in the later part of this chapter is based on the analysis and acceptance of CBR as the most common index of human fertility.

**Table 5.8**: India: Trend of Rural-Urban Differentials in Birth Rates, 1971-91

| *Year* | *Persons per 1000 Population* | | |
|---|---|---|---|
| | *Total* | *Rural* | *Urban* |
| 1971-81* | –3.0 | –3.5 | –2.3 |
| 1981-91* | –4.7 | –4.7 | –4.1 |

*Sources:*

(i) Premi (1982), *Demographic Situation in India*, pp. 35, 64.

(ii) *Sample Registration Bulletin* (1998), 32, 1, Registrar General, India, New Delhi.

* Based on three years moving averages, 1971-73, 1981-83 and 1991-93 respectively.

Since 1971, the SRS data on fertility are available separately for rural and urban areas. The rural societies have differing fertility levels just as in other parts of the world, in India too, rural farm population is usually more fertile than rural non-farm population. The data at the state level indicate the varying fertility trends and their rural-urban differentials among different states by taking CBR as a suitable indicator of fertility trends. Seen as rural-urban component, it is observed that the rural-urban differential is declining continuously over time. It was 8.8 per 1000 in 1971, 7.6 per 1000 in 1981 and 7.0 per 1000 in 1991. (Table 5.9).

**Table 5.9:** India: Rural-Urban Differentials in Crude Birth Rates, 1971-73 and 1991-93

*(Based on 3-years moving averages)*

| *Country/ State* | *Crude Birth Rate (Per Thousand)* | | *Birth Rate, 1991-93* | | *Rural-Urban Differential* | |
|---|---|---|---|---|---|---|
| | 1971-73 | | 1991-93 | | 1971-73 | 1991-93 |
| | Rural | Urban | Rural | Urban | | |
| **India** | **37.7** | **30.0** | **30.7** | **23.7** | **7.0** | **8.8** |
| *States* | | | | | | |
| Meghalaya | DNA | DNA | 33.0 | 17.1 | 15.9 | DNA |
| West Bengal | DNA | DNA | 28.9 | 17.7 | 11.2 | DNA |
| Sikkim | DNA | DNA | 24.3 | 13.3 | 11.0 | DNA |
| Madhya Pradesh | 39.6 | 33.4 | 36.7 | 26.8 | 9.9 | 6.2 |
| Himachal Pradesh | 36.8 | 23.5 | 28.5 | 19.6 | 8.9 | 13.3 |
| Assam | 36.8 | 28.7 | 31.2 | 22.5 | 8.7 | 8.1 |
| Uttar Pradesh | 44.6 | 34.0 | 37.5 | 29.6 | 7.9 | 10.6 |
| Tripura | 35.0 | 22.5 | 24.6 | 16.7 | 7.9 | 12.5 |
| Rajasthan | 42.4 | 34.3 | 36.0 | 28.6 | 7.4 | 8.1 |
| Haryana | 42.5 | 32.0 | 33.6 | 26.3 | 7.3 | 10.5 |
| Bihar | DNA | DNA | 32.5 | 25.3 | 7.2 | DNA |
| Nagaland | DNA | DNA | 20.5 | 14.0 | 6.5 | DNA |
| Orissa | 34.8 | 32.5 | 28.6 | 22.2 | 6.4 | 2.3 |
| Maharashtra | 32.0 | 29.0 | 27.5 | 22.5 | 5.0 | 2.9 |
| Arunachal Pradesh | 35.8 | DNA | 29.0 | 24.4 | 4.6 | DNA |
| Punjab | 35.1 | 30.4 | 28.2 | 24.1 | 4.1 | 0.7 |
| Karnataka | 32.3 | 26.4 | 27.3 | 23.4 | 3.9 | 5.9 |
| Gujarat | 40.1 | 34.2 | 28.9 | 25.5 | 3.4 | 5.9 |
| Andhra Pradesh | 34.3 | 33.1 | 25.4 | 23.4 | 2.0 | 1.2 |
| Manipur | 31.7 | 24.1 | 20.5 | 18.9 | 1.6 | 7.6 |
| Tamil Nadu | 33.4 | 26.2 | 20.5 | 20.0 | 0.5 | 7.2 |
| Kerala | 3.0.7 | 29.2 | 17.8 | 17.8 | 0.0 | 1.5 |
| Goa | 27.0 | 21.0 | 14.8 | 16.4 | –1.6 | 6.0 |

*Source:* Registrar General of India (1999), *Compendium of India's Fertility and Mortality Indicators*, 1971-1997, Vital Statistics Division, Ministry of Home Affairs, New Delhi, pp. 4-338.

DNA—Data Not Available.

*Notes:* (i) Data for Jammu and Kashmir and Mizoram are not available.
(ii) States are arranged in descending order of differential in 1991.

Despite the prevailing CBR differentials between rural and urban areas as well as their inter-state variations, there have been noticeable trends in CBR declining during the last 20 years. This decline is observed in almost half of the states, though its degree varied. In 1971, the maximum and minimum CBR in rural areas was 44.6 in Uttar Pradesh and 21.3 in Nagaland respectively, with a difference of 23.3 per 1000. In 1991, the maximum rural CBR was 36.7 in Madhya Pradesh while the minimum was 14.8 in Goa, with a difference of 21.9 per cent per 1000. Similarly, the maximum urban CBR in 1971 was 34.3 in Rajasthan while the minimum was 18.2 in Meghalaya, making a difference of 16.1 per 1000. In 1991, the maximum urban CBR was 29.6 in Uttar Pradesh and minimum was 13.3 in Sikkim. This represents a difference of 16.3 per 1000. Thus, as a whole, the declining fertility trend in the country caused only a slight tendency of reducing the difference between the maximum and minimum CBRs.

Infact, the declining fertility trends in various states have encouraged among them the inconsistency and disparity in crude birth rate and over time values of this rate have shown growing variations both in rural and urban areas of the state. As is evident from the values of the coefficient of variation (CV) of rural and urban crude birth rates for 1971 and 1991 the variation in urban crude birth rate was much higher (17.89) than rural (12.33) in 1971. However, in 1991, both the areas had shown increased CV, being 21.77 in the rural areas and 21.08 in the urban areas. It is evident that the increase in the variation was more marked in rural areas. It appears that the socio-economic attributes which regulate the fertility trends and determine its level, have shown increasing regional disparity. Although in urban areas an already very high CV emphasizes the traditional existence of this disparity, the increasing trend associated with socio-economic development among various states during the last 20 years is particularly seen in the sharply increased CV of rural CBR. On a single index this characteristic is also reflected in terms of growing disparity in per capita income among various states (Mohan and Pant, 1985). These emerging features indicate that the elements of modernization and process of socio-economic development in the country which are responsible for not only to cause fertility to decline but to reduce its regional variations are still confined in their spatial influence and hence regional fertility differentials exist.

Thus, in the north Indian states of Haryana and *BIMARU* states — Uttar Pradesh, Bihar, Rajasthan and Madhya Pradesh, and Assam and Meghalaya in north-east, the CBR in both the areas is among the highest in the country. On the contrary, in the north-eastern states of Nagaland and Manipur, and Tamil Nadu, Goa and Kerala in the south, the CBR is among the lowest in the country chiefly because of high literacy, a superior status of women and their greater participation in the work force as well as a high female mean age at marriage.

The areal differences in CBR, therefore, reflect the social and economic characteristics of local population. These differences are themselves a function of different social classes and cultural characteristics of the concerned areas or their industrial structure, of the nature and accessibility, of the dwelling stocks and also of certain traditions associated with different areas, which are more difficult to quantify.

For an understanding of the rural-urban differential between 1971-91, data are divided in various categories for the purpose of explanation (Table 5.10 and Map 5.2).

**Table 5.10:** India: Trend of Rural-Urban Differentials in Birth Rates, 1971-73 to 1991-93

*(Based on 3 years moving averages)*

| *Rural-Urban Differential Categories* | | |
|---|---|---|
| 1 | 2 | 3 |
| Orissa (+ 4.1) | Tamil Nadu (–6.7) | Goa (–7.6) |
| West Bengal (+3.8) | Manipur (–5.0) | |
| Madhya Pradesh (+3.7) | Tripura (–4.6) | |
| Punjab (+3.4) | Himachal Pradesh (–4.4) | |
| Maharashtra (+2.1) | Haryana (–3.2) | |
| Bihar (+1.0) | Uttar Pradesh (–2.7) | |
| Andhra Pradesh (+0.8) | Gujarat (–2.5) | |
| Assam (+0.6) | Karnataka (–2.0) | |
| | Kerala (–1.5) | |
| | Meghalaya (–1.4) | |
| | Rajasthan (–0.7) | |

*Source*: Calculated from, Registrar General of India (1999), *Compendium of India's Fertility and Mortality Indicators, 1971-1997*, Vital Statistics Division, Ministry of Home Affairs, New Delhi, pp. 4-338

*Note:* The trend of differentials is calculated for states only.

## Category and Nomenclature

1. Areas with rural birth rate more than urban with increasing differential trend.

2. Areas with rural birth rate more than urban with decreasing differential trend.
3. Areas with rural birth rate more than urban in 1971 but reverse became true in 1991.

### *1. Areas with Rural Birth Rate More than Urban with Increasing Differential Trend*

It is clear from Map 5.2 and Table 5.10 that the rural-urban differential increased in the states of Orissa, West Bengal, Madhya Pradesh, Punjab, Maharashtra, Bihar, Andhra Pradesh and Assam between 1971 and 1991. In Punjab, the rural-urban differential increased from 0.7 in 1971 to 4.1 in 1991. In central highlands and eastern plateaus, the states of Madhya Pradesh and Orissa respectively are important. Among these states, Orissa shows a significant increase in rural-urban differential (4.1) in 1971-91, while on the other end of the scale is Assam with 0.6 differential. In Orissa, with the decline in the rural and urban birth rates from 34.8 and 32.5 in 1971 to 28.6 and 22.2 respectively in 1991. The rural-urban differential increased from 2.3 to 6.4 during 1971-91, because the reduction in birth rate in urban areas was almost double than what it was in rural areas. In West Bengal, the trend of differential is showing an increase with 31.4 and 24.0 in rural and urban areas in 1971 and 28.9 and 17.7 in both the areas respectively in 1991. This differential is more due to a rapid decline of urban fertility between 1971-91. In Maharashtra also the rural and urban fertility rates declined but the rural-urban differential became almost double between 1971-91. Among these states, both the rural and urban fertility rates are declining but the differential between them is increasing owing to the fact that urban fertility decline in all these states is higher than rural fertility decline. The rate of decline in urban areas is higher than rural by more than 3 points in Orissa, West Bengal, Punjab and Madhya Pradesh, above 2 points in Maharashtra, and below one point in Bihar, Andhra Pradesh and Assam. In all these states, with the exception of Punjab (where female mean age at marriage is about 19 years) and Assam (data not available), the female mean age at marriage is low (about 17 years). In all these states, except Punjab and Maharashtra, the level of economic development is also low.

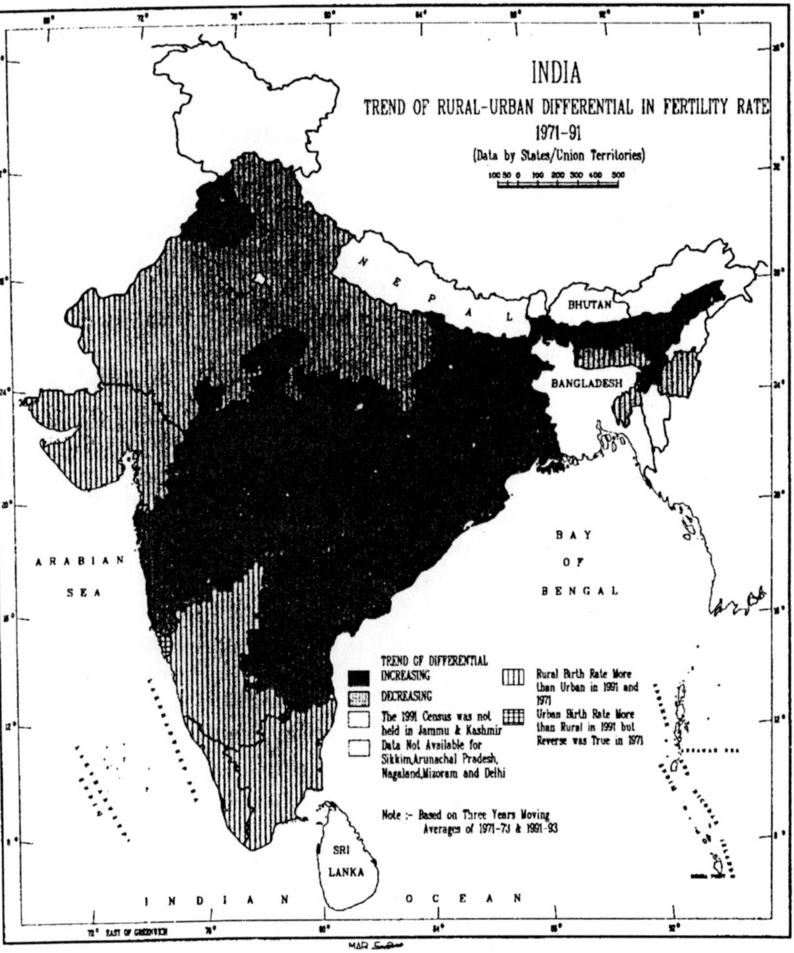


**Map 5.2**: India: Trend of Rural-Urban Differential in Fertility Rate, 1971-91 (Data by States/Union Teritories)

*2. Areas with Rural Birth Rate More than Urban with Decreasing Differential Trend*

The states which fall in this category are Tamil Nadu, Karnataka and Kerala in south, Rajasthan and Gujarat in western India, Haryana, and Uttar Pradesh in upper and middle Ganga plain, Manipur, Meghalaya and Tripura in north-eastern hill region and Himachal Pradesh. In all these areas, rural-urban differentials in fertility are declining.

Among the major regions, Tamil Nadu, Himachal Pradesh, Haryana, Uttar Pradesh, Gujarat and Karnataka are showing maximum decrease in rural-urban differential. All these areas show a decline of more than 2.0 per thousand population in rural-urban differential between 1971-91. Areas of low decrease in rural- urban differential, *i.e.* below 2.0 per thousand population are Kerala, Meghalaya and Rajasthan. In Kerala, the lower fertility in rural and urban areas is associated more with greater equity in education and health facilities. Besides, the state government's efforts on various socio-economic fronts have largely helped Kerala having one of the lowest fertility rates in the country alongwith very low rural-urban differential (Nag, 1984).

Zachariah *et al.* (1994) rightly list the following determinants of fertility decline in Kerala—reduction in infant and child mortality accompanied by an increase in female education, followed by redistribution policies and finally by the official family planning programme. Kerala, thus, typifies balanced *top-down* and *bottom-up* forces operating for fertility decline.

In Tamil Nadu, the factors of political will and an efficient bureaucracy seem to have played a crucial role in the fertility transition, overcoming the intrinsic cultural barriers imposed by low literacy levels, relatively higher mortality, low standards of living, and high heterogeneity of the population. The *top-down* forces seem to be more dominant than the *bottom-up* forces in expediting the fertility decline in Tamil Nadu.

In most of these states, both rural and urban fertility rates declined with decline in rural rates being sharper. The rate of fertility decline in rural areas is higher than urban by more than 6 points in Kerala and Manipur, more than 3 points in Tripura, Himachal Pradesh and Haryana, above 2 points in Uttar Pradesh, Gujarat and Karnataka and below 2 points in Kerala, Meghalaya and Rajasthan. Nevertheless, it ought to be clear that in determination of levels and trends of urban fertility, urbanization seems to have played a less significant role in influencing urban crude birth rate in various states.

A correlation coefficient between the level of urbanization and urban crude birth rate for the year 1991 shows a highly insignificant inter-relationship as Spearman's correlation coefficient value is –0.1212. It is evident from Table 5.9 that some of the states to record lowest urban CBR are those where level of urbanization is low to lowest such as majority of north-eastern states of India and Orissa. With the simultaneous interplay of several socio-economic and demographic as well as behavioural factors relating to modern outlook, the level of urbanization does not show any direct bearing in regulating urban fertility. Experiences around the world indicate that for having any significant influence on fertility, urbanization requires a substantial high level, which India lacks. Urbanization in India has not been accompanied by industrialization to the same extent. Chiefly due to above mentioned two reasons, the role of the urbanization affecting fertility is still inconsistent.

*3. Areas with Rural Birth Rate More than Urban in 1971 but Reverse became True in 1991 with Declining Trend*

Only one state *i.e.* Goa comes in this category. Here, the rural-urban differential was 6.0 in 1971 and it became negative in 1991 with −1.6. In 1971, Goa was showing a similar trend, as was in rest of the country *i.e.* high rural (27.0 per thousand) and low urban (21.0 per thousand) birth rates. But in 1991, the condition reversed with a birth rate of 16.4 per thousand in urban and 14.8 per thousand in rural areas. In Goa, lower fertility has been attributed to several factors, particularly women's higher status in Goan society because of education, low mortality levels especially of children, higher age at marriage, a higher proportion of women remaining single throughout life, long spells of separation because of husbands leaving Goa for work, and, as a consequence, a pervasive desire for a smaller family and adoption of contraceptive methods, including effective use of traditional and natural methods (Pai Panendikar and Chaudhuri 1983).

**India: Spatial Patterns of Rural-Urban Differentials in Fertility Rates, 1991**

A detailed picture of the rural-urban differential in fertility rates can be observed by looking into the rural and urban birth rates and finally their differential index (Table 5.11) in various states of India. The states are divided into two categories of major and minor states by Registrar General of India for calculation of vital statistics.

The rural-urban differential calculated for birth rates show that this differential is more marked in the north-east India as well as West Bengal, Madhya Pradesh and Himachal Pradesh.

Low differential is found in most of the south Indian states. Due to the non-availability of data on district level, the differential index is

**Table 5.11**: India: Rural-Urban Differential Indices in Fertility Rates, 1991

| *Country/State/Union Territory* | *Differential Index* |
|---|---|
| **India** | **0.1300** |
| *States* | |
| Meghalaya | 0.3250 |
| Sikkim | 0.2881 |
| West Bengal | 0.2405 |
| Tripura | 0.1874 |
| Himachal Pradesh | 0.1846 |
| Nagaland | 0.1811 |
| Assam | 0.1638 |
| Madhya Pradesh | 0.1621 |
| Bihar | 0.1270 |
| Orissa | 0.1259 |
| Haryana | 0.1250 |
| Uttar Pradesh | 0.1234 |
| Rajasthan | 0.1191 |
| Maharashtra | 0.0996 |
| Arunachal Pradesh | 0.0865 |
| Punjab | 0.0785 |
| Karnataka | 0.0641 |
| Gujarat | 0.0629 |
| Andhra Pradesh | 0.0406 |
| Manipur | 0.0391 |
| Tamil Nadu | 0.0119 |
| Kerala | 0.0000 |
| Goa | –0.0484 |
| *Union Territories* | |
| Daman & Diu | 0.2201 |
| Dadra & Nagar Haveli | 0.1119 |
| Chandigarh | 0.0868 |
| Delhi | 0.0733 |
| Lakshadweep | 0.0713 |
| Andaman & Nicobar Islands | 0.0483 |
| Pondicherry | 0.0475 |

*Source:* Calculated from, *Sample Registration Bulletin* (1998), 32, 1, Registrar General, India, New Delhi.

*Notes:* (i) Data for Mizoram is not available.

(ii) States and union territories are arranged in descending order of differential index in 1991.

calculated for 23 states (excluding Jammu & Kashmir where census was not held in 1991 and Mizoram where SRS does not exist) and 7 union territories. On the basis of differential index calculated for birth rate in rural and urban areas, the differential indices range between 0.0119 in Tamil Nadu to 0.3250 in Meghalaya. Kerala is the only state where no rural-urban differential exists, because both the rural and urban birth rates are same *i.e.*, 17.8 per thousand population. Goa is the only state where differential index is negative (–0.0484) which is the result of higher urban birth rate (16.4 per thousand population) than the rural birth rate (14.8 per thousand population).

On correlating differentials in fertility rates with various factors affecting these rates, we observe that rural-urban differentials are correlated negatively (Table 5.12) with percentage of family planning programme acceptors, female mean age at effective marriage, rural female literacy rate, level of urbanization, per capita income and percentage of rural female non-agricultural workers to total rural workers.

The expansion of national family planning programmes has influenced the fertility rates in the country and proved as an important means to control it. The couple protection rate improved considerably in the major states of the country during 1981-90 to reach 42 per cent in 1988-89 of which 30 per cent is due to sterilization alone. Similarly, mean age at marriage is an important determinant of fertility as it is directly related to the duration of likelihood of conceiving and carrying pregnancy. Therefore, a lower female age at marriage besides having high fertility potential, also lengthens the span of marital union. In contrast, a relatively higher female age at marriage causes a shortening of reproductive span which accompanied by factors like higher female literacy and work force participation ultimately contributes towards lowering fertility. India in this regard falls into the former group. These states of high differential index have low mean age at marriage. The differentials are also positively correlated with infant mortality rates in rural areas. If unfortunately the infant mortality rate in rural areas increases, the rural-urban differential will also increase.

Although, there does not exist a wide range of rural-urban differentials in birth rate, but for an understanding of differentials in fertility by residence, all the states and union territories are divided into 3 major categories, which is depicted on Map 5.3.

1. States with rural birth rate higher than urban with:
    (a) High rural-urban differential index (0.21 and above).
    (b) Moderate rural-urban differential index (0.10 to 0.20).
    (c) Low rural-urban differential index (0.9 and below).
2. States with urban birth rate higher than rural.
3. States where rural-urban differential does not exist.

**Table 5.12**: India: Coefficients of Correlation of Rural-Urban Differential in Fertility, 1991

| *Indicator* | *Coefficient of Correlation* |
|---|---|
| Percentage of family planning programme acceptors | −0.3610 |
| Per capita income | −0.3571 |
| Female mean age at effective marriage | −0.2062 |
| Percentage of rural female non-agricultural workers to total rural workers | −0.2033 |
| Rural female literacy rate | −0.1932 |
| Level of urbanization | −0.1212 |
| Rural infant mortality rate | +0.3791 |

*Source:* Computed from, Publications made by Registrar General of India (1994, 1995, 1997, 1998) and Economic Intelligence Service (1991, 1993, 1994, 1997).

*1. States with Rural Birth Rate Higher than Urban*

Keeping in view the national average (0.1300) of rural-urban differential index, the states with rural birth rate higher than urban are discussed under three sub-categories:

*(a) High Rural-Urban Differential Index (0.21 and above)*

The states which fall in this category are eastern hill states of Meghalaya (0.3250) and Sikkim (0.2881). The state of West Bengal (0.2405) in eastern plains is also a part of this category of high rural-urban differential. In the eastern hill states, the birth rate in rural areas is almost double than what it is in urban areas and is quite high from national average (30.7). The reasons being early age at marriage, low level of literacy especially among females, and a large proportion of population residing in rural areas belonging to reproductive age-group. The most typical case is Sikkim where despite a low level of urbanization (9.1 per cent) urban crude birth rate (13.3 per 1000) is also very low.

*(b) Moderate Rural-Urban Differential Index (0.10 to 0.20)*

The areas attributed with moderate level of rural-urban differential indices of fertility are northern plains (including Haryana and Uttar Pradesh), north-eastern and southern parts of central highlands (comprising Madhya Pradesh), eastern plateaus (covering Orissa) and in Assam valley. In this category, the rural-urban differential index is

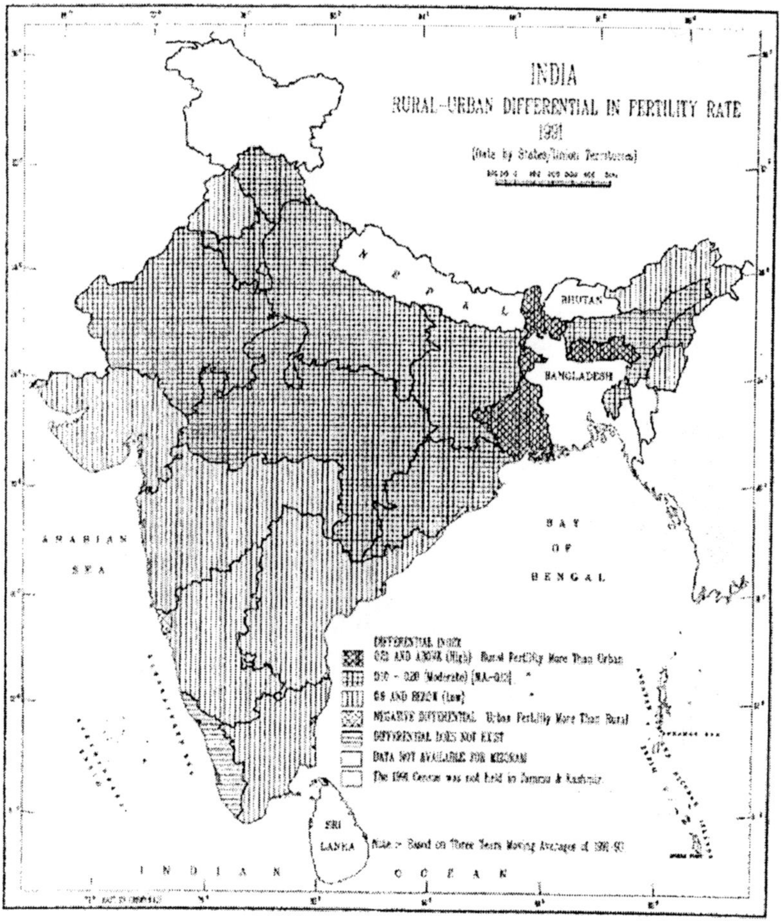


**Map 5.3:** India: Rural-Urban Differential in Fertility Rate, 1991 (Data by States/Union Territories)

maximum in Himachal Pradesh (0.19) and Tripura (0.19). It is followed by Nagaland (0.18), Assam (0.16), Madhya Pradesh (0.16), Bihar (0.13), Haryana (0.13), Orissa (0.13), Rajasthan (0.12) and Uttar Pradesh (0.12). In all these states, rural-urban differential in birth rate is between 6.4 to 9.9 live births per thousand population which, in turn, results in moderate rural-urban differential index. All these areas are agricultural regions as far as their economy is concerned. A majority of people in rural areas depend on the traditional occupations by adopting labour intensive technologies with less inclination to the idea of modernization of these occupations and motivated high fertility aspirations among these poor illiterate rural people. So, the children, more or less, are considered as their assets useful for their vocations (Reddy, 1996). Further, the prevalence of high infant and childhood moralities in the rural areas compel the couples to aspire to have more number of children in their families to assure the survival of a few of them. Male sex preference seems to be another predominant factor in rural areas mainly because patriarchal society exists in north India. Most of the couples in rural areas want to have, at least, two male living children in their families and in some families, especially among the rural people, they continued and aspired to have at least a male child in the event of not having male living children in their families. These expectations deliberately stimulate higher fertility among the couples in rural areas. The cost of rearing children in the rural areas is low. In some rural areas, there are no proper educational facilities and in some cases parents do not send their children to schools, also they are utilized as a contributory labour in their parents' productive activities. But, the situation is entirely different in urban areas, because most of the people in urban areas are involved in non-traditional, modern occupations. Under this environment, children are considered to be consumer products and liabilities. They invest large sums of money in educating their children and these children cannot give any help to their parents in their professional activities. So, the cost of bearing and rearing of children in the urban areas puts pressure upon the people to limit their family size. So, the ways of life in rural and urban areas influence the people towards having children and this, in turn, influences their fertility rates also. The imbalanced sex ratio also contributes to this. The level of urbanization and literacy is also low in comparison to south. Uttar Pradesh and Madhya Pradesh are among *BIMARU* states and are a real cause of worry.

Haryana presents an interesting case. Despite being a fairly rich state with high per capita income (Rs. 3380) and where literacy rates are also comparable with national average, it shows high fertility rates (33.6 per thousand population) in rural areas. Besides *BIMARU* states (Bihar, Madhya Pradesh, Rajasthan and Uttar Pradesh), Haryana constitutes one of the demographically vulnerable states because of the inferior status of women, which partly explains the high level of fertility inspite of economic prosperity (Bose, 1991).

*(c) Low Rural-Urban Differential Index (0.09 and below)*

The entire peninsular India (barring Kerala and Goa), Arunachal Pradesh and Manipur in north-east and Punjab and Gujarat are the areas which cover almost 60 per cent of the country's area, constitute this category of low rural-urban differential index. In all these areas, the rural and urban birth rates are above 20 per thousand and are somewhat similar to each other. So, the resultant rural-urban differential is low. The rural-urban differential index is minimum in Tamil Nadu (0.0119 live births per thousand). In south Indian states, level of status of women is high because of matrilineal society. In all these states, sex ratio is above national average (927 females per thousand males) except in Punjab (888). Per capita income is fairly high.

*2. States with Urban Birth Rate Higher than Rural*

A minor state Goa (–0.0056) comes in this category of negative rural-urban differential. Here, the urban fertility rate exceeds the rural one. The state ranks high in rural literacy rate (72.31 per cent) including rural female literates (62.87 per cent). Despite a high level of urbanization (41.0 per cent), level of economic development (index above 2.51) and status of women, the urban birth rate is more (16.4 live births per thousand), whereas the rural birth rate is 14.8 live births per thousand.

*3. States where Rural-Urban Differential does not exist*

The only state that falls in this category is Kerala. Here, both the rural and urban birth rates are the same (17.8 per thousand). Hence, rural-urban differential does not exist in this coastal state of south India. The impact of Christian missionaries in creating awareness, wide acceptance of family planning programmes, a large number of the population engaged in secondary and tertiary activities, very high literacy rates among both the sexes in rural and urban areas, a high status enjoyed by women and lesser gender inequalities explain the phenomenon.

**India: Rural-Urban Differentials in Mortality**

Mortality, besides, fertility, is the second component of vital rates. It is defined as permanent disappearance of all evidence of life at any time after birth has taken place (United Nations, 1953). The study holds immense importance because the increase of population depends not only upon the birth rate in the country but also on the death rate therein. In the past, the size of population fluctuated mainly in response to variations in mortality (Bhende and Kanitkar, 1985). The developing countries, including India, which are undergoing demographic transition, have also been affected initially by the fall in the death rates. It is revealed that the sharp decline in mortality is more important for rapid growth of population, rather than any rise in fertility rates.

In order to measure the rate of mortality, the simplest measure of mortality, crude death rate, indicating the number of death in a particular year per thousand of population is used. It is expressed as:

$$CDR = \frac{\text{Total number of deaths in a year}}{\text{Total population at the mid - point of the year}} \times 1000$$

Here, the number of deaths is obtained from three years' moving averages from Sample Registration Bulletin. It is crude because it does not take into account the age distribution of the population.

## Trend of Rural-Urban Differentials in Mortality

Mortality is an important demographic variable influencing the growth of the population of a country. Although death has always been a major target of human concern and efforts to bring a decline in it are a matter of worldwide human strategy, India in this regard has a poor reputation in terms of health and disease since nearly all major diseases and causes of death commonly encountered in pre-industrial societies, have been endemic to the country. Frequent attacks of famines, epidemics, influenza and plague mark its modern history from the late nineteenth to the early twentieth century (Thompson, 1935). This experience, accompanied by poverty, deprivation, dirt and ignorance created conditions in which mortality was bound to be very high. Infact, as Table 5.1 and Fig. 5.1 show, due to these factors between 1901-11 and 1911-21, there was a marked increase in the crude death rate in the country. It was only since 1921 that through the control of famines and epidemics, improved storage and distribution facilities for food and by public health measures with no great improvement in socio-economic habit of the people (Ambannavar, 1975) which resulted in decline in CDR. It was only the result of the Government of India's health programme and measures from time to time especially after independence that mortality and infant mortality started declining in the country and its most impressive forms were shaped up only a few decades ago (Table 5.13 and Fig. 5.2)

**Table 5.13:** India: Crude Death Rate, 1911-2000

| *Year* | *CDR* | *Year* | *CDR* |
|---|---|---|---|
| 1911 | 42.6 | 1961 | 22.8 |
| 1921 | 47.2 | 1971 | 18.9 |
| 1931 | 36.3 | 1981 | 12.5 |
| 1941 | 31.2 | 1991 | 10.1 |
| 1951 | 27.4 | 2000 | 8.5 |

*Sources:* (i) 1911 to 1941 from Davis (1968).
(ii) 1951 to 1971 from Actuarial reports of the Census Actuary.
(iii) 1981 to 1991 from *Sample Registration Bulletin* (1998), 32, 1.
(iv) 2000 from *Sample Registration System Bulletin* (2001), Table I, Vol. 35, No. 2, p. 1.

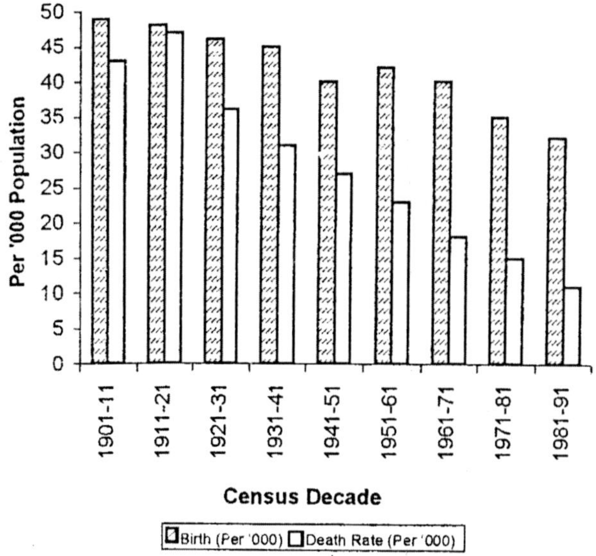


**Fig. 5.1:** 00India: Estimated Birth and Death Rates, 1901-91

The death rate declined from 42.6 in 1901 to around 27 at the time of Independence. This significant decline in the mortality rate has played an important role in accelerating the growth rate of India's population. In fact the socio-economic progress that India has achieved during almost past four decades, perhaps nothing has had a more salutary effect on the condition of everyday life than the decline in death rate. This

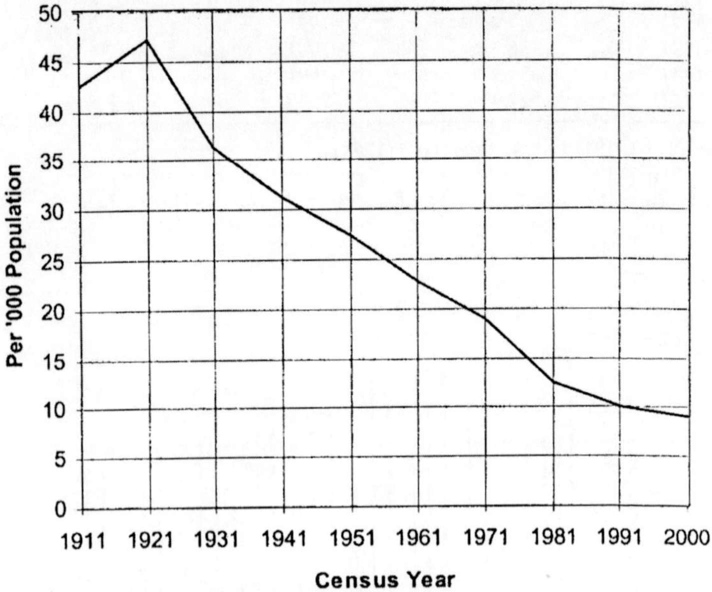


**Fig. 5.2:** India: Crude Death Rate, 1911-2000

phenomenon has been so marked that whereas in the early 1950's Chandrasekhar (1952) lamented on the slow pace of mortality decline, by the late 1960s, its pace gained momentum and became quite rapid (Ruzieka, 1984). However, data given in Table 5.12 also reveal that once the crude death rate had stabilized around 15 in the 1970's, it declined to reach around 9 in the 1990's, though at a slower pace.

The infant mortality rate dropped sharply from 133.6 to 91.2 between 1971-90. The expectation of life at birth recorded an increase of roughly 8 years from an estimated level of 49.7 years during 1971-75, to 57.8 years during 1986-90 (Table 5.14).

The separate figures for both rural and urban areas again reveal declining mortality trend in line with the country as a whole. However, higher decline in the rural as compared to urban areas has resulted in somewhat reducing the rural-urban gap. In rural areas, the crude death rate fell from 15.5 in early seventies (1971-75) to 10.6 in late eighties (1986-90) as compared to corresponding decline from around 9.8 to 7.3 in urban areas. The decline recorded in infant mortality rate in rural areas during the same period was from 143.6 to 99 as compared to from 82.8 to 58.8 in urban areas. Likewise, the improvement revealed in expectation of life at birth was larger in rural areas (from 48 to 56) as compared to urban areas (from 59 to 64).

**Table 5.14:** India: Trends in Mortality Level, 1971-90

| Year | *Total* | | | *Rural* | | | *Urban* | | |
|---|---|---|---|---|---|---|---|---|---|
| | *Crude Death Rate* | *Infant Mortality Rate* | *Expectation of Life at Birth* | *Crude Death Rate* | *Infant Mortality Rate* | *Expectation of Life at Birth* | *Crude Death Rate* | *Infant Mortality Rate* | *Expectation of Life at Birth* |
| 1971-75 | 15.5 | 133.6 | 49.7 | 17.10 | 143.6 | 48.0 | 9.8 | 82.8 | 58.9 |
| 1976-80 | 13.9 | 124.0 | 52.3 | 15.08 | 134.0 | 50.6 | 8.86 | 74.4 | 60.1 |
| 1981-85 | 12.1 | 104.2 | 55.5 | 13.34 | 113.4 | 53.7 | 7.9 | 63.6 | 62.8 |
| 1986-90 | 10.6 | 91.2 | 57.8 | 9.46 | 99.0 | 56.3 | 7.32 | 58.8 | 64.1 |

*Source:* Calculated from, Goyal (1995), *Demography India*, 24, 1, Table 1, p. 104.

These characteristics emphasize that for a further rapid decline in mortality rate in the country, there should be further basic improvements in the living conditions of the people, which in turn imply greater availability of preventive and curative health services on the one hand and elimination of contagious diseases, malnutrition and infant mortality on the other. As Vallin (1968) has suggested that no country can attain a life expectancy of more than 60 years without having made very substantial progress out of the category *less developed* although deaths from a number of chronic and degenerative diseases have been declining for a considerable period the emerging epidemiological and public health evidences suggest that there is still significant potential for further decline in mortality rates in the country.

During the entire post-Independence period, mortality trends seem to have followed a two-phased transition. In the first phase, which was operational up to the 1960s, mortality decline, was also accompanied by the corresponding control of some of the chronic diseases. The second phase began from the early 1970's with mortality though declining, morbidity often increasing.

Inspite of the steep fall in death rate in India since 1980, the infant, child and maternal mortality, though declined, continued to be at alarmingly higher levels. The infant mortality according to 1995 estimates is 74 per thousand live births and the maternal mortality in 1991 is as high as 400-500 for 1,00,000 pregnant women. The main reason, among others, is attributed to ignorance, poverty and poor per capita nutritional availability.

The mortality rates significantly vary between urban and rural areas. Urban mortality rates are lower than rural. This phenomenon is partly attributed to the age structure of urban population where the proportion of people in the working age group is higher, in which mortality is, in any case lower (Agarwala, 1985). But part of the difference is also because of better sanitary conditions, availability of safe drinking water, better sewerage disposal system and better medical facilities and health care in urban areas. Whereas more than 85 per cent of the urban population in the country is now having piped water supply, despite massive efforts thousands of villages still do not have even elementary water supply system. This feature, accompanied by lack of proper sewerage disposal system and scarcity of hospitals are responsible for higher rural mortality rates than urban. Besides, as studies on mortality in various parts of the world have shown, those populations or classes of populations which are in relatively favourable position from economic and social points of view, tend to have lower mortality rates than the less developed populations. Therefore, some of these differences between rural and urban mortality rates are also the outcome of socio-economic gaps between these two areas and these rates are influenced by overall social as well as economic conditions of the people, in which they live and work. This characteristic makes mortality a status-dependent component of the population which ultimately leads towards lower urban mortality rates.

The traditional existence of rural-urban mortality differential in the country has long been recognized (United Nations, 1961; Mehta, 1978). National Sample Survey (NSS) for the first time provided reliable data on the rural and urban mortality trends since the country's Independence through its various rounds of survey from 1950 to 1967. Table 5.15 using sample registration bulletin data presents the mortality rates for rural and urban areas which indicate the prevalence of a noticeable differential between the mortality rates of these two populations between 1970 and 1996. The analysis of this data on mortality shows that the rural-urban differentials in mortality are at decline in India.

**Table 5.15**: India: Rural-Urban Differentials in Mortality Rates, 1971-1999.

| *Year* | *Death Rates (Per thousand)* | | *Rural-Urban Differential* |
|---|---|---|---|
| | *Rural* | *Urban* | |
| 1971 | 16.4 | 9.7 | 6.7 |
| 1973 | 17.0 | 9.6 | 7.4 |
| 1975 | 17.3 | 10.2 | 7.1 |
| 1977 | 16.0 | 9.4 | 6.6 |
| 1979 | 13.9 | 8.4 | 5.5 |
| 1981 | 13.7 | 7.8 | 5.9 |
| 1983 | 13.1 | 7.9 | 5.2 |
| 1985 | 13.0 | 7.8 | 5.2 |
| 1987 | 12.0 | 7.4 | 4.6 |
| 1989 | 11.1 | 7.2 | 3.9 |
| 1991 | 10.6 | 7.1 | 3.5 |
| 1993 | 10.6 | 5.8 | 4.8 |
| 1995 | 9.8 | 6.6 | 3.2 |
| 1997 | 9.6 | 6.5 | 3.1 |
| 1999 | 9.4 | 6.3 | 3.1 |

*Sources*: Calculated from,
(i) Registrar General of India (1999), *Compendium of India's Fertility and Mortality Indicators*, 1971-1997, Table I, p. 3.
(ii) Registrar General of India (2001) *Sample Registration System Bulletin*, Vol. 35, No. 2, Table 2, p. 2.

An examination of mortality trends among major states reveals that mortality trend in each state and also in both urban and rural areas of each state is in line with the whole country and show a continued fall (Table 5.16).

The extent of all, however, differed from state to state, it is generally steeper in states with initial higher levels of mortality. The decline in crude death rate over the period of twenty years varied between 10.6 points in Uttar Pradesh to 2.5 points in the state of Kerala. The fall in infant mortality rate varied between the highest 94 points again in Uttar Pradesh and to 24 points in the state of Karnataka and 35 points in Orissa. The improvement in the life expectancy at birth during the period 1971-75 and 1991-95 for which the figures are available reveal the highest 13.8 years improvement in Uttar Pradesh, from 43.0 to 56.8 years and the lowest 5.9 years in Haryana, from 57.5 to 63.4 years. The notable feature of changes in different states over the period is that the comparative position of states in respect of the level of mortality initially and at the end of the period remained materially unchanged. Kerala and Uttar Pradesh have the lowest and the highest levels of mortality

**Table 5.16**: India: Trends in Mortality Rates by Rural-Urban Residence, 1971-73 to 1991-93

*(Based on 3 years moving average)*

| *Country/State Union Territory* | *Crude Death Rate (Per Thousand)* | | | | | |
|---|---|---|---|---|---|---|
| | *1971-73* | | | *1991-93* | | |
| | *Total* | *Rural* | *Urban* | *Total* | *Rural* | *Urban* |
| **India** | **15.9** | **17.4** | **9.9** | **9.7** | **10.7** | **6.6** |
| *Major States* | | | | | | |
| Andhra Pradesh | 15.8 | 17.0 | 10.3 | 9.2 | 10.1 | 6.0 |
| Assam | 17.3 | 18.1 | 9.7 | 10.7 | 11.1 | 6.9 |
| Bihar | DNA | DNA | DNA | 10.5 | 11.0 | 5.9 |
| Gujarat | 15.7 | 17.0 | 12.1 | 8.6 | 9.1 | 7.6 |
| Haryana | 11.3 | 11.9 | 8.3 | 8.3 | 8.8 | 6.5 |
| Karnataka | 12.4 | 14.2 | 7.9 | 8.5 | 9.5 | 5.9 |
| Kerala | 8.9 | 9.1 | 7.8 | 6.1 | 6.2 | 5.9 |
| Madhya Pradesh | 17.1 | 18.1 | 10.9 | 13.1 | 14.2 | 8.4 |
| Maharashtra | 12.9 | 14.5 | 9.3 | 7.8 | 9.2 | 5.5 |
| Orissa | 17.9 | 18.5 | 11.0 | 12.2 | 12.9 | 6.6 |
| Punjab | 11.7 | 12.4 | 9.1 | 8.0 | 8.7 | 5.9 |
| Rajasthan | 16.2 | 17.6 | 9.6 | 9.9 | 10.6 | 6.7 |
| Tamil Nadu | 14.5 | 16.9 | 8.8 | 8.5 | 9.4 | 6.7 |
| Uttar Pradesh | 21.7 | 22.9 | 13.5 | 11.9 | 12.7 | 8.5 |
| West Bengal | DNA | DNA | DNA | 8.0 | 8.8 | 5.9 |
| *Smaller States* | | | | | | |
| Arunachal Pradesh | DNA | 20.9 | DNA | 10.5 | 11.5 | 2.3 |
| Goa | 8.8 | 9.9 | 5.8 | 7.2 | 7.9 | 5.8 |
| Himachal Pradesh | 14.6 | 15.1 | 6.9 | 8.8 | 9.1 | 5.2 |
| Manipur | 7.9 | 8.0 | 6.6 | 5.3 | 5.3 | 5.2 |
| Meghalaya | DNA | DNA | DNA | 8.0 | 9.1 | 3.1 |
| Nagaland | DNA | DNA | DNA | 3.9 | 4.5 | 1.5 |
| Sikkim | DNA | DNA | DNA | 6.7 | 7.4 | 2.5 |
| Tripura | 13.4 | 14.0 | 8.0 | 7.1 | 7.4 | 5.1 |
| *Union Territories* | | | | | | |
| Andaman & Nicobar Islands | 8.0 | 8.8 | 3.4 | 5.5 | 6.0 | 3.9 |
| Chandigarh | DNA | DNA | DNA | 3.5 | 4.5 | 3.4 |
| Dadra & Nagar Haveli | DNA | 14.8 | DNA | 11.7 | 11.7 | DNA |
| Daman & Diu | DNA | DNA | DNA | 8.4 | 8.4 | 8.3 |
| Delhi | 7.8 | 12.0 | 7.3 | 5.6 | 7.7 | 5.4 |
| Lakshadweep | DNA | 14.5 | DNA | 5.7 | 6.5 | 4.7 |
| Pondicherry | 9.5 | 9.6 | 8.6 | 6.6 | 7.5 | 5.9 |

*Sources*: Registrar General of India (1999), *Compendium of India's Fertility and Mortalty Indicators, 1971-1997,* Vital Statistics Division, New Delhi, pp. 4-410.

DNA = Data Not Available

respectively amongst the spectrum of Indian states both at the beginning as well as at the close of this twenty year period from 1971 to 1991.

However, a great variation in death rates is found among various states (Table 5.17). The states with low level of socio-economic development have comparatively high rural and urban death rates, for example, Madhya Pradesh, Uttar Pradesh, Rajasthan and Orissa. This trend continued between 1971-91. In a large number of states socio-economic as well as medical and health attributes seem to have been collective determinants of crude death rate levels which makes it difficult to correlate the impact of the varying degree of socio-economic development of the concerned state with the variation in mortality. Moreover, the direct effects of social and economic development on mortality like the ones that were experienced by the western nations in the nineteenth century and later are not so pronounced in India (Kohli, 1977). This phenomenon has caused different reasons for existing mortality trends in the states.

Besides, the urban death rates are generally lower than rural in all the states and union territories. The reasons being the younger age structure of the urban population, better sanitary conditions, protected drinking water and easy access to life saving drugs. For example, on the eve of seventh Five-Year Plan, glaring disparities were noticed in the provision of medical facilities to rural and urban people. About two-third of all hospitals with 84 per cent of hospital beds and 66 per cent of all dispensaries are found in urban areas. The picture is more glaring at disaggregated spatial scale.

Further, the entire rural area as well as most of the medium and smaller towns are without proper sewage facilities and availability of safe drinking water is also minimal in them. Another reason for high mortality rate in rural areas is the proportion of population living below poverty line. In 1987-88, the population below poverty line was 20.1 per cent in case of urban areas, whereas it was 33.4 per cent in rural areas.

Table 5.17 also clarifies that with sharp variations there has been a large area of overlap between rural and urban crude death rates prevailing among different states which impinge on the general process of demographic development. For example, in 1971, the urban CDR varied from the maximum of 13.5 in Uttar Pradesh to the minimum of 5.8 in Goa, while in rural areas it ranged from the maximum of 22.9 in Uttar Pradesh to the minimum of 8.0 in Manipur. Coming to 1991 in urban areas, the highest and lowest values were 8.5 in Uttar Pradesh and 1.5 in Nagaland respectively. In the same year, these figures for rural areas

**Table 5.17:** India: Rural-Urban Differentials in Mortality Rates, 1971-73 and 1991-93

*(Based on 3-year moving average)*

| *Country / State / Union Territory* | *Mortality Rate (Per Thousand)* | | | | *Rural – Urban Differential* | |
|---|---|---|---|---|---|---|
| | *1971-73* | | *1991-93* | | *1971-73* | *1991-93* |
| | *Rural* | *Urban* | *Rural* | *Urban* | | |
| **India** | **17.4** | **9.9** | **10.7** | **6.6** | **7.5** | **4.1** |
| *Major States* | | | | | | |
| Andhra Pradesh | 17.0 | 10.3 | 10.1 | 6.0 | 6.7 | 4.1 |
| Assam | 18.1 | 9.7 | 11.1 | 6.9 | 8.4 | 4.2 |
| Bihar | DNA | DNA | 11.0 | 5.9 | 6.7 | 5.1 |
| Gujarat | 17.0 | 12.1 | 9.1 | 7.6 | 5.1 | 1.5 |
| Haryana | 11.9 | 8.3 | 8.8 | 6.4 | 3.6 | 2.4 |
| Karnataka | 14.2 | 7.9 | 9.5 | 5.9 | 6.3 | 3.6 |
| Kerala | 9.1 | 7.8 | 6.2 | 5.9 | 1.3 | 0.3 |
| Madhya Pradesh | 18.1 | 10.9 | 14.2 | 8.4 | 7.2 | 5.8 |
| Maharashtra | 14.5 | 9.3 | 9.3 | 5.4 | 5.2 | 3.9 |
| Orissa | 18.5 | 11.0 | 12.9 | 6.6 | 7.5 | 6.3 |
| Punjab | 12.4 | 9.1 | 8.7 | 5.9 | 3.3 | 2.8 |
| Rajasthan | 17.6 | 9.6 | 10.6 | 6.7 | 8.0 | 3.9 |
| Tamil Nadu | 16.9 | 8.8 | 9.4 | 6.7 | 8.1 | 2.7 |
| Uttar Pradesh | 22.9 | 13.5 | 12.7 | 8.5 | 9.4 | 9.4 |
| West Bengal | DNA | DNA | 8.8 | 5.9 | DNA | 2.9 |
| *Smaller States* | | | | | | |
| Arunachal Pradesh | 20.9 | DNA | 11.5 | 2.3 | DNA | 9.2 |
| Goa | 9.9 | 5.8 | 7.9 | 5.8 | 4.1 | 2.1 |
| Himachal Pradesh | 15.1 | 6.9 | 9.1 | 5.2 | 8.2 | 3.9 |
| Manipur | 8.0 | 6.6 | 5.3 | 5.2 | 1.4 | 0.1 |
| Meghalaya | DNA | DNA | 9.1 | 3.1 | DNA | 6.0 |
| Nagaland | DNA | DNA | 4.5 | 1.5 | DNA | 3.0 |
| Sikkim | DNA | DNA | 7.4 | 2.5 | DNA | 4.9 |
| Tripura | 14.0 | 8.0 | 7.4 | 5.1 | 6.0 | 2.3 |
| *Union Territories* | | | | | | |
| Andaman and Nicobar Islands | 8.8 | 3.4 | 6.0 | 3.9 | 3.4 | 2.1 |
| Chandigarh | DNA | DNA | 4.5 | 3.4 | 1.8 | 1.1 |
| Dadra & Nagar Haveli | 14.8 | DNA | | | | |
| Daman & Diu | DNA | DNA | 8.4 | 8.3 | DNA | 0.1 |
| Delhi | 12.0 | 7.3 | 7.7 | 5.4 | 3.8 | 2.3 |
| Lakshadweep | 14.5 | DNA | 6.5 | 4.7 | DNA | 1.8 |
| Pondicherry | 9.6 | 8.6 | 7.5 | 5.9 | 1.0 | 1.6 |

*Source:* Calculated from, Registrar General of India (1999), *Compendium of India's Fertility and Mortality Indicators, 1971-1997,* Vital Statistics Division, Ministry of Home Affairs, New Delhi, pp. 4-410.
DNA : Data Not Available.

were 14.2 in Madhya Pradesh and 4.5 in Nagaland. This overlap, can be explained, at least in part by the fact that in many states certain areas, particularly belonging to lower urban class hierarchy, may be designated urban according to census criteria whereas only a fraction of the population of the area benefits from such urban amenities as clean water supply, sanitation and health.

The decline in rural-urban differentials is evident in all the states and union territories (for which data are available) except the union territory of Pondicherry where it increased between 1971-91. These states and union territories are grouped into four categories to look into the trend of differentials among states (Table 5.18 and Map 5.4).

**Category and Nomenclature**

1. Areas with rural death rate more than urban with high decline in differential.
2. Areas with rural death rate more than urban with moderate decline in differential.
3. Areas with rural death rate more than urban with low decline in differential
4. Areas with rural death rate more than urban with increase in differential.

*1. Areas with Rural Death Rate More than Urban with High Decline in Differential*

The states which fall in this category are Tamil Nadu, Uttar Pradesh, Himachal Pradesh, Assam and Rajasthan. The decline in rural mortality rate is 3.5 times (Tamil Nadu), 2.5 times (Himachal Pradesh), and 2.0 times (Assam, Rajasthan, Uttar Pradesh) as compared to urban mortality rate. All this is the result of diffusion of health facilities, safe drinking water facilities and improvement in sanitation. The infant mortality rate got reduced in rural areas to 64 in Tamil Nadu, 93 in Uttar Pradesh, 80 in Assam, 89 in Rajasthan and 63 in Himachal Pradesh in 1993-95.

*2. Areas with Rural Death Rate More than Urban with Moderate Decline in Differential*

Tripura (–3.7), Gujarat (–3.6), Karnataka (–2.7) and Andhra Pradesh (2.6) are the states which fall in this category.

**Table 5.18:** India: Trend of Rural-Urban Differentials in Mortality Rates, 1971-73 to 1991-93

*(Based on 3-year moving average)*

| *Rural-Urban Differential Categories* | | | |
|---|---|---|---|
| 1 | 2 | 3 | 4 |
| Tamil Nadu (–5.4) | Tripura (–3.7) | Goa (–2.0) | Pondicherry (+0.6) |
| Uttar Pradesh (–5.2) | Gujarat (–3.6) | Bihar (–1.6) | |
| Himachal Pradesh (–4.3) | Karnataka (–2.7) | Delhi (–1.5) | |
| Assam (–4.1) | Andhra Pradesh (–2.6) | Madhya Pradesh (–1.4) | |
| | | Andaman & N. Islands (–1.3) | |
| | | Maharashtra (–1.3) | |
| | | Orissa (–1.2) | |
| | | Kerala (–1.0) | |
| | | Chandigarh (–0.7) | |
| | | Punjab (–0.5) | |

*Sources*: Computed from, Registrar General of India (1999), *Compendium of India's Fertility and Mortality Indicators, 1971-1977*, Vital Statistics Division, Ministry of Home Affairs, New Delhi, pp. 4-410.

### 3. *Areas with Rural Death Rate More than Urban with Low Decline in Differential*

Goa (–2.0), Bihar (–1.6), Delhi (–1.5), Madhya Pradesh (–1.4), Andaman & Nicobar Islands (–1.3), Maharashtra (–1.3), Orissa (–1.2), Kerala (–1.0), Chandigarh (–0.7) and Punjab (–0.5) fall in this category of low rural-urban differential. Because the death rates in all these states and union territories have reached a stationary stage *i.e.* below 10 per thousand in both rural and urban areas. So, they are declining at a somewhat stable rate in both rural as well as urban areas. For example, in Punjab, low mortality rates in both rural and urban areas are attributed to some important improvements in environmental hygiene (especially safe drinking water and sanitation), in health care facilities and education. These substantial improvements in environmental hygiene resulting from the state's investment in infrastructure and public health standards of food and housing seem to have been the two most important components (Chaudhari and Gupta, 1985). In Kerala, despite a low level of economic development, higher literacy rate, better status of women and governmental incentives to improve the health and general

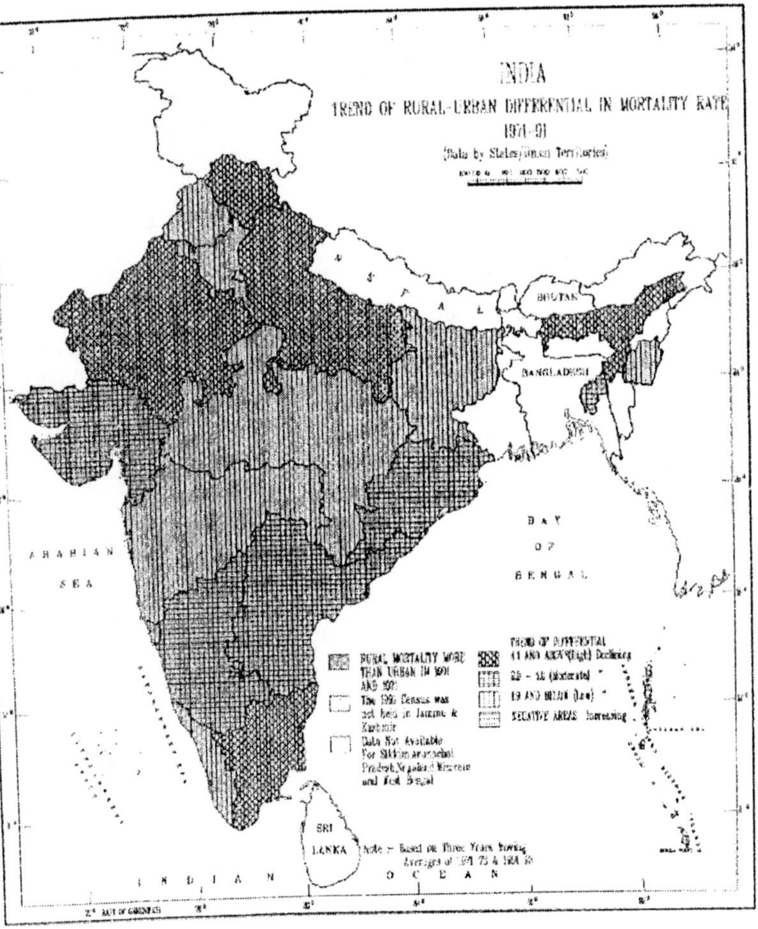


**Map 5.4:** India: Trend of Rural-Urban Differential in Mortality Rate, 1971-91 (Data by States.Union Teritories)

welfare of the population including, simple preventive measures have been significant factors in considerably lowering death rates in both rural and urban areas.

*4. Areas with Rural Death Rate More than Urban with Increase in Differential*

Pondicherry, a union territory, is the only one that comes in this category. Here, both rural (9.6) and urban (9.6) mortality rate in 1971 declined to 7.5 in rural and 5.9 in urban areas in 1991. The increase in differential is the result of low decline in rural mortality rate in comparison to the urban.

**India: Spatial Patterns of Rural-Urban Differential in Mortality Rates, 1991**

As in the case of fertility, there exist wide differentials in mortality between rural and urban areas in the country since urban mortality rates are lower than rural. It is evident from the data that any appreciable decline in crude death rate can be attributed to a significant fall in infant mortality rate, without which mortality decline would be rather limited. This factor has contributed appreciably, in India also, in lowering the overall mortality rate. Although improvements in the life expectancy of women, children and other age groups have also been supportive elements in the achievement of ongoing mortality trends.

It is clear from Table 5.19 and Map 5.5 that the rural-urban differentials are substantially higher in some states. It is because of the socio-economic and medical as well as health related factors which create differences between the vital rates of these two populations, and influence the crude death rates strongly.

However, with the declining crude death rates among the rural and urban population these differentials have also observed a decline such as in Manipur and in the union territory of Daman and Diu, the rural and urban death rates reached 5.3 and 5.2 (Manipur) and 8.4 and 8.3 (Daman & Diu) respectively with the differential index value of 0.01 point. In Kerala also the crude death rates recorded are 6.2 and 5.9 in rural and urban areas respectively. However, in some states such as Arunachal Pradesh, Meghalaya, Nagaland, Sikkim and Orissa these differential index values reached above 0.30.

**Table 5.19:** India: Rural-Urban Differential Indices in Mortality Rates, 1991

| *Country/State/Union Territory* | *Differential Index* |
|---|---|
| India | 0.2192 |
| *States* | |
| Arunachal Pradesh | 0.7197 |
| Nagaland | 0.4837 |
| Sikkim | 0.4822 |
| Meghalaya | 0.4811 |
| Orissa | 0.3054 |
| Bihar | 0.2821 |
| Himachal Pradesh | 0.2518 |
| Maharashtra | 0.2449 |
| Madhya Pradesh | 0.2414 |
| Andhra Pradesh | 0.2354 |
| Assam | 0.2160 |
| Karnataka | 0.2150 |
| Rajasthan | 0.2081 |
| Uttar Pradesh | 0.1840 |
| West Bengal | 0.1802 |
| Punjab | 0.1750 |
| Tripura | 0.1668 |
| Tamil Nadu | 0.1532 |
| Haryana | 0.1437 |
| Goa | 0.1389 |
| Gujarat | 0.0816 |
| Kerala | 0.0222 |
| Manipur | 0.0085 |
| *Union Territory* | |
| Dadra & Nagar Haveli | 0.4119 |
| Andaman & Nicobar Islands | 0.1918 |
| Delhi | 0.1593 |
| Lakshadweep | 0.1448 |
| Chandigarh | 0.1242 |
| Pondicherry | 0.1078 |
| Daman & Diu | 0.0054 |

*Source*: Calculated from, *Sample Registration Bulletin* (1998), 32, 1, Registrar General, India, New Delhi.

On correlating rural-urban differentials of mortality with various variables, we observe that they are correlated (Table 5.20) negatively with dispensaries per lakh of rural population and rural female literacy rate.

**Table 5.20:** India: Coefficients of Correlation of Rural-Urban Differential in Mortality, 1991

| *Indicator* | *Coefficient of Correlation* |
|---|---|
| Dispensaries per lakh of rural population | –0.2308 |
| Rural female literacy rate | –0.2527 |
| Food security (enhanced agricultural productivity) | +0.1758 |

*Source*: Calculated from, *Sample Registration Bulletin* (1998), 32,1, Registrar General, India, New Delhi.

The spread of education influences the mortality rates, by making people more aware of diseases and health care during pregnancy, child care, diseases prevalent in childhood and prevention of various fatal diseases and also infusing sense of cleanliness and proper sanitation. A study conducted for Greater Bombay in 1966 observed that the levels of infant mortality were highly influenced by the educational attainment of the mothers. The infant mortality rate was the highest for infants of illiterate mothers and the lowest for infants whose mothers had either passed the matriculation or had higher education (Ruzieka and Kanitkar, 1972).

The real difference between rural-urban mortality is partially because of improved sanitary conditions, availability of pure drinking water, better sewerage disposal and better medical facilities and health care in urban areas (Agarwala, 1985) and partially because of the difference in public awareness towards various health hazards which is more in urban areas, the role of varying level of urbanization on urban mortality rates seems to be ineffective in the country and the states attaining high level of urbanization have not been able to create health conditions conducive to relatively higher mortality reduction. This characteristic proves that urbanization may also lower the quality of environment which leads towards higher mortality trends (Cumper, 1985). On the other hand, the rural-urban differentials in mortality are correlated positively with increasing food security (enhanced agricultural productivity) implying that a decline in rural mortality will be caused by increasing food security and in turn the rural-urban differential would decrease.

On the basis of rural-urban differential index values, various states and union territories are divided into three categories, keeping in view that rural mortality rates are higher than urban. These are:

1. Areas with high differential index (0.31 and above)
2. Areas with moderate differential index (0.15 - 0.30)
3. Areas with low differential index (0.14 and below)

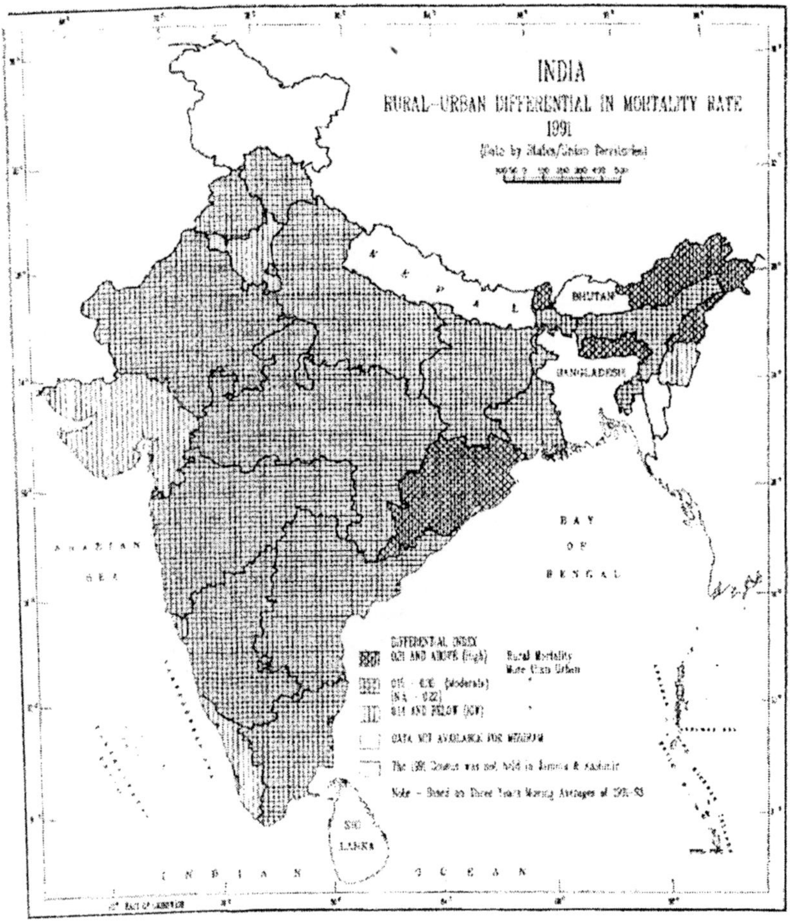


**Map 5.5:** India: Rural-Urban Differential in Mortality Rate, 1991 (Data by States / Union Territories)

## *1. Areas with High Differential Index (0.31 and above)*

The areas of high rural-urban differentials are Orissa and north-eastern hill states, including Arunachal Pradesh, Meghalaya, Nagaland and Sikkim. The maximum rural-urban differential is found in Arunachal Pradesh (0.72 deaths per 1000) followed by Meghalaya (0.48), Nagaland (0.48), Sikkim (0.48) and Orissa (0.31). In 1991, the rural death rate in

Arunachal Pradesh was 9.1 and urban 3.1 per thousand population. In Nagaland, these rates were 4.5 and 1.5 in rural and urban areas respectively. In Sikkim, Meghalaya and Orissa these rates were 7.4, 9.1 and 12.9 (rural), 2.5, 3.1 and 6.6 (urban) respectively. This high differential is attributed to very low death rates in urban areas, because of young urban population in areas where people in working age-group dominate and in this age group mortality rates are comparatively low. Part of the difference is due to a highly illiterate rural population, inadequate health and sewage facilities. In these five states, only 4.74 per cent of the population is accepting family planning programmes, the lowest percentage is in Orissa (0.14 per cent).

*2. Areas with Moderate Differential Index (0.15-0.30)*

Majority of India comprises this category covering lower half of western Himalayas, whole of northern plains, upper half of eastern plains, central highlands of India, north-western half of eastern plateau, the Deccan region, northern half of eastern and western coastal plains.

The maximum differential is observed in Bihar, where rural-urban differential is 0.28, followed by Maharashtra (0.25), Himachal Pradesh (0.25), Andhra Pradesh (0.24), Madhya Pradesh (0.24), Assam (0.22), Karnataka (0.22), Rajasthan (0.21), Punjab (0.18), Uttar Pradesh (0.18), West Bengal (0.18), Tripura (0.17) and Tamil Nadu (0.15), and among the union territories of Andaman and Nicobar Islands (0.19) followed by Delhi (0.16).

In north Indian states, where a major proportion of country's population lives and has a high and constant trend of decline in rural mortality. But the rural-urban differential values are still large because of high rural mortality rates (above 10) in most of these states. However, in most of the south Indian states both the rural and urban mortality rates have reached to an almost stationary stage (below 10). In north India, the states like Madhya Pradesh, Uttar Pradesh, Rajasthan and Bihar fall under the category of *BIMARU* states (comprising a large proportion of the Indian population) where facilities are at a very low level in rural as well as in urban areas. In Madhya Pradesh, high infant mortality rates in rural areas (109 deaths per 1000 live births) are indicative of high mortality rate in rural areas.

In the hill states of Himachal Pradesh and Assam, the rural birth rates are 9.1 and 11.8 and for urban areas 5.2 and 6.9 respectively. The female mean age at marriage is also low (around 16 years) in most of the north Indian states except in Himachal Pradesh and Punjab where it is around 19 years and in south India where it is around 16.5 years except in Tamil Nadu where it is around 18.5 years.

*3. Areas with Low Differential Index (0.14 and Below)*

The states and union territories which fall in this category are found scattered here and there all over India as northern half of western coastal plains (Gujarat), northern part of northern plains (Haryana), southern part of western coastal plains (Kerala). The maximum differential in this category is found in Haryana (0.14) followed by Goa (0.14), Gujarat (0.08), Kerala (0.02) and Manipur (0.01). Among union territories this differential is maximum in Lakshadweep (0.14) followed by Chandigarh (0.12), Pondicherry (0.11) and Daman & Diu (0.01). Not only have crude death rates declined in these areas but so also the differentials. Particularly in Kerala, Manipur and Daman & Diu the crude death rates have almost become equal in rural as well as in urban areas in 1991. These are 6.2 and 5.9 in Kerala, 5.3 and 5.2 in Manipur, 8.4 and 8.3 in Daman and Diu for the rural and urban areas respectively.

## CONCLUDING REMARKS

1. In India, with the decline in birth rates from 36.3 in early seventies to 29.1 per thousand in early nineties and a drop in death rate from 15.9 to 9.7 during the corresponding period ultimately resulting in decline in natural growth rate, the performance in controlling death was much better than that in checking birth. With this, India entered in late expanding stage of demographic transition in case of birth rates (crude birth rate around 30) and in late stationary stage in case of death rates (crude death rate under 10) according to Jone's Model of Demographic Transition.
2. Not only have the rural-urban differentials in fertility existed ever since but the rural fertility rates have remained higher than urban throughout the present century. The low urban fertility is caused by unbalanced sex ratio, high living standards, economic insecurity and unemployment, social capillarity, occupational status, female employment, educational facilities and the availability of clinical aids towards family planning and so on. The rural areas are denied many of these. The latter drenched in poverty, ignorance and insecurity result in high fertility. Not all the regions are alike. In

the north Indian states of Haryana, Uttar Pradesh, Bihar, Rajasthan and Madhya Pradesh, the crude birth rate in both the areas is among the highest in the country. In Maharashtra, Punjab and south Indian states of Tamil Nadu, Karnataka and Kerala, these rates are relatively lower. In Hilly northern and north-eastern states, the crude birth rate is among the lowest in the country chiefly because of high literacy, a superior status of women, their greater participation in work force as well as higher female age at marriage. The different measures of human fertility based on varied standards of reproduction such as crude birth rate (CBR), general fertility rate (GFR), total fertility rate (TFR) and gross reproduction rate (GRR) indicate that although there exist differentials in rural-urban fertility, it is declining over time. The different rates of fertility are continuously declining over time despite the fact that with growing population in the country, increasing number of women are entering the reproductive age-group and the aggregate number of live births is continuously increasing.

3. The sharp difference between rural and urban GFR testifies that besides change in marital customs, mainly higher mean age at marriage in urban areas, more urban women are practicing family planning than rural women. The magnitude of difference between rural and urban GFR is, to a certain extent, a reflection of fertility trend effected by birth control measures.
4. Similarly, the state-level estimates of TFR in urban areas suggest a sharp decline in urban fertility to near replacement level in Kerala, Tamil Nadu, Assam and West Bengal. This decline in urban fertility, with the urban sector having a total population of nearly 230 million by 1995, has considerable significance for the demographic situation in the country as a whole, because continuing interaction between urban and rural population is likely to generate a fairly strong demographic effect. However, the inter-state difference in the TFR cannot be explained in terms of the conventional indicators of modernization such as urbanization, industrialization or the female worker-population ratios.
5. Infant mortality rates and crude death rates have substantially declined both in rural and urban areas as a result of improvement in the living standards, but more so in urban areas. These tendencies are likely to impact upon the rural areas as well.
6. It must be noted that fertility has declined in almost all parts of the country to a greater or lesser extent. Also, the pace of decline is not

necessarily the highest in states with the highest per capita income (*i.e.*, Punjab or Haryana) or in the poorer states (such as Bihar or Orissa). So, neither a rapid rise in living standards nor poverty seem to have led to a substantial fall in fertility. By looking into the age-specific fertility rates between 1970-92, it is observed that there has been a clear shift in the pattern of childbearing age, the peak fertility now occurs in the age group 20-24 instead of in the age group 25-29. More importantly, fertility declines are evident in all age groups, but particularly at ages 30 and above.

7. The crude birth rate, which is the most common index of human fertility taken for analysis reveals that the trend of rural-urban differentials in birth rates are showing a continuous decline in rural areas. Interestingly, a very strong positive relationship is seen between rural and urban crude birth rate, the correlation coefficient being .7290 in 1991, implying that the states having high or low urban crude birth rates are also having high or low rural crude birth rates. However, in low crude birth rate states urban-rural continuum is helping in minimizing these fertility rates in both the areas. In high crude birth rate states it seems that the dominant presence of values attributed to high rural crude birth rate on the one hand and lack of industrial and occupational structure as well as exposure to many aspects of modernization and development conducive to reduce urban fertility, have contributed in keeping the crude birth rates in both the areas at relatively higher levels.
8. Despite the prevailing differentials between rural and urban areas as well as their inter-state variations, there have been noticeable trends in CBR declining during the last 20 years. This decline is observed in almost half of the states, though its degree varied. Infact, the declining fertility trends in various states have encouraged among them inconsistency and disparity in crude birth rate and over time, values of this rate have shown growing variation both in rural and urban areas of the state. The increase in the variation was more marked in rural areas. It appears that the socio-economic attributes which regulate the fertility trends and determine its level, have observed increasing regional disparity. Although, in urban areas an already very high coefficient of variability emphasizes the traditional existence of this disparity, the increasing trend associated with socio-economic development among various states, during the last 20 years is particularly seen in the sharply increased coefficient of variability of rural crude birth rate. These emerging features

indicate that the elements of modernization and the process of socio-economic development in the country which are responsible for not only to cause fertility decline but also to reduce its regional variations are still confined in their spatial influence and hence regional fertility differentials exist.

9. The rural-urban differential in fertility is increasing in the states of Orissa, West Bengal, Madhya Pradesh and Assam and declining in the states of Tamil Nadu, Manipur, Tripura, Himachal Pradesh, Haryana, Uttar Pradesh, Gujarat, Karnataka, Kerala, Meghalaya, and Rajasthan between 1971-91, although the rural birth rates are more than urban in all these states. Only Goa has urban birth rates more than rural with declining differential trend.
10. The rural-urban fertility differentials are correlated negatively with percentage of family planning programme acceptors, female mean age at effective marriage, rural female literacy rate, level of urbanization, per capita income and percentage of rural female non-agricultural workers to total rural workers. On the other hand, it is correlated positively with infant mortality rate in rural areas. A balanced *top-down*, and *bottom-up* forces, therefore, would operate for minimizing rural-urban fertility differentials.
11. Spatially speaking, the rural-urban differential calculated for birth rates show that this differential is more marked in the north-east India as well as West Bengal, Madhya Pradesh and Himachal Pradesh, whereas, low differential is found in most of the south Indian states.
12. Mortality besides fertility, is the second component of vital rates, which is defined as permanent disappearance of all evidence of life at any time after birth has taken place. India has a poor reputation in terms of health and disease. It was only the result of the Government of India's health programmes and measures from time to time especially after its Independence that mortality and infant mortality started declining in the country and its most impressive forms were shaped up only a few decades ago.
13. The mortality trends for states are declining in line with the country as a whole. However, higher decline in the rural as compared to urban areas has resulted in somewhat reducing the rural-urban gap.
14. During the entire post-Independence period, mortality trends seem to have followed a two phase transition. In the first phase, which was operational upto 1960s, mortality decline, was also accompanied by the corresponding control of some of the chronic diseases. The

second phase began from the early 1970's with mortality though declining, morbidity often increasing. Notwithstanding the traditional existence of rural-urban mortality differential in the country, the rural-urban differentials in mortality are at decline in India, which is evident in all the states and union territories except the union territory of Pondicherry where it increased between 1971-91. The notable feature of changes in infant mortality rates and life expectancy at birth in different states over the period is that the comparative position of states in respect of the level of mortality initially and at the end of the period (1971-91) remained materially unchanged. Kerala and Uttar Pradesh have the lowest and the highest levels of mortality respectively amongst the spectrum of Indian states both at the beginning as well as at the close of this twenty-year period from 1971 to 1991. However, a great variation in death rates is found among various states. The states with low level of socio-economic development have comparatively high rural and urban death rates. In a large number of states, socio-economic as well medical and health attributes seem to have been collective determinants of crude death rate levels which make it difficult to correlate the impact of the varying degree of socio-economic development of the concerned state with the variation in mortality.

15. There has been a large area of overlap between rural and urban crude death rates, with sharp variations, prevailing among different states which impinge on the general process of demographic development. This overlap can be explained, at least in part by the fact that in many states certain areas, particularly belonging to lower urban class hierarchy, may be designated urban according to census criteria whereas only a fraction of the population of the area benefits from such urban amenities as clean water supply, sanitation and health. It is observed that the rural-urban differentials in mortality are correlated negatively with dispensaries per lakh of rural population and rural female literacy. This shows that the spread of education influences the mortality rates by making people more aware of diseases, health care during pregnancy, child care, diseases prevalent in childhood and prevention of various fatal diseases and also infusing a sense of cleanliness and proper sanitation.
16. On the other hand, it is correlated positively with enhanced agricultural productivity, implying that a decline in rural mortality will be caused by increasing food security and in turn the rural-urban differential would decrease.

17. Spatially speaking, the rural-urban differentials are high in Orissa and north-eastern hill states including Arunachal Pradesh, Meghalaya, Nagaland and Sikkim. The maximum rural-urban differential is found in Arunachal Pradesh. Low differential is typical of advanced states like Gujarat, Haryana, Kerala, Goa and Manipur alongwith the union territory of Lakshadweep, Chandigarh, Pondicherry and Daman & Diu. In rest of India, the differential is moderate.
18. Broadly speaking, the rural-urban differentials in vital rates alongwith overall fertility and mortality rates are continuously declining throughout India, albeit at varied pace.

# 6

# SIZE OF HOUSEHOLD

The household that exists in almost all the societies of the world in one form or the other, is a significant unit in the comparison and analysis of human societies. It is a basic unit in any society for social, economic, political, and socialization purposes. The household, basically is a co-residential socio-economic unit regardless of kinship ties. It is likely to be influenced by kinship rules, demographic factors, and socio-economic conditions in a society. Changes in the type of economy and in demographic factors *e.g.* migration, sex ratio, death rate, birth rate are also likely to have an effect on the size of household in a society. Process of industrialization and urbanization, which are a result of change in an economy, have also been recognized as important factors affecting the size of household in societies with changing economies.

A household in the Indian census is a group of persons who commonly live together and would take their meals from a common kitchen unless the exigencies of work prevented them from doing so. A household may comprise of persons related with blood or of unrelated persons or having a mix of both (Census of India, 1991). On the basis of the principle of co-residence, it is a demographic unit composed of related or unrelated persons, who share some physically or socially defined space for everyday life (Curson, 1978). It must have a common kitchen as the nucleus as per requirements of the Indian census.

A family by comparison, is a social unit based on marriage and united by ties of kinship (Clarke, 1972). The household and the family are not equivalent. Whereas, a household entails co-residence of related or unrelated individuals, the family can comprise individuals who have particular economic or religious connections but who do not co-reside (Caldwell *et al.*, 1982). So, the household is not necessarily a family, but in the Indian context the two are almost the same. It is not surprising that a tendency to use words *family and household* interchangeably still persists in the Indian sociological literature (Shah, 1973). The number and size of families and households greatly influence the character of settlement, and that is of considerable geographical significance.

While the individuals are important units of a society, household constitutes its molecular unit holding immense importance in several aspects of human life (United Nations, 1972). Census enumeration and a variety of studies in social science adopt the household as the primary unit of their investigations. Economists in their inquiry of income and expenditure patterns, sociologists in examination of various social phenomena and processes, demographers in the analysis of housing situation and problems use data generally at the level of individual households. The household can be used in projecting the future population (United Nations, 1981) and is an important economic unit useful for planning purposes. The geographical significance of making a study of household lies in understanding the spatial variations in family organization (relative representation of nuclear and joint families), mode of production (whether it demands pooling together of family resources or permits individual efforts), degree of modernization, represented by attitude towards family size and demographic situation in respect of natural increase, migration and marital status (Krishan, 1980).

Indeed, the household is an important demographic unit in its own. Investigation of the household is perhaps the least developed of the demographic fields in India. Whereas leading geographical journals of the country, for instance, *Annals of NAGI, Transactions of IIG* and *Geographical Journal of India* are replete with research papers on fertility, mortality, migration, sex ratio, urbanization, etc., the household is left virtually untouched. It may find explanation among other things, in the way data on the household have been presented in the censuses. Another reason could be that the importance of the household as a demographic unit in its own right is often overlooked (Bose *et al.*, 1977; United Nations, 1980). There has been a long standing interest in the Indian household by sociologists, but not by demographers and geographers.

Size and composition are the two dimensions of a household. The Census of India normally provides data only on the size of the household. Information on composition of households (number of families/ generations in the household, age-sex structure of the family members and relationship of each member to the head of the household) is generally not given. Hence, any study of the household based on census data has to confine itself to the aspect of size alone.

## The Rural-Urban Factor

It is true that India lives in its villages. According to 1991 census, 74.28 per cent of the total population in India resides in rural areas. The proportion of persons living in rural areas has declined by only 14.88 per cent points in 90 years from 89.16 per cent in 1901 (Table 6.1).

From the results available for various census decades, it is observed that though the proportion of urban population has grown over the years, it is the rural India which controls and determines the overall pattern. Hence, it is important to study the population of India by rural or urban area of residence.

**Table 6.1:** India: Rural-Urban Population, 1901-91

| *Census Year* | *Rural Population Per cent* | *Urban Population* | |
|---|---|---|---|
| | | *Per cent* | *Per cent Change* |
| 1901 | 89.16 | 10.84 | — |
| 1911 | 89.71 | 10.29 | 0.35 |
| 1921 | 88.82 | 11.18 | 8.27 |
| 1931 | 88.01 | 11.99 | 19.11 |
| 1941 | 86.14 | 13.86 | 31.97 |
| 1951 | 82.71 | 17.29 | 41.42 |
| 1961 | 82.03 | 17.97 | 26.41 |
| 1971 | 80.09 | 19.91 | 38.22 |
| 1981* | 76.69 | 23.31 | 46.38 |
| 1991** | 74.28 | 25.72 | 36.19 |

*Sources*: Calculated from,

(i) Census of India (1981), *Final Population Totals*, Paper 1 of 1982, Series-1, Office of the Registrar General and Census Commissioner, India, New Delhi.

(ii) Census of India (1991), *General Population Tables* (Tables A-1 to A-3), Series-1, India, Part II-A (i), Office of the Registrar General and Census Commissioner, India, New Delhi.

* Includes the projected population of Assam.

** Excludes Jammu & Kashmir where census was not held in 1991.

## Size of the Household in India and Other Countries

The average size of the household in India is 5.57 persons per household in 1991, which is one of the largest among the countries of the world. The average household size for the world as a whole is 4.54 persons with 5.33 persons in developing countries and 3.54 persons in developed countries.

The regional pattern of rural-urban differential in size of the household did not conform to that of household size. The differential was the largest in the Latin American countries, relatively large in the developed realm, insignificant or even negative in the Muslim world and marginal in most of the remaining countries (Krishan and Rana, 1980).

**India: Average Size of the Household, 1951-1991**

According to 1991 census, a total of 846 million population of India is found to be distributed over 152 million households. Therefore, the average size of a household comes to 5.57 persons per household. Whereas the rural size of household is 5.63 persons with a population of 629 million persons residing in 112 million households, the urban size of household stands at 5.38 persons with 218 million population living in 41 million households. A comparison of the average household size in India for 1991 census with those of previous decades reveals that the average size of the Indian household is gradually increasing over time. Since Independence in 1947, it is observed that average size of the household has increased from 4.88 persons per household in 1951 to 5.57 in 1991 (Table 6.2 and Fig. 6.1). The maximum increase is

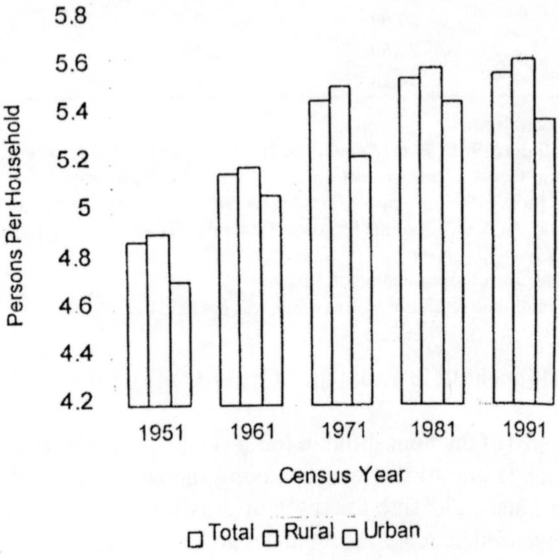


Fig. 6.1: India : Average Size of the Household, 1951-91

witnessed for the period 1951-71. The recent decade shows some signs of stabilization.

Seen as rural-urban break-up, average size of the rural household is continuously increasing since 1951. The maximum increase in rural areas could be witnessed during 1951-71 when the average size of household registered an increase from 4.91 to 5.52 which was similar to the increase in total size of household during the same period. However, 1971-91 period has seen a small increase in size of the household of rural areas.

On the other hand, in case of urban size of the household, the maximum increase was during the decade of 1951-61. Between 1961-81, the size of household increased at slow rate, but, it declined during 1981-91 (Table 6.2). It shows that the urban household size reached its culmination point because many migrants were forced to take residence in their peripheral villages rather than within the cities to avail themselves of the lower cost of living, including rent. Secondly, the frequency of the territorial extension of existing towns was less visible during the 1980's. The net addition of towns/urban agglomerations during 1981-91 was only 390 as compared with 788 during 1971-81. Thirdly, rural development and the associated decline in the incidence of rural poverty appears to have had a moderating effect on rural-urban migration (Krishan, 1993). All these factors account for the slowing down of urban growth and the resultant slow rate of increase in size of the household.

**Table 6.2**: India: Average Size of the Household, 1951-91

| *Census Year* | *Size of the Household* | | | *Rural-Urban Differential* |
|---|---|---|---|---|
| | *Total* | *Rural* | *Urban* | |
| 1951 | 4.88 | 4.91 | 4.71 | + 0.20 |
| 1961 | 5.16 | 5.19 | 5.07 | + 0.12 |
| 1971 | 5.46 | 5.52 | 5.23 | + 0.29 |
| 1981 | 5.55 | 5.59 | 5.45 | + 0.14 |
| 1991 | 5.57 | 5.63 | 5.38 | + 0.25 |

*Sources*: (i) Krishan, G. (1980), "Size of Household in Rural India" in Singh R.L. & Singh R.P.B. (eds.), *Rural Habitat Transformation in World Frontiers*, Table 4, NGSI, Publication 30, Varanasi, p. 359.

(ii) Computed from, Census of India (1991), *Primary Census Abstract: General Population*, Series 1, India, Part II-B(i), Vols. I & II, Office of the Registrar General and Census Commissioner, India, New Delhi.

One of the salient revelations of the Indian census data was that there was not much to distinguish between the average size of the rural household (5.63 persons/household) and the urban household (5.38 persons/household) in 1991. More than 50 per cent of the districts in India had, on an average, a household size of 5.5 persons and above (Table 6.3 and Map 6.1). The figure for rural areas (57.85 per cent) (Map 6.2) was only marginally higher than that for urban areas (47.96 per cent) (Map 6.3).

**Table 6.3:** India: Distribution of Districts by Number of Persons per Household, 1991

| *Type of Area* | *Percentage of Districts with Persons per Household* | | | | *Entirely Rural or Urban* |
|---|---|---|---|---|---|
| | *3.4 to 4.5* | *4.5 to 5.5* | *5.5 to 6.5* | *6.5 & above* | |
| All Areas | 5.09 (23) | 40.04 (181) | 44.91 (203) | 9.96 (45) | 16 |
| Rural areas | 5.15 (23) | 37.00 (165) | 46.86 (209) | 10.99 (49) | 6 |
| Urban areas | 5.43 (24) | 46.61 (206) | 34.61 (153) | 13.35 (59) | 10 |

*Source*: Computed from, Census of India (1991), *Primary Census Abstract: General Population*, Series-1, India, Part II-B(i), Vols. I & II, Office of the Registrar General and Census Commissioner, India, New Delhi.

*Note*: Figures in parentheses indicate the number of districts.

By contrast, size of the household in more than one-third of the Class-I cities of India was larger than the average size of the rural household (5.63 persons/household). Even, out of 23 metropolitan cities in 1991, one-fourth of them have an average size of the household larger than the average for the country (5.57 persons/household) (Table 6.4).

Table 6.4 reveals that Varanasi stands at the top with 7.33 persons as average size of the household. Besides Varanasi, the metropolitan cities of Patna (6.57 persons/household), Kanpur (5.57 persons/household) and Lucknow (5.69 persons/household) also have size of the household even larger than the average size of the rural household (5.63 persons/household) in India. This is mainly because of that most of the cities of Indo-Gangetic plain have a long history of settlement and majority of them are characterised with industries and services as the main functional character. It had been observed in the past that the incidence of joint families in urban areas was almost as high as in rural areas. The observation was supported by several empirical studies and it was revealed that small joint family is now the most typical form of family life amongst the middle and upper middle urban classes in India (Ross, 1973).

**Table 6.4:** India: Size of the Household in Metropolitan Cities, 1991

| *Metropolitan City* | *State/Union Territory* | *Functional Character* | *Average Size of Household* |
|---|---|---|---|
| Varanasi | Uttar Pradesh | Industry | 7.33 |
| Patna | Bihar | Service | 6.57 |
| Kanpur | Uttar Pradesh | Service-cum-Industry | 5.75 |
| Lucknow | Uttar Pradesh | Service | 5.69 |
| Indore | Madhya Pradesh | Industry-cum-Service | 5.62 |
| Jaipur | Rajasthan | Industry-cum-Service | 5.58 |
| Hyderabad | Andhra Pradesh | Industry-cum-Service | 5.54 |
| Ludhiana | Punjab | Industry | 5.38 |
| Bhopal | Madhya Pradesh | Service-cum-Industry | 5.37 |
| Surat | Gujarat | Industry | 5.34 |
| Ahmedabad | Gujarat | Industry | 5.16 |
| Nagpur | Maharashtra | Industry-cum-Service | 5.15 |
| Kolkata | West Bengal | Industry-cum-Trade and Commerce | 5.11 |
| Kochi | Kerala | Services-cum-Industry | 5.11 |
| Delhi | Delhi | Industry | 4.98 |
| Bangalore | Karnataka | Industry | 4.98 |
| Pune | Maharashtra | Industry-cum-Service | 4.85 |
| Vadodara | Gujarat | Industry-cum-Service | 4.82 |
| Chennai | Tamil Nadu | Service | 4.76 |
| Mumbai | Maharashtra | Industry | 4.75 |
| Madurai | Tamil Nadu | Industry-cum-Trade and Commerce | 4.72 |
| Visakhapatnam | Andhra Pradesh | Service-cum-Industry | 4.59 |
| Coimbatore | Tamil Nadu | Industry | 4.31 |

*Sources*: Computed from,

(i) Census of India (1991), *Primary Census Abstract: General Population*, Series-1, India, Part II-B(i), Vols. I & II. Office of the Registrar General and Census Commissioner, India, New Delhi.

(ii) Census of India (1991), *Functional Classification of Urban Agglomerations/Towns of India, 1991*. Occasional Paper 3 of 1994. Office of the Registrar General and Census Commissioner, India, New Delhi.

## India : Rural–Urban (Differentials in Size of the Household, 1951-1991)

The rural-urban differential has not been consistent but varying from decade to decade. It was 0.20 persons in 1951, 0.12 in 1961, 0.29 in 1971, 0.14 in 1981 and 0.25 in 1991 (Table 6.2). It shows that the overall gap between size of the rural and urban households has widened. The increased differential is because the size of rural household has increased constantly at a faster rate than the urban one. The rural household size increased continuously between 1951-91 but this increase shows a declining trend since 1971. The increase in the size of household was 0.28 points in 1951-61, it reached 0.33 in 1961-71, but thereafter it

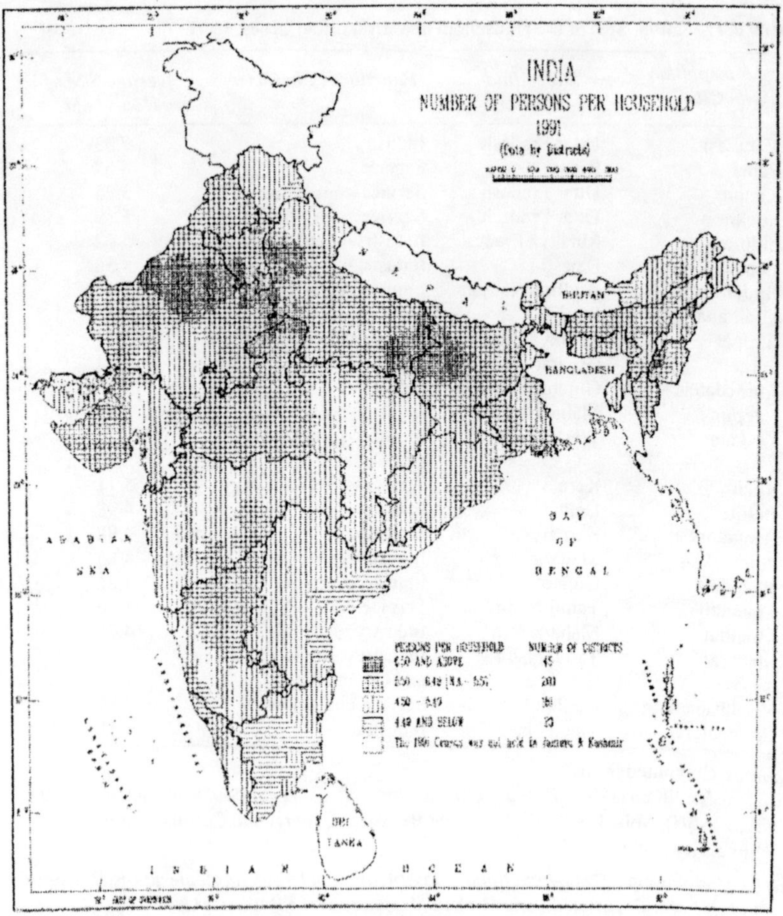


**Map 6.1:** India. Number of Persons per Household, 1991 (Data by Districts)

declined to 0.04 points in 1981-91 (Table 6.5 and Fig. 6.2).

Its urban counterpart also displays a continuous increase except in the decade of 1981-91 where it is showing a decline in size of the household. The increase in household size was more in urban areas in comparison to rural both in 1951-61 and 1971-81 decades. During 1961-71, the rural household size recorded maximum increase.

Among the various states of India (Table 6.6), Himachal Pradesh was noted for the largest difference (+1.30 persons) in average size of its rural (5.48 persons) and urban (4.18 persons) household. The large differential was related to an unusually small size of the urban household, the rural household being close to the national average (5.57 persons).

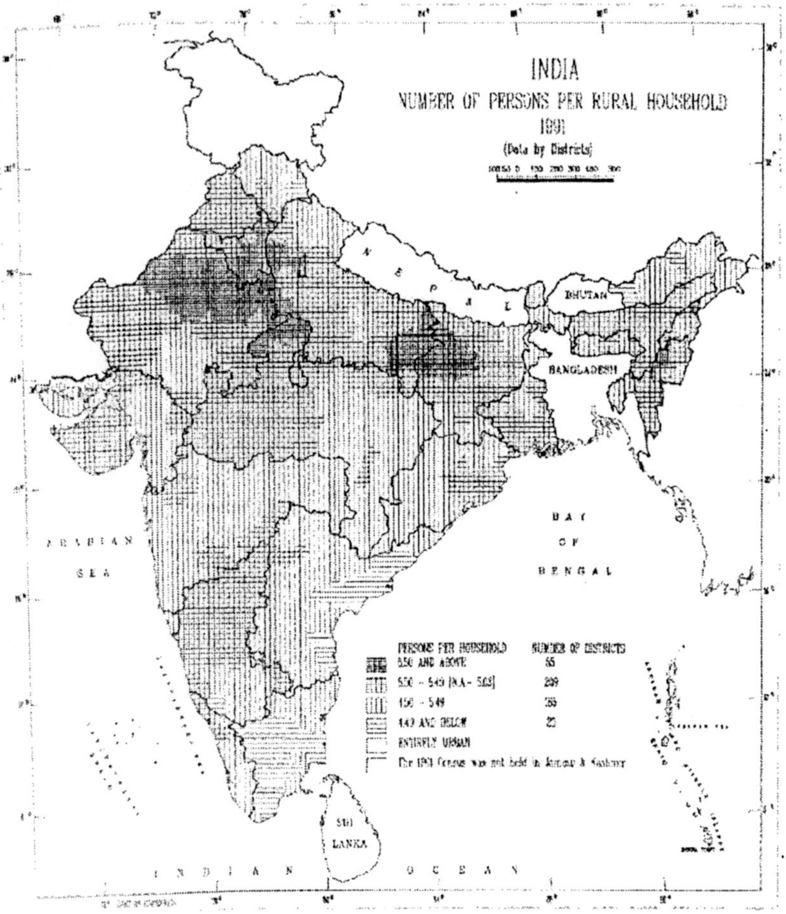


**Map 6.2**: India : Number of Persons per Rural Household, 1991

The functional structure of towns, most of which were administrative centres, along with recency of migration to them, explained this phenomenon. In-migration was largely of educated persons with small families (Krishan and Rana, 1980).

The Punjab and Haryana plain was also noted for a large differential in size of the rural (over 6 persons) and urban (about 5.50 persons) households. The difference in this case was associated with a distinctly large size of the rural household explained by a strong tradition of joint family system which historically has been a more salient feature of joint villages (with a joint tenure of land) as previously typical of north-western India (Powell, 1972). The region's urban community with

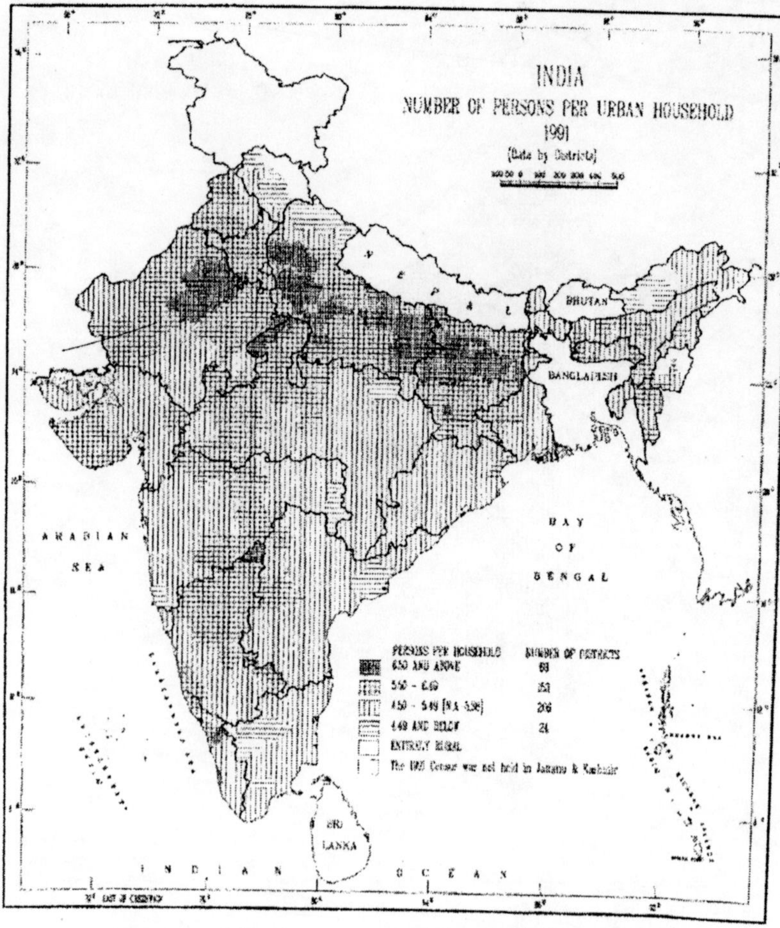


**Map 6.3**: India – Number of Persons per Urban Household, 1991

predominance of the Punjabi-Hindus in service, trade and modern industry, had a lower proportion of joint families.

In Assam and Arunachal Pradesh also, with an average size of rural households as 5.92 and 5.02 persons and urban households as 5.18 and 4.37 persons respectively, wide rural-urban differential exists. These states experienced a rapid growth of population due to a decline in death rate accompanied by a stable high birth rate and sizeable in-migration.

On the other hand, the state of Meghalaya has the lowest rural-urban differential (+0.09 persons) in average size of its rural (5.44 persons) and urban (5.35 persons) households. The prevalence of nuclear

**Table 6.5:** India: Decadal Change in Size of the Household by Rural-Urban Residence, 1951-91

| *Census Decade* | *Decadal Change in Size of Household* | | *Rural-Urban Differential* |
|---|---|---|---|
| | *Rural* | *Urban* | |
| 1951-61 | + 0.28 | + 0.36 | − 0.08 |
| 1961-71 | + 0.33 | + 0.16 | + 0.17 |
| 1971-81 | + 0.07 | + 0.22 | − 0.15 |
| 1981-91 | + 0.04 | − 0.07 | + 0.11 |

*Source:* Computed from, Census of India (1991), *Primary Census Abstract: General Population*, Series-I, India, Part II-B(i), Vols. I & II, Office of the Registrar General and Census Commissioner, India, New Delhi.

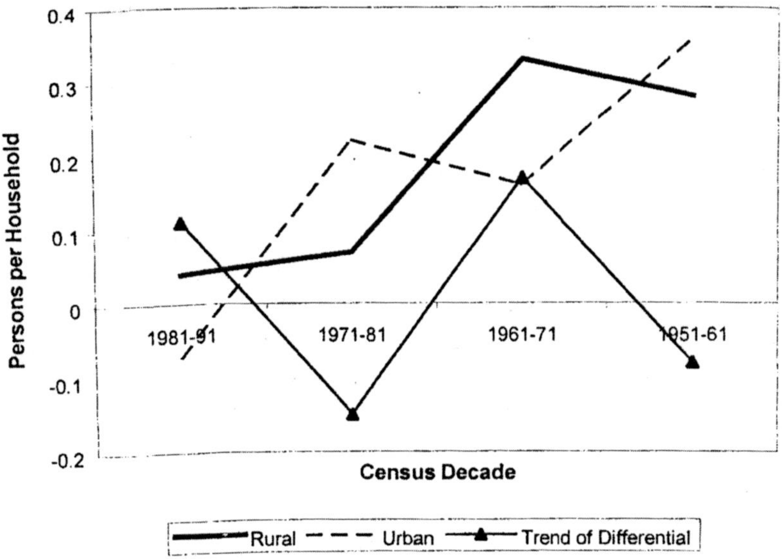


**Fig. 6.2:** India – Decadal Change in Size of the Household by Rural-Urban Residence, 1951-91

family system kept its rural as well as urban households small (about 5 to over 5.50 persons), and the resultant rural-urban differential index was also small (0.007).

Nine out of 31 states and union territories have urban household size bigger than rural. These, in ascending order are Chandigarh (–0.86), Lakshadweep (–0.35), Pondicherry (–0.32), Tamil Nadu (–0.28), Andhra Pradesh (–0.24), Kerala (–0.22), Uttar Pradesh (–0.15), Manipur (–0.08), and Bihar (–0.02). The factors of local endogamy and prevalence of joint family system in urban areas play their role in south Indian states. Joint family system and migration characterise the situation in

**Table 6.6**: India: Average Size of the Household by Residence and its Rural-Urban Differential, 1971-91

| *Country/State/ Union Territory* | *Number of Persons per Household in 1991* | | | *Rural-Urban Differential* | |
|---|---|---|---|---|---|
| | *All Areas* | *Rural* | *Urban* | *1991* | *1971* |
| **India*** | **5.52** | **5.58** | **5.34** | **+0.24** | **+0.29** |
| *States* | | | | | |
| Himachal Pradesh | 5.34 | 5.48 | 4.18 | +1.30 | +1.39 |
| Haryana | 6.30 | 6.59 | 5.54 | +1.05 | +0.22 |
| Nagaland | 5.57 | 5.73 | 4.92 | +0.81 | –0.14 |
| Assam | 5.83 | 5.92 | 5.18 | +0.74 | +0.52 |
| Arunachal Pradesh | 4.93 | 5.02 | 4.37 | +0.65 | +0.85 |
| Punjab | 5.92 | 6.07 | 5.60 | +0.47 | +0.76 |
| Tripura | 5.24 | 5.30 | 4.91 | +0.39 | +0.04 |
| Delhi | 5.02 | 5.35 | 4.98 | +0.37 | +1.08 |
| West Bengal | 5.44 | 5.54 | 5.19 | +0.35 | +0.55 |
| Gujarat | 5.51 | 5.63 | 5.30 | +0.33 | +0.29 |
| Mizoram | 4.75 | 5.84 | 5.55 | +0.29 | +0.35 |
| Karnataka | 4.99 | 5.60 | 5.37 | +0.23 | –0.33 |
| Goa | 5.52 | 5.08 | 4.86 | +0.22 | +0.18 |
| Orissa | 5.28 | 5.31 | 5.09 | +0.22 | +0.43 |
| Rajasthan | 6.04 | 6.09 | 5.87 | +0.22 | +0.20 |
| Maharashtra | 5.14 | 5.23 | 5.02 | +0.21 | +0.49 |
| Madhya Pradesh | 5.65 | 5.68 | 5.54 | +0.14 | +0.27 |
| Sikkim | 5.33 | 5.34 | 5.20 | +0.14 | DNA |
| Meghalaya | 5.42 | 5.44 | 5.35 | +0.09 | –0.04 |
| Bihar | 6.16 | 6.16 | 6.18 | –0.02 | +0.32 |
| Manipur | 6.19 | 6.17 | 6.25 | –0.08 | –0.50 |
| Uttar Pradesh | 6.22 | 6.19 | 6.34 | –0.15 | +0.22 |
| Kerala | 5.28 | 5.22 | 5.44 | –0.22 | –0.43 |
| Andhra Pradesh | 4.77 | 4.71 | 4.95 | –0.24 | –0.08 |
| Tamil Nadu | 5.45 | 4.36 | 4.64 | –0.28 | –0.32 |
| *Union Territories* | | | | | |
| Dadra & Nagar Haveli | 5.28 | 5.33 | 4.75 | +0.58 | DNA |
| Daman & Diu | 5.30 | 5.50 | 5.08 | +0.42 | +0.43 |
| A & N Islands | 5.70 | 4.82 | 4.56 | +0.26 | +0.22 |
| Pondicherry | 4.97 | 4.77 | 5.09 | –0.32 | –0.53 |
| Lakshadweep | 6.23 | 6.04 | 6.39 | –0.35 | DNA |
| Chandigarh | 4.38 | 3.63 | 4.49 | –0.86 | +0.39 |

*Source:* Computed from, Census of India (1991), *Primary Census Abstract: General Population*, Series-1 India, Part II-B(I), Vols. I and II, Office of the Registrar General and Census Commissioner, India, New Delhi.

DNA – Data Not Available

* Excludes Jammu & Kashmir where census was not held in 1991.

*Notes:* (i) Data for the states/union territories of Sikkim, Dadra & Nagar Haveli and Lakshadweep are not available in 1971.

(ii) States and union territories are arranged in descending order of rural-urban differential in 1991.

north India. The overall differential ranges from –0.86 to + 1.30 persons per household.

**India: Trend of Rural-Urban Differentials in Size of the Household, 1971-91**

The trend in rural-urban differentials in size of the household has been observed using state-wise data for two-decades, from 1971 to 1991. The overall picture shows that the rural-urban differentials in almost half of India are squeezing but at a slow rate.

Some of the rural areas are adopting small size of household norms, under the influence of urban areas and many of the urban areas, while facing the housing and costly city life problems, are adopting joint family systems. Recent years have also seen a rise in the middle class families in urban areas with aptitude towards maintaining small, joint family system initially. These areas broadly fall under six categories (Table 6.7 and Map 6.4).

**Table 6.7**: India: Trend of Rural-Urban Differentials in Size of the Household, 1971-91

| *Rural-Urban Differential Categories* | | | | | |
|---|---|---|---|---|---|
| 1 | 2 | 3 | 4 | 5 | 6 |
| Andhra Pradesh (+0.16) | Manipur (–0.42) | Tripura (+0.35) | Delhi (–0.71) | Chandigarh (+1.25) | Nagaland (+0.95) |
| | Pondicherry (–0.21) | Assam (+0.22) | Punjab (–0.29) | Uttar Pradesh (+0.37) | Goa (+0.55) |
| | Kerala (–0.21) | Mizoram (+0.07) | Maharashtra (–0.28) | Bihar (+0.34) | Meghalaya (+0.13) |
| | Tamil Nadu (–0.04) | Karnataka (+0.05) | Orissa (–0.21) | | |
| | | Gujarat (+0.04) | Arunachal Pradesh (–0.20) | | |
| | | Rajasthan (+0.02) | West Bengal (–0.20) | | |
| | | | Haryana (–0.17) | | |
| | | | Madhya Pradesh (–0.13) | | |
| | | | Andaman & Nicobar Islands (–0.09) | | |
| | | | Himachal Pradesh (–0.09) | | |
| | | | Daman & Diu (–0.01) | | |

*Source*: Computed from, Census of India (1991), *Primary Census Abstract: General Population*, Series-1, India, Part II-B(i), Vols. I & II, Office of the Registrar General and Census Commissioner, India, New Delhi.

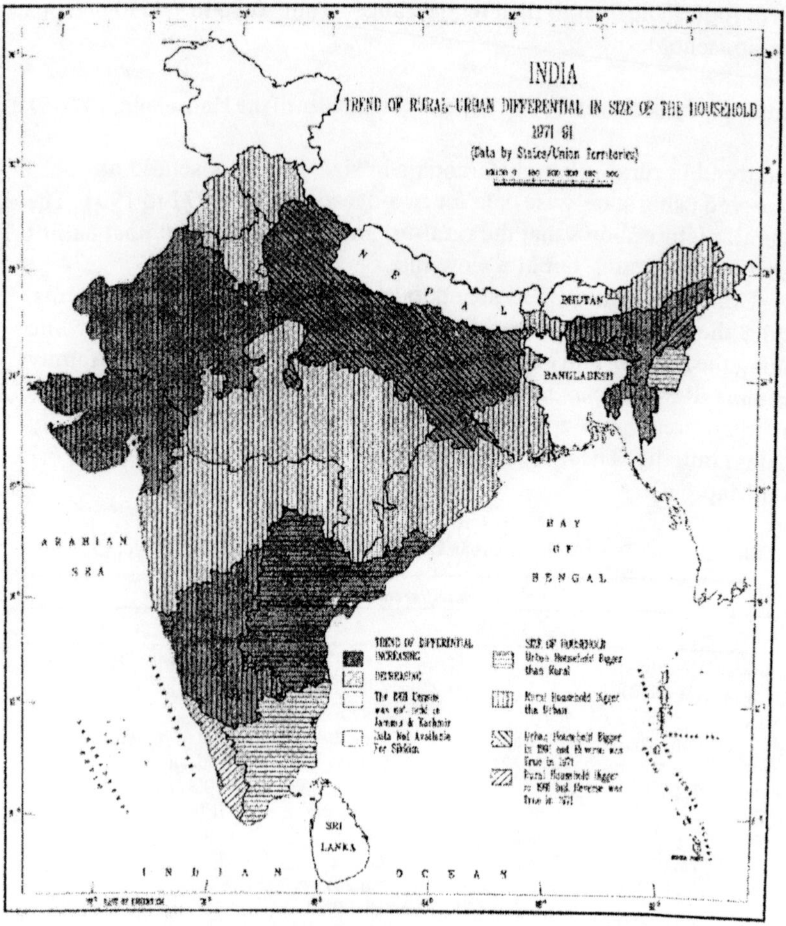


Map 6.4: India: Trend of Rural-Urban Differential in Size of the Household, 1971-91 (Data by States/Union Territories)

## Category and Nomenclature

1. Areas where urban household size was bigger than rural with increasing differential trend.
2. Areas where urban household size was bigger than rural with declining differential trend.
3. Areas where rural household size was bigger than rural with increasing differential trend.

4. Areas where rural household size was bigger than urban with declining differential trend.
5. Areas where urban household size was bigger in 1991 but reverse was true in 1971.
6. Areas where rural household size was bigger in 1991 but reverse was true in 1971.

### *1. Areas where Urban Household Size was Bigger than Rural with Increasing Differential Trend*

Only one state, *i.e.*, Andhra Pradesh (+0.16) falls in this category. The state is characterised by a high rate of natural increase of urban population (21.0 and 17.7 per 1000 persons in 1981 and 1991 respectively) which is more than the national average. Low mortality in urban areas (6.7 per thousand) than in rural (10.5 per thousand) and family migration to cities are other factors.

The better employment opportunities through industrialization and modernization in the districts of Kurnool, Guntur, Krishna, Prakasam, Nellore, Hyderabad and Ranga Reddy, are able to attract majority of the scheduled tribes who migrate with families towards these urban centres (Reddy, 1996). Such type of migration trends have been helpful in increasing the urban size of household in Andhra Pradesh.

### *2. Areas where Urban Household Size was Bigger than Rural with Declining Differential Trend.*

Manipur (–0.42), Kerala (–0.21), Pondicherry (–0.21) and Tamil Nadu (–.04) have urban household size bigger than rural but it is revealing a declining trend of differential. In southern states of Tamil Nadu and Kerala, high caste groups in urban places tend to have a larger proportion of joint families and display a greater degree of family solidarity. Besides it, local endogamy is also common (Karve, 1953). Now, the size of urban household is declining but it is still larger than the rural household size. The natural increase rate has declined considerably from 19.9 in 1981 to 12.3 in 1991 in Manipur.

Availability of job opportunities in rural areas motivate people to stay in their villages with their families and the male-selective migration towards urban areas decreased.

### 3. *Areas where Rural Household Size was Bigger than Urban with Increasing Differential Trend*

The rural-urban differential was maximum in Tripura (+0.35) followed by Assam (+0.22), Mizoram (+0.07), Karnataka (+0.05), Gujarat (+0.04) and Rajasthan (+0.02). Owing to the fact that the north-eastern states particularly have witnessed large scale family migration to rural areas from across the border in addition to high birth rate. In villages, cottage industries have been set up for young unemployed persons. Several districts in Gujarat and Rajasthan have been declared as industrially backward by the Government and qualified for special incentives and attracted considerable large-scale industries to their rural parts along the main transport routes, for instance, Panch Mahal in Gujarat and Alwar in Rajasthan. Such areas attracted significant migration to their rural areas in response to employment opportunities made available by new industry. So, a lot of rural-urban migration took the form of rural to rural migration (Krishan, 1993). Besides, a strong tradition of joint family system also worked in rural areas of Rajasthan and Gujarat, In Karnataka, the endogamous system of marriages between close kins and within the locality was typical.

North-eastern states witnessed large scale family migration in rural areas from across the border in addition to high birth rate. In Assam Valley, rural household size is increasing due to stable birth rate in rural areas (33.8 in 1981 and 31.7 in 1991) and a fast fall in urban birth rate (33.2 in 1981 and 21.3 in 1991) accompanied by sizeable in-migration.

### 4. *Areas where Rural Household Size was Bigger than Urban with Declining Differential Trend*

Data for 4 states/union territories not being available, 11 out of 28 states/ union territories fall in this category of declining differential trend with rural household size bigger than urban. The maximum differential exists in Delhi (–0.71) which is followed by Punjab (–0.29), Maharashtra (–0.28), Orissa (–0.21), Arunachal Pradesh (–0.20), West Bengal (–0.20), Haryana (–0.17), Madhya Pradesh (–0.13), Himachal Pradesh (–0.9), Andaman and Nicobar Islands (–0.9), and Daman and Diu (–0.01). All these states have experienced high rate of rural-urban male-selective migration. The states particularly in the north-west and west have a strong hold of joint family system both in rural and urban areas.

Also due to the impact of urbanization, the rural household size is declining and male-selective migration is taking the form of family migration.

*5. Areas where Urban Household Size was Bigger in 1991 but Reverse was True in 1971*

The states and union territories which come in this category are Chandigarh (+1.25), Uttar Pradesh (+0.37) and Bihar (+0.34). Chandigarh being the capital of two states, attracted a lot of migrants with their families to work in administrative offices. In Bihar, predominance of single families among the tribals, coupled with a high mortality rate, explained the small size of the household in their predominantly rural habitats (Vidyarthi and Rai, 1977). In the hill districts of Uttar Pradesh, out-migration from rural areas had depleted the size of rural households. In north-western as well as in central Uttar Pradesh and north Bihar Plain also, the urban household size surpassed the rural household in 1991. Because many of the towns in these areas are overgrown villages characterised by large households associated with a high proportion of joint families, while out-migration from the countryside caused reduction in size of the rural household. A considerable number of the Muslim families in towns were also responsible for making the urban household large.

*6. Areas where Rural Household Size was Bigger in 1991 but Reverse was True in 1971*

The states which falls in this category are Nagaland (+0.95), Goa (+0.55) and Meghalaya (+0.13). In these states, the urban household was bigger in 1971 but the rural household size surpassed it in 1991 and became larger than urban. Initially, the prevalence of nuclear family system in rural areas kept their household small (about 5 to over 5.50 persons). While the frequency of institutional household such as defence establishments, convents and boarding houses were responsible for raising urban household size (5 to 6 persons) in Nagaland and Meghalaya. But, now by facilitating rural areas with transport and communication and basic amenities like electricity, water supply, etc. rural-urban migration is checked to some extent and villages simultaneously rendered the attraction of urban facilities as less critical for rural migrants than before (Krishan, 1993). In hilly areas, incentives are given by government to unemployed youths for setting-up of small scale and cottage industries. In Meghalaya and Nagaland, there is a stable high birth rate in rural areas. In Goa, the urban mortality rate increased to 6.4 in 1991 as compared to 4.3 in 1981 which was far more in comparison to rural one (8.0 in 1991 and 7.7 in 1981) while the birth rates were almost stable.

## India: Spatial Patterns of Rural-Urban Differentials in Size of the Household, 1991

Notwithstanding small differential in the average size of rural and urban households in India, striking regional variations can be seen in this regard (Table 6.8). It clearly depicts that the maximum differential is found in Himachal Pradesh (+0.121) and minimum in Meghalaya (+0.007). In these states and the states falling in between, the rural household size is bigger than urban. Besides, there are states and union territories where urban household size is bigger than rural in 1991 and differential ranges between –0.001 in Bihar to –0.094 in Chandigarh.

When rural-urban differential index was correlated with some indicators for states and union territories of India (Table 6.9), it was observed that the rural-urban differential in size of the household is correlated negatively with level of urbanization, per cent population in class-I cities, percentage of urban population in primary activities, household industry, manufacturing, per cent agricultural labourers in rural areas, Muslim population as per cent to total urban population, rural literacy, rural female literacy and urban natural growth rate.

It is observed that the rural-urban differential is low in areas where the level of urbanization is high. It gives an interesting commentary on the popular notion that the rural-urban differential will be high if urbanization level is high. Thus, our hypothesis which says that rural-urban differential will find a strong association with the degree of urbanisation proves invalid. Because the nature of urbanization or modernization is traditional with urban places retaining a number of rural attributes. Similarly, the differential is low in areas where urban population is engaged in primary activities, household industry and manufacturing. It is also low in areas where high proportion of agricultural labourers are found in rural areas. The urban areas with high proportion of Muslim population also have low differential index. Similarly, the index is low in areas of high rural female literacy and total rural literacy. The natural growth rate in urban areas also has a

**Table 6.8**: India: Rural-Urban Differential Indices of Size of the Household, 1991

| *Country/State/Union Territory* | *Differential Index* |
|---|---|
| **India*** | **+0.020** |
| *States* | |
| Himachal Pradesh | +0.121 |
| Haryana | +0.078 |
| Nagaland | +0.068 |
| Arunachal Pradesh | +0.062 |
| Assam | +0.060 |
| Punjab | +0.036 |
| Tripura | +0.034 |
| West Bengal | +0.029 |
| Gujarat | +0.027 |
| Mizoram | +0.023 |
| Goa | +0.020 |
| Karnataka | +0.019 |
| Maharashtra | +0.018 |
| Orissa | +0.018 |
| Rajasthan | +0.017 |
| Madhya Pradesh | +0.012 |
| Sikkim | +0.012 |
| Meghalaya | +0.007 |
| Bihar | –0.001 |
| Manipur | –0.006 |
| Uttar Pradesh | –0.011 |
| Kerala | –0.019 |
| Andhra Pradesh | –0.023 |
| Tamil Nadu | –0.028 |
| *Union Territories* | |
| Dadra & Nagar Haveli | +0.052 |
| Daman & Diu | +0.035 |
| Delhi | +0.031 |
| Andaman & Nicobar Islands | +0.025 |
| Lakshadweep | –0.026 |
| Pondicherry | –0.029 |
| Chandigarh | –0.094 |

*Source*: Computed from, Census of India (1991), *Primary Census Abstract: General Population*, Series-1, India, Part II-B(i), Vols. I & II, Office of the Registrar General and Census Commissioner, India, New Delhi.

* Excludes Jammu & Kashmir where census was not held in 1991.

*Note*: States and union territories are arranged in descending order of differential index in 1991.

negative correlation with size of household which means that the differential index is low in areas of high urban birth, death and natural growth rates. So, all the hypotheses except the first prove valid and give same results as were our assumptions.

The index is correlated positively (Table 6.9) with the percentage of urban population in trade and commerce and urban female literacy rate. Thus, the areas where more urban population is engaged in trade and commerce and in areas of high urban female literacy the differential is more. The increase in urban female literacy does not yield a proportionate increase in rural literacy implying widening up of the rural-urban differential in size of the household.

**Table 6.9:** India: Coefficients of Correlation of Rural-Urban Differentials in Size of the Household, 1991

| *Indicator* | *Coefficient of Correlation* |
|---|---|
| Percentage of urban population in household industry | –.4612 |
| Population of class-I cities as per cent to total population | –.4081 |
| Level of urbanization | –.3687 |
| Agricultural labourers as per cent to total rural population | –.3549 |
| Muslim population as per cent to total urban population | –.3005 |
| Percentage of urban population in primary activities | –.2003 |
| Urban natural growth rate | –.1007 |
| Percentage of urban population in manufacturing | –.0747 |
| Rural female literacy | –.0210 |
| Rural literacy | –.0131 |
| Percentage of urban population in trade and commerce | +.1063 |
| Urban female literacy rate | +.1313 |

*Source:* Computed from Publications made by Census of India (1991) and *Economic Intelligence Service* (1991, 1993, 1994, 1997).

The rural-urban differentials become more pronounced when examined at district level. Out of 436 districts, 55.05 per cent districts recorded bigger rural household size than urban and the rest 44.95 per cent had urban household size bigger than rural.

Out of 240 districts, where rural household size was bigger than urban, 20 districts showed highest rural-urban differential index which was above 0.100; in 48 districts, this differential index ranged from 0.050 to 0.099 and the rest 172 districts displayed differential index below 0.049 persons. On the other hand, 196 districts recorded urban household size larger than the rural.

The rural-urban differential index ranged from +0.176 in Faridabad district (where rural household size was 7.2 persons and urban size of household was 4.8 persons) of Haryana to +0.001 in Shivpuri (where rural household size was 6.0 persons and urban household size was also 6.0 persons) and Shajapur (where both rural and urban size of household

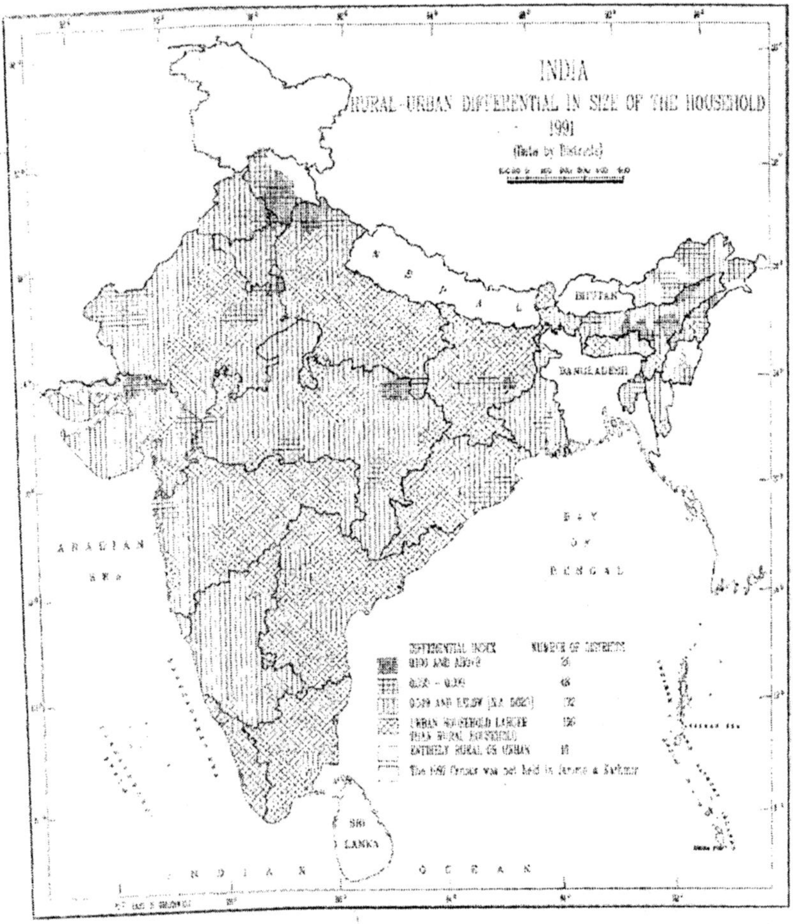


**Map 6.5**: India : Rural-Urban Differential in Size of the Household, 1991
(Data by Districts)

was 5.9 persons) districts of Madhya Pradesh, Chittorgarh district of Rajasthan and Birbhum district of West Bengal. There also existed a few districts, where there was no rural-urban differential. These districts, scattered in different parts of the country, were: Gopalganj in Bihar, Tumkur in Karnataka, Satara and Kolhapur in Maharashtra, Ajmer in Rajasthan and Mainpuri, Bareilly and Varanasi in Uttar Pradesh.

The spatial patterns of rural-urban differentials in size of the household are not uniform throughout the country (Map 6.5). Keeping in view the national average of rural-urban differential index (+0.020

persons) and to obtain a comprehensive regional picture of the rural-urban differentials in size of the household in 1991, all the districts of India can be grouped in the following three categories:

1. Areas where rural household size is bigger than urban with differential distinctly larger (+0.050 and above).
2. Areas where rural household size is bigger than urban with differential marginally larger (+0.049 and below).
3. Areas with larger urban households than rural households.

*1. Areas where Rural Household Size is Bigger than Urban with Differential Distinctly Larger (+0.050 and above)*

There are a total of 68 districts which fall in this category. It comprised of 20 districts confined to north and north-eastern India (Map 6.5), where differential index is more than +0.100 persons. Faridabad in Haryana state was noted for the maximum rural-urban differential. Its rural size of household is 7 persons and urban household size is 4.8 persons, accounted by a predominance of joint family system in rural areas and large scale labour migration in this industrial town which, in turn, leads to the creation of single person households, thereby, decreasing the size of urban household. The overall differential is also high in the state of Himachal Pradesh. It ranks the highest among states owing to the fact that 6 out of 12 districts experience very high rural-urban differential. These districts are Shimla (rural household size 5.5 and urban 3.7), Kullu (rural household size 5.4 and urban 3.4), Solan (rural household size 5.6 and urban 4.0), Bilaspur (rural size of household 5.7 and urban 4.4), Mandi (rural household size 5.5 and urban 4.2), and Sirmaur (rural household size 6.0 and urban 4.6). The large differential is related to an unusually small size of urban household, while the size of rural household remains close to the national average. The functional structure of towns, most of which were administrative centres, along with migration largely of educated persons with small families explained this phenomenon. In Himachal region, Chamba, Kangra and Hamirpur have small urban households of about 4.53 persons on an average. The size of rural household (about 5.40 persons) was close to the national average. The resultant differential is obviously large.

The districts of Uttar Pradesh Himalayas such as Uttar Kashi (0.110), Tehri Garhwal (0.127), Pithoragarh (0.092), Ghaziabad (0.096), Chamoli (0.076), Dehradun (0.056) are similarly situated in this category. In these districts, the average size of rural households being 5.56 persons and of urban households 4.54 persons, the resultant rural-urban differential is obviously high.

Kamrup, Dhemaji, Marigaon, Karbi Anglong and Lakhimpur districts in Assam with fairly large size of rural household and distinctly low size in urban areas are characterised by large differential. Rural areas in Assam Valley experienced rapid growth of population due to higher natural growth rate of 19.9 per thousand in comparison to 14.4 per thousand in urban areas and sizeable in-migration. The natural increase rate in urban areas is much lower than the average for the country (17.2 per thousand).

Similarly, the districts of Sidhi in Madhya Pradesh and Banas Kantha in Gujarat also fall in this category with +0.124 and +0.101 as value of differential index respectively. Another zone of high rural-urban differential extends in an elongated tract from Chandigarh union territory to Jaipur and Alwar in Rajasthan. Rupnagar, Ludhiana, Patiala, Ambala, Kurukshetra, Yamunanagar, Karnal, Sonipat, Ghaziabad and Gurgaon also come in this tract. In these districts, rural household size is above 6 persons per household and urban household size is around 5 persons per household. The rural-urban differential in this region is associated more with a distinctly large size of the rural household explained by a strong tradition of joint family system which historically has been a more salient feature of joint families (with a joint tenure of land) as previously typical of north-western India (Powell, 1972).

*2. Areas where Rural Household Size is Bigger than Urban with Differential Marginally Larger (+0.049 and below)*

A total of 172 districts comprise this category. Western Punjab-Haryana plains, large parts of Rajasthan plain, Madhya Pradesh, Gujarat, Western Maharashtra, Karnataka Plateau, West Bengal, a few adjoining districts of Orissa and some districts scattered in the North-Eastern Hill states fall in this category (Map 6.5).

The Punjab-Haryana plain, Rajasthan, Madhya Pradesh and Gujarat zone is of high natural growth rate both in rural and urban areas. The average size of rural households in these districts is 6 to 6.5 persons and urban household is 5.5 to 6 persons. The traditional life style and high incidence of joint families due to varying social, economic and historic reasons is common.

The proportion of scheduled castes in Punjab, Haryana and a few districts of Rajasthan is fairly high. The tribal districts in Madhya Pradesh too recorded a small differential. Despite a high level of economic development, the size of both rural and urban households is large in Punjab and Haryana.

Gujarat also recorded a larger size of rural household (5.63 persons) but the urban household is also not very small (5.30 persons) although it is smaller than the national average. Thus, this is again an area, where, both the rural and urban households were relatively large. The hold of joint family system here could be compared with that in Punjab-Haryana plain. The level of economic development measured in terms of per capita income too is high. But, the stress on joint families has remained strong on the Gujarati community inspite of its economic development (Shah, 1973).

In the districts of Karnataka and Maharashtra, endogamous system of marriages between close kins and within the locality is typical. Such a marriage pattern mitigated the conflict between mother-in-law and daughter-in-law and thereby strengthened the patrilineal joint family (Gazetteer of India, 1973). Level of economic development is very high in Maharashtra and is fairly high in Karnataka. Rural-urban growth rates are also matching each other in these states.

In West Bengal the size of both the rural and urban households is between 5 to 6 persons, while in Orissa it ranges between 4.5 to 5.5 persons per household. These constituted another area of marginal rural-urban differential. Towns in this area have retained rural character to a significant degree. These towns are small in size, with a high proportion of their workers in primary activities and household industries (Krishan, 1980). Joint family system is prevalent in all the urban areas as well. Natural growth rate (21.4 persons) is higher than urban growth rate (11.8 persons per thousand).

Likewise, both rural (about 5.50 persons) and urban (4 to 5 persons) households are close to national average and showed a marginal difference in the hill districts of Uttar Pradesh. Towns, here, had experienced sizeable in-migration during the recent years, resulting in an addition of many small families. Simultaneously, out-migration from rural areas had depleted the size of rural households. Thus, it is under the impact of migration that the differential had narrowed down.

The level of economic development and level of urbanization is low in hill districts of Arunachal Pradesh, Assam, Meghalaya, Manipur, Tripura and Mizoram. Scheduled tribes comprise 75 per cent or more of the population in these hill districts. The average rural household size in these hill districts is 5 to 6 persons and of urban households is 4 to 5 persons.

It follows that a small differential in size of rural and urban households is generally typical of the areas at a low level of development. But many of these areas differed among themselves in terms of average size of the household, it being relatively small in tribal regions and moderate to large in other areas with predominantly rural and agricultural populations. The level of development and urbanization is also low in almost all these districts.

### 3. *Areas with Larger Urban Households than Rural Households*

The maximum number of districts (196) comprise the category, where the size of urban household is much bigger than the rural one. This category comprises almost whole of Tamil Nadu Upland and South Sahyadri, most of the districts of Andhra Plateau, Maharashtra Region, Orissa Highland Region, Chotta Nagpur Region, Upper and Middle Ganga Plain. A few districts in Udaipur-Gwalior Region and Vindhyachal-Baghelkhand Region, also come in this category (Map 6.5). The frequency of such districts where urban household size is bigger than rural was greater in south India where local endogamy was common in contrast to exogamy in north India (Karve, 1953). Endogamy was conducive to persistence of joint family system in the districts of southern India.

In Kerala, average household size was 5.3 persons, which is near to national average (5.5 persons). Here, the average rural household size (5.2 persons) was a little bit smaller than urban household size (5.4 persons). The state is exceptional in matters of family and kinship. The Nayars and some other castes of this region were matrilineal and joint family of several married sisters, their children and their mother and her sisters was the common type in both rural and urban areas (Mandelbaum, 1972). The comparatively small size of the rural households was associated with some out-migration. Most of the population is engaged in secondary and tertiary sector.

In Tamil Nadu, both rural household size (3.5 to 4.5 persons) and urban household size (4 to 5 persons) were comparatively smaller. Natural growth rate is more in urban than in rural areas (13.2 and 11.3 respectively). High castes and groups in urban places tended to have a larger proportion of joint families and displayed a greater amount of family solidarity (Aiyappan, 1955). But the people of low castes, among whom nuclear family was a norm, made a high proportion in rural areas and the resultant household size was small there. Another important factor is migration from rural areas, which also affects the size of household. Similarly, whole of the Eastern Coastal Belt, Rayalseema region shows that there were small rural and comparatively bigger urban households. In these coastal districts, the size of urban household was found between 4.5 to 5.5 persons and rural household size between 4 to 5 persons.

The districts of eastern half of Maharashtra recorded a larger size of urban households (5 to 6 persons) than that of rural households (5 to 5.50 persons). Here, 75 per cent to 80 per cent of total workers population is engaged in primary sector among which 35 per cent to 45 per cent is engaged in cultivation. Four per cent to 8 per cent of total workers population is engaged in secondary sector and about 15 per cent in tertiary sector Level of economic development is low in some districts and moderate in the others. Level of urbanization is in line with national average. Forty five per cent to 75 per cent population is literate. Ten per cent to 24 per cent population is of scheduled castes and 5 per cent to 35 per cent is of scheduled tribes, where nuclear family pattern is more common. These people lived mostly in rural areas, thereby reducing the average household size there. A high proportion of rural households here was in agricultural labour (30 per cent to 50 per cent of total workers) who for the most part remained elementary units (Epstein, 1973).

A relatively high proportion (16.72 per cent) of Muslim population lived in urban areas. Joint families is the basic characteristic of Muslims, which has enlarged the size of urban households. The Muslims were found to be slightly more conservative in respect of joint family living than the non-Muslims even if income, education and other socio-economic variables were controlled and this difference was more noticeable in urban areas than in the rural (Conklin, 1972). So, the specific composition of rural and urban communities of these districts of Maharashtra was responsible for making the urban household bigger than rural.

Among the north Indian states, Uttar Pradesh has the maximum number of districts where urban household size is bigger than rural. Most of the districts of Bihar also come in this category. Here, the urban household size is between 6 to 7 persons and rural household size is 5.5 to 6.5 persons. In these districts, many of the towns were overgrown villages characterized by large households associated with a high proportion of joint families, while out-migration from the countryside caused reduction in size of the rural households. In Uttar Pradesh, a considerable number of urban population is of Muslims. These Muslim families in towns of Bihar and Uttar Pradesh were also responsible for making the urban household large.

In Rajasthan, about one-third districts which are central in location have larger urban household than rural one. In these districts, growth of population is high both in urban and rural areas. The proportion of workers engaged in primary sector is 50 per cent to 80 per cent of the total workers. Out of the total workers, 45 per cent to 75 per cent of workers are engaged in cultivation, whereas 5 per cent to 15 per cent of total workers are agricultural labourers. The proportion of workers engaged in secondary sector is 4 per cent to 16 per cent of total workers. However, the tertiary sector comprises 20 per cent of total workers. Level of economic development is very low. Level of urbanization is moderate. The proportion of scheduled castes is 17 per cent to 24 per cent of the total population, which decrease the size of rural household by creating nuclear families. Scheduled tribes comprise 4 per cent to 15 per cent of the total population of Rajasthan. The partitioned family is the basic characteristic of these tribes and these are responsible for small size of rural households. Status of women is very low here. Muslim population is also dominant in a few districts which increase the urban household size because of the prevalence of joint family system among them.

A few districts of the tribal territories like Sikkim, Meghalaya, Nagaland and Manipur are also noted for a larger size of their urban households over that of the rural. The prevalence of nuclear family system in rural areas kept their households small (5 to 6 persons), while the frequency of institutional households, such as defence establishments, convents and boarding houses, raised the urban household size upto 6 to 6.5 persons. On the whole, these areas are noted for relatively small size of households.

In brief, we can say that local endogamy in southern districts and dominance of Muslim population in urban areas of northern districts is responsible for big urban households and comparatively small rural households. Sizeable amount of migrants from rural areas is another noticeable factor for smaller rural households than their urban counterparts.

## CONCLUDING REMARKS

1. A comparison of the average household size in India for 1991 census with those of previous decades reveals that the average size of the Indian household is gradually increasing over time which reached to 5.57 persons per household in 1991 from 4.88 in 1951.
2. Contrary to the popular notion that the rural household would be distinctly larger than the urban, the urban household in India is only marginally smaller than the rural suggesting a virtual continuation of the traditional family patterns in urban India as well. Ryan's assertion that urban atomization theory in regard of kinship has proven incorrect seems to be true in case of India (Ryan, 1975). In the urban as well as in rural areas, the incidence of joint family is very common resulting in only slight difference between the two. However, striking regional variations can be observed.
3. The size of household and its rural-urban differential did not show any consistent relationship. Regional differences in the urban household size are found to be more pronounced in comparison to rural household size. Thus, the rural-urban differential is determined more by urban size of household than the rural.
4. The rural-urban differential has not been consistent but varying from decade to decade. The overall gap between size of the rural and urban households has widened over the decades. The increased differential is because the size of rural household has increased constantly at a faster rate than the urban one.
5. The trend of rural-urban differentials in size of the household indicates that the rural-urban differentials in almost half of the India are squeezing but at a slow rate. Some of the rural areas are adopting small size of household norms under the influence of urban areas and many of the urban areas, while facing the housing and costly city life problems, are adopting joint family systems, resulting into the squeezing of rural-urban differentials in size of the household.
6. The rural-urban differential in size of the household is correlated negatively with level of urbanization, per cent population in Class-I cities, percentage of urban population in primary activities, household industry, manufacturing, per cent agricultural labourers in rural areas, Muslim population as in urban areas, rural literacy, rural female literacy and urban natural growth rate. By contrast, it is positively correlated with percentage of urban population in trade and commerce and urban female literacy. Further, it is observed

that the rural-urban differentials in almost half of India are narrowing but slowly, over time.

7. Striking regional variations in terms of rural-urban differential index have been observed both at the state and district levels. At state level, the maximum value of differential index, where the rural household size is bigger than urban is found in Himachal Pradesh (+0.121) and minimum in Meghalaya (+0.007). However, in the states and union territories where urban household size is bigger than rural in 1991, the rural-urban index ranges between –0.001 in Bihar to –0.094 in Chandigarh.

   At district level, the rural-urban differential index ranged from +0.176 in Faridabad district (where rural household size was 7.2 persons and urban size of household was 4.8 persons) of Haryana to +0.001 in Shivpuri (where rural household size was 6.0 persons and urban household size was also 6.0 persons) and Shajapur (where both rural and urban size of households was 5.9 persons) districts of Madhya Pradesh, Chittorgarh district of Rajasthan and Birbhum district of West Bengal.

8. Furthermore, more than two-fifth of the districts recorded urban household size bigger than rural. Most of these districts were concentrated in south India where local endogamy accounted for large size of urban household. On the other hand, some of the tribal territories and areas of sizeable rural out-migration of Uttar Pradesh and Bihar in north India were noted for a large size of the urban household than the rural. In eastern half of Rajasthan, illiteracy and early marriages of girls in most of rural and urban areas was responsible for joint families.

9. In nutshell, the rural-urban differentials, where the rural household size is bigger than urban, are more marked in relatively developed areas because of a strong tradition of joint family system and sizeable in-migration of educated persons with small families and marginal in backward regions which are at a low level of development and urbanisation.

   By contrast, the negative rural-urban differentials, where the urban household size is bigger than its rural counterpart, are more peculiar of the areas where local endogamy is prevalent as in south India and dominance of Muslim population in urban areas exists as in north India particularly in the states of Uttar Pradesh and Bihar. Sizeable out-migration from the countryside is another noticeable factor for smaller rural households than their urban counterparts.

# 7

# SUMMARY OF CONCLUSIONS

The present study aimed at describing and interpreting the trends in and regional aspects of rural-urban differentials of social variables of the Indian population, on the basis of statistical analysis and mapping of the 1991 census data for all the 452 districts (excluding the state of Jammu & Kashmir where census was not held in 1991) in the country. In 1991, there were 25 states, 7 union territories and 466 districts in the country.

It is primarily an empirical investigation of the rural lag in literacy, urban lag in sex ratio, size of household, etc. in relation to the economy, society, urbanization, industrialization, modernization and educational history of different parts of India. Rural-urban differences are essentially a function of the differential rates of change occurring in towns and villages. Keeping in consonance with the purpose, only those aspects for which the data were available, were chosen for the study. These were size of household, vital rates (only state level data were available), sex ratio and literacy.

For calculating rural-urban differentials and their trends of the social variables, secondary sources of data were tapped. Census of India (1991 and 2001) and Vital Statistics Division, different publications of Economic Intelligence Service, Centre for Monitoring Indian Economy Private Limited, New Delhi provided most of the data required for the study. But the analysis of these factors was constrained by the nature of available data. Most of the data required for the study were on district level and due to non-availability of district level data on vital rates, they were examined for state level. The data were then processed to find the relevant ratios.

To measure the rural-urban differentials in size of the household, vital rates, sex ratio and literacy rates, an index that satisfied all the four axioms of additive and multiplicative monotonicity, redistribution and repetitive transfers was employed. This was Sopher's index which was further modified by Kundu and Rao (1982).

$$D_s = log\ (X_2 / X_1) + log\ (200-X_1)/(200-X_2)$$

where $X_2 \geq X_1$ and $X_1$ and $X_2$ are various demographic aspects of *alphas* and *non-alphas* respectively.

The differential index for various demographic attributes for districts of India was computed on the basis of disparity index given by Kundu and Rao (1982). Since spatial concept occupies a central position in every geographic inquiry, map is an important tool. On calculating differential index for various demographic indicators, the districts of India were lassified into various categories and represented cartographically so as to present regional patterns of rural-urban differentials in size of the household, vital rates, sex ratio and literacy. The Census Maps of India for 1991 and 2001 showing district boundaries have been adopted as the base maps. Hypotheses framed were tested through Spearman's correlations.

As far as size of the household is concerned, it is observed that contrary to the popular notion that the rural household would be distinctly larger than the urban, the urban household in India is marginally smaller than the rural suggesting a virtual continuation of the traditional family patterns in urban India as well. In the urban as well as in rural areas, the incidence of joint family is very common resulting in only slight difference between the two. It is observed that there is marginal rural-urban differential in size of the household in more than four-fifth of the districts irrespective of the fact, whether urban household size is bigger or the rural. It is interesting to note that the urban places in India have not only retained a high degree of rural life style, but also maintained their cultural heritage. The size of the household and its rural-urban differential did not show any consistent relationship. Regional differences in the urban household size are found to be more pronounced in comparison to rural household size. Thus, the rural-urban differential is determined more by urban size of household than the rural.

The rural-urban differentials are correlated negatively with level of urbanization, percentage of population in Class-I cities, percentage of urban population in primary activities, household industry, manufacturing, percentage of agricultural labourers in rural areas, Muslim population as per cent to total urban population, rural literacy, rural female literacy and urban natural growth rate. By contrast. These are correlated positively with percentage of urban population in trade and commerce and urban female literacy. The rural-urban differentials are narrowing down slowly with time in almost half of India. Spatially speaking, the high differential is accounted for by a predominance of joint family system in rural areas contrasted with its weakening in urban places. Male-selective migration from rural to urban areas has its own impact in decreasing urban household size. The rural-urban differential is moderate in areas of traditional urbanization with towns retaining a number of rural attributes.

In more than two-fifth of the districts, most of which were concentrated in south India, the urban household size is bigger than rural. Prevalence of local endogamy accounted for this large size of urban household. Broadly speaking, the rural-urban differences are more marked in relatively developed areas and marginal in backward regions (with a few exceptions) with traditional urbanization.

Vital rates are an essential component of population growth. In India, the death rates declined at a faster rate than the birth rates, revealing that our performance in controlling death was much better than that in checking birth. It was found that the rural-urban differentials in fertility existed ever since and rural fertility always remained higher than urban. The low urban fertility was caused by unbalanced sex-ratio, high living standards, economic insecurity and unemployment, social capillarity, occupational status, female employment, educational facilities and the availability of clinical aids towards family planning and so on. The rural areas are denied many of these. The latter drenched in poverty, ignorance and insecurity result in high fertility. It is noted that fertility has declined in almost all parts of the country to a greater or lesser extent. Also the pace of decline is not necessarily the highest in states with the highest per capita income (*i.e.* Punjab or Haryana) or in the poorer states (such as Bihar or Orissa). So, neither a rapid rise in living standards nor poverty seems to have led to a substantial fall in fertility. The gap between aspirations and the achieved level of living and the awareness of the gap might be a more potent force in bringing about a decline in fertility. Continuing on this line of argument, one can propose a hypothesis for exploration and testing that an acceleration of the rate of development, with or even without an accentuation of the inequalities in the level of living or even the recognition of the latter, resulting from the success of a sufficiently large number of enterprising persons in escaping the poverty trap could be an important factor contributing to an accelerated decline in fertility. If this hypothesis holds, the liberalization of the Indian economy during the past four years is likely to generate forces that would accelerate the fertility decline. The different measures of human fertility based on varied standards of reproduction such as crude birth rate, general fertility rate, total fertility rate and gross reproduction rate indicate that although there exists differential in rural-urban fertility, it is declining over time, despite the fact that with growing population in the country, increasing number of women were entering the reproductive age-group and the aggregate number of live births is continuously increasing. Infant mortality rates and crude death rates have substantially declined both in rural and urban areas as a result of improvement in the living standards, but more so in urban areas. These tendencies are likely to impact upon the rural areas as well. The trend of rural-urban differentials in birth rates are showing a continuous decline in rural areas. Interestingly a very strong positive relationship is seen between rural and urban crude birth rate, the correlation coefficient being .7290 in 1991, implying that the states having high or low urban crude birth rates are also having high or low rural crude birth rate. The decline in rural-urban differential was observed in almost half of the states, though its degree varied. Infact, the declining fertility trends in various states have encouraged among them inconsistency and disparity in crude birth rate and over time, values of this rate have shown growing variation both in rural and urban areas of the states. The increase in the variation was more marked in rural areas. The fertility rate is increasing in the states of Orissa, West Bengal, Madhya Pradesh and Assam and declining in the rest of the states. The rural-urban fertility differentials are correlated negatively with percentage of family planning programme acceptors, female mean age at effective marriage, rural female literacy rate, level of urbanization, per capita income and percentage of rural female non-agricultural workers to total rural workers. On the other hand, it is correlated positively with infant mortality rate in rural areas. A balanced *top-down*, and *bottom-up* strategies and forces, therefore, would minimize rural-urban fertility differentials. Spatially speaking, the rural-urban differentials are more marked in north-east India as well as West Bengal, Madhya Pradesh and Himachal Pradesh, whereas, low differential is found in most of the south Indian states.

Notwithstanding the traditional existence of rural-urban mortality differentials in the country, they are at decline in India, which is evident in all the states and union territories. Kerala and Uttar Pradesh have the lowest and the highest levels of mortality amongst the spectrum of Indian states both at the beginning as well as at the close of twenty-year period from 1971 to 1991. There exists a great variation in death rates among various states. The states with low level of socio-economic development have comparatively high rural and urban death rates. There has been a large area of overlap between rural and urban crude death rates, with sharp variations prevailing among different states which impinge on the general process of demographic development. It is observed that the rural-urban differential in mortality is correlated negatively with dispensaries per lakh of rural population and rural female literacy. On the other hand, it is correlated positively with enhanced agricultural productivity. Spatially speaking, the rural-urban differentials are high in Orissa and north-eastern hill states including Arunachal Pradesh, Meghalaya, Nagaland and Sikkim. Whereas, the low differential is typical of advanced states like Gujarat, Haryana, Kerala, Goa and Manipur alongwith the union territory of Lakshadweep, Chandigarh, Pondicherry and Daman and Diu, the differential is moderate in rest of India. Broadly speaking, the rural-urban differentials in vital rates alongwith overall fertility and mortality rates are continuously declining throughout India, albeit at varied pace.

An examination of the sex ratio reveals that right from the beginning of the census operations, the sex ratio in India has been adverse to women. Not only that, it suffered a consistent decline all through the present century except during the decades of 1941-51 and 1971-81. The sex ratio got precariously reduced to from 972 females per 1000 males in 1901 to 927 females per 1000 males in 1991. Obviously, male mortality rates have declined much faster than female mortality rates. The rural-urban differential are declining continuously but at varying rate.

After 1961 there was increase in urban sex ratio and decline in rural sex ratio. The increase in urban sex ratio is a good symbol of social change in women's status but decline in rural sex ratio is a painful scene of rural areas and is a matter of serious concern. The rural-urban differential declined in nearly three-fifth of the states/union territories particularly in areas which had shown a large rural-urban differential in 1971. Infact greater the differential, more rapid was the decline over the decades. Some states witnessed a slight fall in rural sex ratio along with increase in its urban counterpart. Instances are that of West Bengal, Tripura, Nagaland and Haryana. There are others such as Meghalaya, Maharashtra, Kerala and Assam where both the rural and urban sex-ratios improved but the rise in urban sex ratio was more, thereby, declining the rural-urban differential. The rural-urban differentials in sex ratio are correlated negatively with rural female mortality rates, road density and positively with urban female mortality, rural male mortality and rural female literacy rates. Spatially speaking, it was found that a decline in rural sex ratio is commensurate with increase in sex ratio in urban areas. The result, however, is the decline in rural-urban differential. There are wide regional variations in rural-urban differentials in sex ratio. The differential is high primarily due to male-selective migration from rural areas, in north-west and north-east Himalayan region, Orissa highland region and Chota Nagpur region. The areas of low differential constitute one broad belt running through the sub-continent from north of Rajasthan plain, most of the Gujarat region, western half of central India, Malwa region, Maharashtra, northern part of Karnataka plateau and north-western Andhra plateau, Tamil Nadu upland, south Sahyadri, a few scattered districts of middle and lower Ganga plain and Meghalaya-Mikir region. A higher urban sex ratio than rural is typical of eastern half of Andhra Pradesh, upper Ganga plain, major parts of Haryana and adjoining districts of Punjab and a few districts scattered in Gujarat, Kerala, Maharashtra, Tamil Nadu and to the south of eastern hill states. Feminization of rural-urban migration streams, decreasing female mortality rates, greater longevity of life of urban females and better medical facilities in urban areas are some of the reasons. Male-selective migration now-a-days is less crucial a factor. One redeeming feature of sex-composition of India's population is that the regional disparity has got reduced over time. In 1901, the urban sex ratio's coefficient of variability (65.37) was much higher than rural (31.46) implying that urban sex ratio had a greater variation and inconsistency. However, in 1991 not only both the areas displayed a decline in disparity, coefficient of variability being 7.81 in rural and 8.70 in the urban areas but a tremendous decline in disparity within urban areas was noticeable. In fine, family migration as a result of increased social approval for out-of-home female mobility, large number of avenues for females towards nuclear families, improved mortality rates, feminization of cities, commuting, index of relative advancement of society in terms of housing facilities, finance and culture in urban areas indicate a healthy trend of minimizing the rural-urban differential in sex ratio in the country.

In case of literacy, it is observed that despite India's rich ancient tradition of universal literacy and education, about half of the country's population still continues to live in the darkness of illiteracy. The rural-urban differential index of literacy for the country is 0.3013 with literacy rates being 44.69 and 73.08 per cent in rural and urban areas respectively. This gap can be attributed to general poverty, primarily agricultural economy, limited facilities for getting education, deep rooted caste structure, feudalistic attitudes of the society and limited development of the secondary sector of economy and sex prejudices. The urban literacy rates, being rather high everywhere, do not account much for the differential. The rural-urban differential is influenced more by rural literacy rates. The rural-urban differentials in literacy are negatively correlated with rural literacy, rural female literacy, percentage of rural population in other services, percentage of non-agricultural workers to total workers in rural areas, percentage of urban population and rural Christian population. By contrast, it is positively correlated with rural Muslim population and percentage of scheduled caste and scheduled tribe population to urban population as well as total population. After Independence both the rural and urban rates increased and this increase being sharper in rural areas has resulted in decline of rural-urban differential in the country. The decline is, however, not uniform everywhere. It is maximum (above 5 per cent) in a few northern and north-eastern hill states, Haryana plain and in lower Ganga plain and minimum (below 1 per cent) in Rajasthan plain, Orissa highland region and Chhota Nagpur plateau region. Spatially speaking, there are marked regional variations in rural-urban literacy differentials in the country. Low differential is found in coastal, near coastal, peripheral and in and around the highly urbanized, industrialized, commercialized areas and in metropolitan cities or areas. High literacy differential is found in interior areas, particularly those previously ruled by princely states and mountainous districts of Himalayas. Elsewhere, it is moderate and in two coastal districts of Kerala, it is negative. The low rural-urban differential is characteristic of those areas where there is a relatively high degree of urbanization, commercialization of agriculture, dense road network or transportation network, exposure to external influences through coastal location and emigration, school facilities are more in rural areas, status of females is high and prejudice against female education in rural areas is less. The differential is also low in many of the less urbanized areas, provided that their rural literacy is stimulated by missionary efforts, diversification of the rural economy and efficient administration. By contrast, high rural-urban differential is found generally in non-Christian tribal tracts, areas of predominantly subsistence agriculture, former princely states, areas of low level of urbanization, less developed transportation and communication network, low status of women and where prejudice against female mobility exists, lack of general awareness about benefits of literacy, inadequate educational facilities and high proportion of Muslim, scheduled caste and scheduled tribe population which are socially and economically less developed groups of population. Literacy in India, thus, has uneven development with urban bias.

A declining trend of rural-urban differentials albeit at varying rates in majority of areas with south India distinctly displaying lesser differential between its rural and urban counterparts is seen as typical feature of Indian demographic scenario.

Let us enunciate some research questions which emerge from the discussion in the present study. The impact of liberalization of economy on rural-urban differentials of various aspects of demography calls for a detailed study for future research. The second agenda for research pertains to development process *vis-a-vis* rural-urban differentials. Finally, the role of political economy and culture in promoting or diminishing rural-urban differentials.

# BIBLIOGRAPHY


Agarwala, S.N. (1985), *India's Population Problems,* 3rd Ed., Tata McGraw-Hill Publishing Co. Ltd., New Delhi.

Ahmad, A. and Nuna, S.C. (1986), "Inequity in the Literacy Levels of Population in Maharashtra" in Raza, M. (ed.), *Educational Planning: A Long Term Perspective,* NIEPA (National Institute of Educational Planning and Administration), Concept Publishing Co., New Delhi, pp. 129-161.

Ahmad, S.S. (1992), *India's Population — A Demographic Profile with Special Reference to Urban Areas (1961-1981),* An Unpublished Ph.D. Thesis, CSRD, J.N.U., New Delhi.

Aiyappan, A. (1955), In Tamilnad" in "Symposium on Caste and Joint Family, *Sociological Bulletin,* **4**, p. 21.

Alam, S.M. (1965), *Hyderabad and Secunderabad: Twin Cities: A Study in Urban Geography,* Allied Publishers Pvt. Ltd., New Delhi, pp. 77-93.

Ali, I. and Reddy, R. (1995), "India's Population Problem: A Sociological Study", *Indian Journal of Regional Science,* 27, 1 and 2.

Alonso, W. (1968), "Urban and Regional Imbalances in Economic Development", *Economic Development and Cultural Change,* 17, 1.

Ambannavar, J.P. (1975), *Population (Second India Studies),* Macmillan Co. of India Ltd., New Delhi, pp. 1-25.

Andorka, R. (1978), *Determinants of Fertility in Advanced Societies,* The Free Press, New York.

Anker, R. (1987) "An Analysis of Fertility Differential in Developing Countries" *Review of Economic Statistics,* 60, 1, pp. 58-69.

Arriaga, E.E. (1995), "Rural-Urban Mortality in Developing Countries: An Index for Detecting Rural Under-registration", *Demography,* 32, · pp. 98-107.

Arriaga, E.E. and Peter, O.W. (1988), "Determinants of Excess Female Mortality", *Population Bulletin of the United Nations,* pp. 21-22.

Askhem, J. (1975), *Fertility and Deprivation,* Cambridge University Press, Cambridge.

Baden Powell, B.H. (1972), *Indian Village Community* (Indian Reprint), Cosmo Publications, Delhi.

Baker, J. (1986), *The Rural-Urban Dichotomy in the Developing World: A Case Study from Northern Ethiopia*, Norwegian University Press, Oxford.

Bala, R. (1986), *Trends in Urbanisation in India, 1901 to 1981*, Rawat Publications, Jaipur.

Balfour, M.C. (1956), "Some Considerations regarding the Performance of Recent Declines in Mortality in Under-Developed Areas", in *Trends and Differentials in Mortality*, Milbank Memorial Fund.

Banerjee, M. (1975), "Literacy in Singhbhum, Bihar", *Geographical Review of India*,· 37, 2, pp. 151-157.

Bhardwaj, K. (1982), "Regional Differentiation in India, A Note", *Economic and Political Weekly*, 17, pp. 14-16.

Bhende, A. and Kanitkar, T. (1985), *Principles of Population Studies*, 3rd Ed., Himalaya Publishing House, Bombay.

Bhende, A.A. and Kanitkar, T. (1985), *Principles of Population Studies*, 3rd Ed., Himalaya Publishing House, Bombay.

Bhutani, S. (1995), *Demographic Dynamism in India*, Discovery Publishing House, New Delhi.

Bongaarts, J. (1978), "A Framework for Analysing Proximate Determinants of Fertility", *Population and Development Review*, 4,1, pp. 105-132.

Bongaarts, J. (1983), "The Formal Demography of Families and Households: An Over-view", *International Union for the Study of Population Newsletter*, 17, pp. 27-42.

Borooah, G.L. (1985), *Population Geography of Assam: A Study of Dibrugarh District* (1872-1971), Mittal Publications, Delhi.

Bose, A. (1991), *Demographic Diversity of India: 1991 Census State and District Level Data*, B.R. Publishing Corporation, Delhi.

Bose, A. (1991), *Demographic Diversity of India: 1991 Census State and District Level Data*, B.R. Publishing Corporation, Delhi. Bose, A. *et al.* (eds.) (1977), *Population Statistics in India*, Vikas Publishing House Pvt. Ltd., New Delhi.

Bose, S. (1991), "Urban Sex Ratio in West Bengal", *Geographical Review of India*, 52, 3, pp. 75-80.

Bulatao, R.A. (1984), *Reducing Fertility in Developing Countries*, World Bank, Washington.

Burch, T.K. (1967), "The Size and Structure of Families: A Comparative Analysis of Census Data", *American Sociological Review*, 32, pp. 347-363.

Burch, T.K. (1970), "Some Demographic Determinants of Average Household Size: An Analytic Approach", *Demography*, 7, 1, pp. 61-69.

Burnight, R.G. *et al.* (1956), "Differential Rural-Urban Fertility in Mexico", *American Sociological Review*, 31, 1, pp. 1-8.

Caldwell, J.C. *et al.* (1982), " Illustrative Analysis: Family Structure and Fertility." *World Fertility Survey Scientific Report No. 39*, International Statistical Institute, London.

Caldwell, J.C. *et al.* (1982), "Determinants of Fertility Decline in India", Paper to British Society for Population Studies Conference on Indian Population, Oxford, Mimeographed.

Caldwell, J.C. *et al.* (undated), *The Determinants of Family Structure in Rural South India*, Department of Demography, Australian National University.

Cassen, R.H. (1978), "India-Population Economy", *Society*, Macmillan, Hong Kong, p. 51.

Census of India (1951), *Literacy and Education Standard*, Paper 5 of 1954.

Census of India (1971), *Housing Tables*, Part IV-B, Office of the Registrar General and Ex-Officio Census Commissioner, India, New Delhi, p. xv.

Census of India (1981), *Child Mortality Estimates of India*, Occasional Paper 5 of 1988, Office of the Registrar General and Census Commissioner, India, New Delhi.

Census of India (1981), *Fertility in India*, Occasional Paper 13 of 1988, Office of the Registrar General and Census Commissioner, India, New Delhi.

Census of India (1981), *Final Population Totals*, Paper 1 of 1982, Series-1, India, Office of the Registrar General and Census Commissioner, India, New Delhi.

Census of India (1991), *Census-Based Estimates of Fertility by Rural-Urban Residence and Religion*, Occasional Paper No. 3 of 1993, Office of the Registrar General and Census Commissioner, India, New Delhi.

Census of India (1991), *Census Atlas*, National Vol. I, Office of the Registrar General and Census Commissioner, India, Map Division, New Delhi.

Census of India (1991), *Census-Based Estimates of Fertility by Rural-Urban Residence and Religion*, Occasional Paper No. 3 of 1993, Office of the Registrar General and Census Commissioner, India, New Delhi.

Census of India (1991), *Emerging Trends of Urbanisation in India: An Analysis of 1991 Census Results,* Occasional Paper No. I of 1993, Office of the Registrar General and Census Commissioner, India, New Delhi.

Census of India (1991), *Emerging Trends of Urbanization in India: An Analysis of 1991 Census Results*, Occasional Paper No. I of 1993, Office of the Registrar General and Census Commissioner, India, New Delhi.

Census of India (1991), *Final Population Totals*, Paper-1 of 1992, Vols. 1 & 2, Series – 1, India, Office of the Registrar General and Census Commissioner, India, New Delhi.

Census of India (1991), *Final Population Totals,* Paper-I of 1992, Vols. I & II, Series-1, India, Office of the Registrar General and Census Commissioner, India, New Delhi.

Census of India (1991), *Final Population Totals: Brief Analysis of Primary Census Abstract,* Pager 2 of 1992, Series-1, India, Office of the Registrar General and Census Commissioner, India, New Delhi.

Census of India (1991), *Functional Classification of Urban Agglomerations/Towns of India* 1991, Occasional Paper No. 3 of 1994, Office of the Registrar General and Census Commissioner, India, New Delhi.

Census of India (1991), *General Population Tables (Tables A-1 to A-3),* Series-1, India, Part II-A(i), Vols. I & II, Office of the Registrar General and Census Commissioner, India, New Delhi.

Census of India (1991), *Primary Census Abstract: General Population,* Series-1, India, Part II-B(i), Vols. I & II, Office of the Registrar General and Census Commissioner, India, New Delhi.

Census of India (1991), *Religion,* Paper 1 of 1995, Series-1, India, Office of the Registrar General and Census Commissioner, India, New Delhi.

Census of India (1991), *Union Primary Census Abstract for Scheduled Castes and Scheduled Tribes,* Paper 1 of 1993, Series-1, India, Office of the Registrar General and Census Commissioner, India, New Delhi.

Census of India (2001), Provisional Population Totals, Paper I of 2001, Series I, Office of the Registrar General and Census Commissioner, India, New Delhi.

Census of India (2001), Provisional Population Totals, Paper I of 2001 (supplement) District Totals, Series I, Office of the Registrar General and Census Commissioner, India, New Delhi.

Chandna, R.C. (1972), "Schedule Caste Population in Rural Haryana: A Geographic Analysis", *The National Geographical Journal of*

*India,* 23, 3 & 4, pp. 177-186.

Chandna, R.C. (1979), "Demographic Characteristics of India's District Headquarters, 1971", *Population Geography,* 1, 1 & 2, pp. 68-90.

Chandna, R.C. (1986), *A Geography of Population: Concepts, Determinants and Patterns,* Kalyani Publishers, New Delhi.

Chandna, R.C. (1989), *Spatial Dimensions of Scheduled Castes in India,* Intellectual Publishing House, New Delhi.

Chandna, R.C. (2000), *Geography of Population: Concepts, Determinants and Patterns,* Fourth Edition, Kalyani Publishers, New Delhi.

Chandna, R.C. and Sidhu, M.S. (1979), "Sex Ratio and Its Determinants", *Transactions, Institute of Indian Geographers,* 1,1, pp. 17-23.

Chandna, R.C. and Kant, S. (1985), "Distribution and Density of Population in India, 1981", *Asian Profile,* Vol. 13, No. 4, pp. 339-351.

Chandna, R.C. and Sidhu, M.S. (1980), *Introduction to Population Geography,* Kalyani Publishers, New Delhi.

Chandrasekhar, S. (1946), *India's Population – Facts and Policy,* Asia Press, New York.

Chandrasekhar, S. (1952), *Hungry People and Empty Lands,* George Allen, & Unwin, London.

Chandrasekhar, S. (1971), *Infant Mortality, Population Growth and Family Planning in India,* George Allen & Unwin, London, pp. 220-239.

Chaubey, P.K. and Chaubey, G. (1998), "Rural-Urban Disparity in Literacy: Inter-State Variation in India", *Indian Journal of Regional Science,* 30, 1, pp. 22-39.

Chaudhari, D.P. and Gupta, A.K. (1985), *Agriculture and Development,* Croom Helm, Kent.

Chaudhari, D.P. and Gupta, A.K. (1985), *Agriculture and Development,* Croom Helm, Kent.

Chaudhari, R.H. (1982), *Social Aspects of Fertility,* Vikas Publishing House, New Delhi.

Chitnis, S. (1972), "Education for Equality: Case of Scheduled Castes", *Economic and Political Weekly,* 7, 31-33, pp. 1675-1681.

Chitnis, S. (1974), "A Study of Evolution of Female Education in Gujarat till Independence", in Buch, M.B. (ed.), *History of Education: Abstract,* Centre of Advanced Studies in Education, M.S. University, Baroda, pp. 57-58.

Clark, J.I. (1960), "Rural and Urban Sex Ratios" *Tijdschrift voor Economische en Sociale Geografie*, 51, p. 29.

Clark, J.I. (1972), *Population Geography*, Pergamon Press, Oxford, p. 83.

Coale, A.J. (1956), "The Effects in Mortality and Fertility on Age Composited", *The Milbank Memorial Quarterly*, 36, pp. 79-114.

Cochrane, S.H. (1979), *Fertility and Education*, World Bank, Washington.

Cochrane, S.H. (1983), "Effects of Education and Urbanisation on Fertility" in Bulatao, R.A. and Lee, R.D. (eds.), *Determinants of Fertility in Developing Countries*, 2, Academic Press, New York.

Conklin, G.H. (1972), "Muslim Family Life and Secularisation in Dharwar, Karnataka", in Ahmad, I. (ed), *Family, Kinship and Marriage among the Muslims in India*, Manohar, New Delhi, p. 132.

Connell, J. *et al.* (1976), *Migration from Rural Areas*, Oxford University Press, New Delhi.

Cumper, G. (1985), "Economic Development Health Services and Health", in Kenneth Lee and Anne Mills (eds.), *The Economics of Health in Developing Countries*, Oxford University Press, Hongkong.

Curson, P.H. (1976), "Household Structure in Nineteenth Century, Auckland", *New Zealand Geographer*, 32, 2, pp. 177-193.

Curson, P.H. (1978), "Households, and Household Structure in Auckland, New Zealand", *New Zealand Geographer*, 34, 2, pp. 97-104.

D'Souza, V.S. (1980), *Educational Inequalities among Scheduled Castes – A Case Study in Punjab*, Occasional Monograph, Department of Sociology, Punjab University, Chandigarh.

D'Souza, V.S. (1982), "Rural-Urban Disparities: Education", *Demography India*, 11, 2, pp. 202-205.

Datt, R. (1996), "Inequalities in Educational Development with Special Reference to Literacy Status and School Education", *Journal of Educational Planning and Administration*, 9, 3, pp. 225-269.

Datta, S. (1961), "Differential Fertility in West Bengal in 1956", *Artha Vijnana*, 1, p. 67.

Davis, K. (1951), *Population of India and Pakistan*, Princeton University Press, Princeton.

Davis, K. (1956), "The Amazing Decline of Mortality in Underdeveloped Areas", *American Economic Review*, 46, pp. 305-318.

Davis, K. (1968), *Population of India and Pakistan*, Russel and Russel, New York.

Davis, K. and Blake, J. (1956), "Social Structure and Fertility: An

Analytical Framework", *Economic Development and Cultural Change,* 4, pp. 211-235.

De, J. (1990), "The Process of Urbanisation in Mauritius", *Geographical Review of India,* 52, p. 3.

Desai, P.B. (1967), "Variation in Population Sex-Ratios in India, 1901-61", in Bose, A. (ed), *Patterns of Population Change in India, 1951-61,* Allied Publishers, New Delhi, pp. 372-388.

Desai, P.B. (1969), *Size and Sex Composition of Population in India 1901-61,* Asia Publishing House, New Delhi.

Devi, D.R. (1991), "Literacy: A Study of South Indian Districts", *Demography India, 20, 1, pp. 103-112.*

Dewey, R. (1960), "The Rural-Urban Continuum: Real but Relatively Unimportant", *The American Journal of Sociology,* 66. pp. 60-66.

Dikshit, K.N. (1970), *Geography of Gujarat,* National Book Trust, New Delhi.

Dubey, K.N. (1981), *Regional Disparities in the Levels of Socio-Economic Development in an Indian State" A Case Study of Uttar Pradesh,* An Unpublished Ph.D. Thesis, Department of Geography, Punjab University, Chandigarh.

Duncan, O.D. (1957), "Community Size and the Rural-Urban Continuum", in Hatt, P. and Reiss, A.J., Jr. (eds). *Cities and Society,* Free Press, Glencoe, pp. 35-45.

Dutta, G. (1982), "Analysis of Literacy Rates in Southern Districts of West Bengal", *Geographical Review of India,* 44, 2, pp. 19-26.

Dyson, T. (1981), "Preliminary Demography of 1981 Census", *Economic and Political Weekly,* 16, pp. 1349-1365.

Economic Intelligence Service (1991), *Basic Statistics Relating to the Indian Economy, States,* 2, Tables 2.1-2.4, Centre for Monitoring Indian Economy Pvt. Ltd., New Delhi.

Economic Intelligence Service (1993), *Basic Statistics Relating to the Indian Economy, States,* 2, Tables 2.1-2.5, Centre for Monitoring Indian Economy Pvt. Ltd., New Delhi.

Economic Intelligence Service (1994), *Basic Statistics Relating to the Indian Economy, States,* 2, Tables 1.14, 1.15, Centre for Monitoring Indian Economy Pvt. Ltd., New Delhi.

Economic Intelligence Service (1997), *Profiles of States,* Centre for Monitoring Indian Economy Pvt. Ltd., New Delhi.

Epstein, S. (1973), *South India: Yesterday, Today and Tomorrow,* Macmillan, London, p. 201.

Franklin, S.H. (1956), "The Pattern of Sex Ratios in New Zealand,

*Economic Geography,* 32, pp. 162-176.

Gazetteer of India (1973), *Indian Union, Volume One: Country and People* (Reprint), Publication Division, Ministry of Information and Broadcasting, Government of India, New Delhi, p. 546.

Gibbs, J.P. (ed.) (1961), *Urban Research Methods,* Affiliated East-West Press, New Delhi, pp. 472-503.

Gill, M.S. and Singh, M. (1986), " Migration to Indian Cities", *Asian Profile,* Vol.14, No. 3, pp. 233 – 247.

Gill, M.S. and Singh, S.B. (1985), "Sex Ratio in Punjab, *Geographical Review of India,* 47, 3, pp. 34-44.

Gist, N.P. (1952), "Ecological Decentralisation and Rural-Urban Relationships", *Rural Sociology,* 17, pp. 328-335.

Goel, N.P. (1994), *Readings in Population Geography,* Mohit Publications, New Delhi.

Goode, W.J. (1963), *World Revolution and Family Patterns,* Collier-Macmillan Limited, London, p. 367.

Gopinath Nair, P.R. (1974), "Decline in Birth Rate in Kerala", *Economic and Political Weekly,* 9, pp. 323-336.

Gosal, G.S. (1961), "The Regionalism of Sex Composition of India's Population", *Rural Sociology,* 26, 2, pp. 122-137.

Gosal, G.S. (1964), "Literacy in India: An Interpretative Study", *Rural Sociology,* 29, 3, pp. 261-277.

Gosal, G.S. (1967), "Regional Aspects of Rural Literacy in India", *Transactions of the Indian Council of Geographers,* 4, pp. 1-15.

Gosal, G.S. (1979), "Spatial Perspective on Literacy in India", *Population Geography,* 1, 1 & 2, pp. 41-67.

Gosal, G.S. (1985), "Spatial Perspective on Literacy in India", in Mukerji, A.B. and Ahmad, A. (eds.), *India-Culture, Society and Economy and Geographical Essays,* Inter-India Publications, New Delhi, pp. 362-379.

Gosal, G.S. and Mukerji A.B. (1970), "The Religious Composition of India's Population – A Spatial Perspective" Tijdschrift voor Economische en Sociale Geografie, 61, pp. 91-100.

Gosal, R.P.S. (1980), *Literacy of the Scheduled Caste Population of India,* An Unpublished M.Phil Dissertation, Department of Geography, Punjab University, Chandigarh.

Gosal, R.P.S. (1988), "Literacy in India's Scheduled Caste Population: A Spatial Analysis", *Population Geography,* 10, No. 1 & 2, pp. 42-60.

Gosal, R.P.S. (1997), "Scheduled Caste Population of India and its Recent

Demographic Dynamism: A Spatial Perspective", in Ahmad, A. *et al.* (eds.), *Demographic Transition*: The Third World Scenario, Rawat Publications, Jaipur, pp. 147-161,

Gould, K. (1968), "Literacy in Kerala", in Goody, J. (ed.), *Literacy in Traditional Societies,* Cambridge University Press, Cambridge, pp. 133-160.

Gould, K. (1983), "Sex Inequalities in the Dual System of Education: The Parsis of Gujarat", *Economic and Political Weekly,* 18, 39, pp. 1668-1676.

Government of India (1985), "Education," in *Statistical Abstract, India,* Central Statistical Organization, New Delhi, pp. 522 – 540.

Government of India (1992), *Statistical Abstract: India,* Central Statistical Organization, Department of Statistics, Ministry of Planning & Programme Implementation, New Delhi.

Government of India (1996-97), *Economic Survey,* Ministry of Finance, Economic Division, New Delhi.

Goyal, R.P. (1984), "Mortality in India: Trend and Prospects", *Demography India*, Vol. 23, Nos. 1 & 2, pp. 103 –116.

Goyal, R.P. (1988), *Marriage Age in India,* B.R. Publishing Corporation, Delhi.

Goyal, R.P. (1994), "Mortality in India: Trend and Prospects", *Demography India,* 23, 1 & 2, pp. 103-116.

Gupta, P.K. (1986), "Are Inter-District Disparities Too", *Yojana,* 30, 4, pp. 9-22.

Gurumurthy, G. (1976), "Fertility Differentials in Andhra Pradesh-1961", *Demography India,* 5, 1 & 2, pp. 153-162.

Heenan, L.D.B. (1967), "Rural-Urban Distribution of Fertilities in South Island: New Zealand", *Annals of the Association of American Geographers,* 57, p. 313.

Hoselitz, B.F. (1960), "The Urban-Rural Contrast as a Factor in Social Change", *The Economic Weekly,* Annual, pp. 145-152.

Hussain, I.Z. (1970), "Educational Status and Differential Fertility in India", *Social Biology,* 17, 2, p. 132.

Jaco, G.E. and Belkamp, I. (1953), "Is a New Family Form Emerging in the Urban Fringe?" *American Sociological Review,* 18, pp. 551-557.

Jain, S.P. (1975), *Democracy: A Status Study on Population Research in India*, Vol. II, Tata McGraw Hill Publishing Co. New Delhi, pp. 128-144.

Jain, S.P. (1975), *Demography: A Status Study on Population Research in India,* Vol. II, Tata McGraw Hill Publishing Co., New Delhi, pp. 128-144.

Jayasree, R. and Audinarayana, N. (1991), "Differential Growth and Characteristics of Population Across the Ecological Regions of Tamil Nadu, 1991", *Demography India,* 20, 1, pp. 35-40.

Jerzy, B. (1970), "Census of Fertility Decline in Eastern Europe and Soviet Union", *Population Studies,* 24, 1, pp. 35-58.

Jolly, K.G. (1991), "Strategies to Attain Universal Literacy in India by 2001", *Demography India,* 20, 1, pp. 141-154.

Jones, H.R. (1981), *Population Geography,* Harper & Row, London, p. 166.

Joshi, P. C. and Rao, M. R. (1965), "Changes in Literacy and Education-Study of Villages in U. P. and Punjab", *The Economic Weekly*, July 3, pp.1061-1068.

Karve, I. (1953), *Kinship Organization in India*, Deccan College Monograph Series No. 11, Poona.

Kashyap, S.S. (1975), "The Changing Pattern of Sex-Ratio in Punjab", *Demography India,* 4, 2.

Kaur, I. (1983), *Trends in Literacy Differential in Patiala District: 1951-71,* An Unpublished M. Phil. Dissertation, Department of Geography, Punjab University, Chandigarh.

Kaur, S. and Chandna, R.C. (1983), "Changes in the Industrial Structure of India's Male Working Force, 1961-81", *Population Geography,* Vol. 5, Nos. 1 & 2, pp. 87-104.

Kobrin, F.E. (1976), "The Fall in Household Size and the Rise of the Primary Individual in the United State", *Demography,* 13, 1, pp. 127-138.

Kohli, K.L. (1977), *Mortality in India*, Sterling Publishers, New Delhi.

Kothari, D.S. (1970), *Economic Guide and Investor's Handbook of India, 1969 – 70*, Kothari & Sons, Madras, pp. 2215 – 2220.

Krishan, G. (1980) "Size of the Household in Rural India", in Singh, R.L and Rana, P.B.S. (eds.) *Rural Habitat Transformation in World Frontiers,* National Geographical Society of India, Varanasi, pp. 354-363.

Krishan, G. (1989), "Fertility and Mortality Trends in India States", *Geography,* 74, pp. 53-56.

Krishan, G. (1989), "Trends in Regional Disparities in India", *Asian Profile,* 17, 3, pp. 243-261.

Krishan, G. (1991), "Urban-Rural Relations in India: A Critique", *IASSI Quarterly,* 10, 1, pp. 92-104.

Krishan, G. (1993), "The Slowing Down of Indian Urbanization", *Geography,* 78, pp. 80-84.

Krishan, G. and Chandna, R.C. (1973), "Sex Composition of Haryana's Population", *Geographical Review of India,* 35, 2, pp. 113-125.

Krishan, G. and Chandna, R.C. (1974), "Patterns of Literacy in Haryana", *Punjab University Research Bulletin (Arts),* 5, 2, pp. 95-104.

Krishan, G. and Kant, S. (1986), "Spurts in India's Population Growth During the Twentieth Century: A Spatial View", *Geoforum,* 17, 1, pp. 57-67.

Krishan, G. and Rana, P. (1980), "Rural-Urban Differential in Size of the Household in India", *Population Geography,* 2, 1 & 2, pp. 21-34.

Krishan, G. and Shyam, M. (1973), "Spatial Perspective on Progress of Female Literacy in India: 1901-71", *Pacific Viewpoint,* 14, pp. 203-206.

Krishan, G. and Shyam, M. (1974), "Literacy Patterns of Indian Cities", *Geoforum,* 19, pp. 77-80.

Krishan, G. and Shyam, M. (1977), "Literacy in India", *Geographical Review of India,* 39, 2, pp. 117-125.

Krishan, G. and Shyam, M. (1978), "Regional Aspects of Urban-Rural Differentials in Literacy in India: 1971", *The Journal of Developing Areas,* 13, 1, pp. 11-21.

Kundu, A. and Rao, J.M. (1982), "Inequality in Educational Development: Issues in Measurement Changing Structure and Its Socio-Economic Correlates with Special Reference to India", Paper Presented at Regional Workshop on Lo*ng-Term Educational Planning,* NIEPA, New Delhi.

Kundu, A. and Rao, J.M. (1986), "Inequity in Educational Development: Issues in Measurement Changing Structure and Its Socio-Economic Correlates with Special Reference to India" in Raza, M. (ed.), *Educational Planning: A Long Term Perspective,* NIEPA and Concept Publishing Co., New Delhi, pp. 435-466.

Lal, H. (1987), *City and Urban Fringe: A Case Study of Bareilly,* Concept Publishing Co., New Delhi.

Lall, A. (1962), "Age and Sex Structure of Cities of India", *Geographical Review of India,* 24, 1, pp. 7-29.

Laslett, P. (1969), "Size and Structure of the Household in England Over Three Centuries", *Population Studies,* 23, pp. 199-223.

Laslett, P. (1970), "The Comparative History of Household and Family",

*Journal of Social History*, 4.

Laslett, P. (1972), *Household and Family in Past Time*, Cambridge University Press, Cambridge, pp. 301-342.

Lewis, O. (1958), *Village Life in Northern-India*, Vintage Books, New York.

Lipton, M. (1977), *Why Poor People Stay Poor: Urban Bias in World Development*, Temple Smith, London.

Lipton, M. (1984), "Household Size and Poverty", in Dyson, T. and Crook, N. (eds.), *India's Demography*, South Asian Publishers Pvt. Ltd., New Delhi, pp. 209-234.

Lipton, M. (1986), "Why Poor People Stay Poor", in Harriss, J. (ed.), *Rural Development: Theories of Peasant Economy and Agrarian Change*, English Language Book Societies, Hutchinson, pp. 66-81.

Mamoria, C.B. (1981), *India's Population Problem: A Sociological Study*, Kitab Mahal, Delhi.

Mandelbaum, D.G. (1972), *Society in India*, Popular Prakashan, Bombay, pp. 54-55.

Mandelbaum, David G. (1974), *Human Fertility in India*. University of California Press, Berkely.

Mathur, B.B. (1982), *Literacy Differentials in Uttar Pradesh: 1971*, An Unpublished M. Phil. Dissertation, Department of Geography, Punjab University, Chandigarh.

Mathur, B.B. (1985), "Geography of Literacy in India, A Bibliographical Note", *The Avadh Journal of Social Sciences*, 2, pp. 148-151.

Maurya, S.D. and Devi, G. (1985), "Changing Pattern of Urban Sex Ratio in Uttar Pradesh", *National Geographer*, 20, 2, pp. 171-182.

Mehta, B.C. (1978), *Regional Population Growth*, Research Books, Jaipur.

Mehta, S. and Kaur, G. (1983), "Rural-Urban Differences in Sex Ratio of Rajasthan", *The Indian Geographical Journal*, 58, 2, pp. 152-161.

Ministry of Information and Broadcasting (1974), *India: 1974*, Government of India, New Delhi, p. 80.

Misra, B.D. (1980), *An Introduction to the Study of Population*, South Asian Publishers Pvt. Ltd., New Delhi.

Mitra, A. (1978), *India's Population: Aspects of Quality and Control*, 1, Abhinav Publications, New Delhi, p. 112.

Mitra, A. (1979), *Implications of Declining Sex-Ratio in India's Population*, Allied Publishers Pvt. Ltd., New Delhi, pp. 1-85.

Mohan, R. and Chandrasekhar, P. (1982), "Morphology of Urbanization in India", *Economic and Political Weekly,* 17, 39, pp. 1579-88.

Morton, J. (1962), "Who'll House the Single"? *New Society,* 25, March, pp. 664-65.

Mukerjee, K. (1962), *Rural-Urban Differences and Relationships with Social Characteristics,* Paper for UNESCO Seminar, p. 85.

Mukerji, A.B. (1968), "Spatial Patterns of Literacy in Andhra Pradesh, India", *Selected Papers,* 21 International Geographical Congress, pp. 181-186.

Mukhopadhyay, A.K. (1983), "Estimates for Sex Differentials in Mortality from Differential Growth of the Two Sexes", in Narain, V. and Prakasham, C.P. (eds.), *Population Policy Perspectives in Developing Countries,* Himalaya Publishing House, Bombay.

Murthi, M. *et al.* (1995), "Mortality, Fertility, and Gender Bias in India: A District-Level Analysis", *Population and Development Review,* 21, 4, pp. 745-782.

Muthiah, S. (1987), *A Social and Economic Atlas of India*, Oxford University Press, Delhi.

Nag, M. (1973), "Tribal-Non-tribal Fertility Differential in India", *Demography India,* 11, 1, pp. 104-120.

Nag, M. (1984), "Fertility Differential in Kerala and West Bengal," *Economic and Political Weekly*, Vol.16, No.1, pp. 33 – 41.

Naik, J.P. (1971), *Education of the Scheduled Castes (1965-66),* Occasional Monograph 6, ICSSR, New Delhi.

Naik, J.P. (1975), *Policy and Performers in India Education: 1947 – 1974*, Orient Longman, New Delhi.

Naik, J.P. (1978), *Education for Our People: A Policy Frame for the Development of Education (1978 – 87),* ICSSR, Allied Publishers, New Delhi, pp. 1 - 7.

Nain, N.S. (1988), *Trends in Urban-Rural Differentials in Select Aspects of Indian Demography, 1951-81: A Spatial View,* An Unpublished M. Phil. Dissertation, Department of Geography, Punjab University, Chandigarh.

Namboodiri, N.K. (1966), "Contribution to the Study of within Urban and within Rural Differentials", *Rural Sociology,* 31, 1, pp. 29-39.

Ogburn, W.F. (1936), "Regions", Social Forces, 15, pp. 6-11.

Ojha, G.K. (1966), *Progress of Compulsory Education in India (1951 – 66),* Universal Publication, Delhi.

Pai Panandikar, V.A. and Chaudhuri, P.N. (1983), *Demographic Transition in Goa and Its Policy Implications,* Uppal Publishing House, New Delhi.

Pal, M.N. (1975), "Regional Disparities in the Level of Development in India", *Indian Journal of Regional Science*, 7, 1, pp. 35-52.

Palm, R. (1976), An Index of Household Diversity, *Tijdschrift voor Economische en Sociale Geografie*, 67, pp. 194-201.

Parulekar, R. V. (1939), *Literacy in India*, Macmillan, London.

Pathak, K.B. and Murty, P.K. (1985), "Socio-Economic Determinants of Fertility and Mortality Decline in India", *Demography India*, 14, 1, pp. 17-33.

Patnaik, M.M. (1985), *Fertility Behaviour*, Janaki Prakashan, Patna.

Paulus, C.R. (1966), *The Impact of Urbanization on Fertility in India*, University of Mysore, Mysore, pp. 82 – 99.

Paulus, C.R. (1966), *The Impact of Urbanization on Fertility in India*, University of Mysore, Mysore, pp. 82-99.

Phadke, V.S. (1983), "Spatial Disparities in Socio-Economic Infrastructure in the Bombay Metropolitan Region", *Indian Journal of Regional Science*, 15, 1, pp. 48-51.

Phednekar, M.M. and Sita, K. (1985), "Spatial Patterns of Sex Ratio in South Konkan (Maharashtra), 1951 and 1971", in Sundram, K.V. and Nangia, S. (eds.) *Population Geography* (Contributions to Indian Geography-VI), Heritage Publishers, New Delhi, pp. 130-135.

Pitirim, S. and Carle, C.Z. (1929), *Principles of Rural-Urban Sociology*, Henry Holt and Co., New York, p. 14.

Pocock, D.F. (1960), "Sociologies: Urban and Rural", *Contributions to Indian Sociology*, 4, p. 63.

Population Foundation of India (1998), *State of India's Population*, Population Foundation of India, New Delhi.

Prakasam, C.P. (1986), *Determinants of Fertility Levels and Trends in Sri Lanka*, Bookwell Publications, Delhi.

Prasad, R. (1990), *Population Geography of India: A Case Study of Rajasthan*, Radha Publications, New Delhi.

Premi, M. K. (1976), " Probable Literacy Rates in India by 1986 under Different Assumptions of Population Growth", *Manpower Journal* ,Vol. X, No. I, pp. 85-116.

Premi, M.K. (1982), *Demographic Situation in India*, East-West Population Institute, Honolulu.

Premi, M.K. (1991), "Education for All: The Concern Areas", *Demography India*, 20, 1, pp. 91-102.

Premi, M.K. (1993), "India's Changing Population Profile and Policy Issues", Paper presented at International Symposium on Population Growth in Developing Countries, Organized by the Centre for the

Study of Regional Development, School of Social Science, J.N.U., New Delhi, Tables 12, 15, pp. 52-55, 58-61.

Premi, M.K. (1997), "India's Changing Population Profile and Policy Issues", in Ahmad, A. *et al.* (eds.), *Demographic Transition: The Third World Scenario*, Rawat Publication, Jaipur, pp. 382 – 419.

Premi, M.K. *et al.* (1983), *An Introduction to Social Demography*, Vikas Publishing House, New Delhi.

Premi, M.K. *et al.* (1983), *An Introduction to Social Demography*, Vikas Publishing House, New Delhi.

Queen, S.A. and Carpenter, D.B. (1953), *The American City*, McGraw Hill Book Co., New York.

Rainia, B.L.(undated) *Family Size Norms in Population Problems in India*, p. 49.

Rakesh, M. and Pant, C. (1982), "Morphology of Urbanization in India," *Economic and Political Weekly*, Vol. 17, No. 39, pp.1579 – 88.

Ram, S. (1981), *Literacy Differential in Punjab: 1971*, An Unpublished M.Phil. Dissertation, Department of Geography, Punjab University, Chandigarh.

Ramasundaram, S. (1995), "Causes for the Rapid Fertility Decline in Tamil Nadu: A Policy Planner's Perspective", *Demography India*, 24, 1, pp. 13-21.

Ramu, G.N. (1988), *Family Structure and Fertility*, Sage Publications, New Delhi.

Ramu, G.N. (1988), *Family Structure and Fertility*, Sage Publications, New Delhi.

Ranjan, A. (1994), "A Comparison of Fertility Transition in India and Madhya Pradesh", *Demography India*, 24, 1 & 2, pp. 29-39.

Raza, M. and Aggarwal, Y.P. (1986), "Inequities in the Levels of Literacy in India: The Regional Dimension", in Shafi, M. and Raza, M. (eds.), *Spectrum of Modern Geography*, Concept Publishing Co., New Delhi. pp. 193-225.

Raza, M. and Aggarwal, Y.P. (1988), An Analysis of Inequalities in the Levels of Literacy in India", in Raza, M. (ed.), *Regional Development* (Contributions to Indian Geography), Heritage Publishers, New Delhi, pp. 385-403.

Raza, M. *et al.* (1985), "Spatial Patterns of Tribal Literacy in India", *The Indian Geographical Journal*, 60, 2, pp. 103-116.

Reddy, M.M.K. (1996), *An Introduction to Demographic Behaviour in India*, Kanishka Publishers, New Delhi, pp. 53-70.

Reddy, U.B. (1985), "Regional Disparities in Educational Development in India: An Inter-State Analysis". *Geographical Review of India*, 47, 2, pp. 22-27.

Registrar General of India (1994), *Sample Registration System: Fertility and Mortality Indicators, 1992*, Fertility and Mortality (SRS) Survey Division, Ministry of Home Affairs, New Delhi.

Registrar General of India (1994), *SRS Based Abridged Life Tables, 1986-90*, Occasional Paper No. I of 1994, Vital Statistics Division, Ministry of Home Affairs, New Delhi.

Registrar General of India (1994), *SRS Based Abridged Life Tables, 1986-90*, Occasional Paper No. 1 of 1994, Vital Statistics Division, Ministry of Home Affairs, New Delhi.

Registrar General of India (1995), *Sample Registration Bulletin*, 29, 1, Vital Statistics Division, Ministry of Home Affairs, New Delhi.

Registrar General of India (1997), *District Level Estimates of Fertility and Child Mortality for 1991 and Their Inter-Relations with Other Variables, Occasional Paper No. 1 of 1997*, Vital Statistics Division, Ministry of Home Affairs, New Delhi.

Registrar General of India (1998), *Sample Registration Bulletin*, Vol. 32, No. 1, Vital Statistics Division, Ministry of Home Affairs, New Delhi, pp. 6, 39 – 53.

Registrar General of India (1998), *Sample Registration Bulletin*, 32, 1, Vital Statistics Division, Ministry of Home Affairs, New Delhi.

Registrar General of India (1999), *Compendium of India's Fertility and Mortality Indicators, 1971 – 1997*, Vital Statistics Division, Ministry of Home Affairs, New Delhi.

Rele, J.R. (1963), "Fertility Differentials in India", *The Milbank Memorial Fund Quarterly*, 41, 2, p. 183.

Richard, J. and Sundar Rao, P.S.S. (1995), "Influence of Age at Marriage and Family Planning on Fertility", *Demography India*, 24, 1, pp. 81-86.

Robinson, W.C. (1961), "Urban-Rural Fertility Differentials," *Population Studies*,Vol.14, No.3, pp. 218 – 234.

Robinson, W.C. (1961), "Urban-Rural Fertility Differentials", *Population Studies*, 14, 3, pp. 218-234.

Robinson, W.C. (1963), "Urbanization and Fertility: The Non-Western Experience, *The Milbank Memorial Fund Quarterly*, 41, 3.

Ross, A.D. (1973), *The Hindu Family in its Urban Setting*, Oxford University Press, Bombay, p. 38.

Rudolph, S.H. and Rudolph, L.I. (1972), *Education and Politics in India*, Harvard University Press, Cambridge, Massachusetts.

Ruzieka, L.T. (1984), "Mortality in India", in Dyson, J. and Cook, N. (eds.), *India's Demography,* South Asian Publishers, New Delhi.

Sagar, P. (1984), *Changes in Female Literacy in India, 1951 – 81,* Unpublished M.Phil. Dissertation of Geography, Panjab University, Chandigarh, p. 73.

Sagar, P. (1990), *Spatial Patterns of Literacy Differentials in India: 1981,* An Unpublished Ph.D. Thesis, Department of Geography, Punjab University, Chandigarh.

Samuel, J.J. (1963), "Culture and Human Fertility in India", *Journal of Family Welfare,* 9, 4, p. 45.

Schultz, T.P. (1976), "Determinants of Fertility", in Coale. A.J. (ed.), *Economic Factors in Population Growth,* Macmillan, London.

Schwartzberg, J.E. (1961), "Observations on the Progress of Literacy in India: 1951-61", *Indian Population Bulletin,* 2, Office of the Registrar General, India, New Delhi, pp. 295-300.

Sdasyuk, G. V. (1971), "Urbanization and Spatial Structure of Indian Economy". *Economic and Socio-Cultural Dimensions of Regionalization.* An Indo-USSR Collaborative Study. Census Centenary Monograph No. 17, New Delhi.

Sen , A. (1973), *On Economic Inequality* , Oxford , Delhi.

Senapati, R.N. (1993), "Sex-Ratio: Trends and Implications in India", *Vision,* 13, 1 & 2, pp. 92-100.

Shah, A.M. (1973), *The Household Dimensions of the Family in India: A Field Study in a Gujarat Village and a Review of Other Studies,* Orient Longman, New Delhi, pp. 148-151.

Shah, A.M. (1974), *The Household Dimensions of the Family in India,* Orient Longman, New Delhi.

Sharma, H.N. (1985), "Sex Disparity in Literacy and Social Topography of Assam", in Mukerji, A.B. and Ahmad, A. (eds.), *India,* Inter-India Publication, New Delhi, pp. 379-401.

Sharma, J.C. (1968), "Literacy in Western Rajasthan ", *Selected Papers,* 21st International Geographical Congress, pp. 230-250.

Shastri, P.S. (1985), "Patterns of Tribal Literacy in Vidarbha", *Population Geography,* 7, 1 & 2, pp. 40-59.

Shyrock, H.S. (ed.) (1976), *The Method and Materials of Demography,* Academic Press, New York, p. 105.

Siddique, M. (1977), "The Geography of Literacy in Uttar Pradesh," *Geographical Review of India,* Vol. 39, pp. 374-388.

Siddiqui, F.A. (1975), "Occupational Structure of Population in Haryana", *The Geographer,* 22, 2.

Siddiqui, F.A. (1982), "Regional Analysis of the Sex-Structure of Population of Uttar Pradesh", *The National Geographical Journal of India,* 28, 1 & 2, pp. 74-85.

Siddiqui, N.A. and Ahmad, Q.M. (1971), "Regional Variation of the Sex-Ratio in the Population of Haryana", *The Geographer,* 18, pp. 99-114.

Singh, A.K. (1980), "Population Growth, Sex-Ratio and Age Structure of Five Cities of West Bengal: A Case Study", *National Geographer,* 15, 1. pp. 83-96.

Singh, C.P. (1979), "Literacy in Rural Population in Meerut District", *Geographical Observer,* Vol.15, pp.32-36.

Singh, K.P. (1988), "Religion and Fertility: A Study in Differentials-Education", *Population Geography,* 10, 1 & 2, pp. 18-27.

Sinha, V.C. (1979), *Dynamics of India's Population Growth,* National Publishing House, New Delhi.

Singh, R.L. (1971), *India: A Regional Geography,* National Geographical Society of India, Varanasi.

Smith, R.M. (1981), "Fertility, Economy and Household Formation in England Over Three Centuries", *Population and Development Review,* 7, 4, pp. 595-622.

Smith, T.L. and Zopf, P.E. (1970), "Education Status", in *Demography,* F.A. Davis Company , Philadelphia , pp. 265 – 282.

Sopher, D.E. (1974), "A Measure of Disparity", *The Professional Geographer,* 26, 4, pp. 389-392.

Sopher, D.E. (1980), "Sex Disparity in Indian Literacy", in Sopher D.E. (ed.), *An Exploration of India Geographical Perspectives on Society and Culture,* Cornell University Press, Ithaca, New York, pp. 130-188.

Sorokin, P and Zimmerman, CC (1929), *Principles of Rural-Urban Sociology,* Henry Holt and Co., New York, p. 14.

Spate, O.H.K. and Learmonth, A.T.A. (1954), *India and Pakistan,* Methuen and Col. Ltd., London.

Srinivasan, K. (1967), "Prospective Study of the Fertility Behaviour of a Group of Married Women in Rural India: Design and Findings of the First Round of Enquiry", *Population Review,* 11, 2, p. 46.

Srinivasan, K. (1991), "Fertility and Proximate Determinants", in Satia, J.K. and Jejeebhoy, S.J. (eds.), *The Demography Challenge,* Oxford University Press, Bombay, pp. 37-76.

Srinivasan, K. (1995), "Lessons from Goa, Kerala and Tamil Nadu: The Three Successful Fertility Transition States in India",

*Demography India,* 24, 2, pp. 163-194.

Steinman, D.L. and Attar, M.E. (1981), "Natural Population Decrease Differentials in Mississippi: An Indicator of Rural Development", *Demography India,* 9, 1 & 2, pp. 18-30.

Stewart, C.T., Jr. (1958), "The Urban-Rural Dichotomy: Concepts and Uses", *The American Journal of Sociology,* 64, pp. 152-158.

Stockwell, E.G. (1963), Fertility, Mortality and Status of Underdevelopment Areas, *Social Forces,* 4, pp. 390-395.

Sundaram, K.V. and Nangia, S. (eds.) (1985), *Population Geography* (Contributions to Indian Geography-VI), Heritage Publishers, New Delhi.

Suri, K.C. *et al.* (1988), *Analysis of Work Force in India,* Occasional Paper No. 8 of 1988, Office of the Registrar General and Census Commissioner, India, New Delhi.

Syamala, T.S. and Roy, T.K. (1994), "Relationship Between Child Mortality and Fertility: A Few Empirical Evidences from Goa, India", *Demography India,* 23, 1 & 2, pp. 117-126.

Taylor, L. and Jones, A.R., Jr. (1964), *Rural Life and Urbanised Society,* Oxford University Press, New York, pp. 49-67.

Thompson, W.S. (1935), *Population Problems,* McGraw Hill Book Company, Englewood.

Thompson, W.S. (1935), *Population Problems,* McGraw Hill Book Company, Englewood.

Tilak, J.B.G. (1981), "Inter-State Disparities in Educational Development", in Nair, K.R.G. (ed.), *Regional Disparities in India,* Agricole Publishing Academy, New Delhi, pp. 33-48.

Tilak, J.B.G., (1978), "Regional Inequality in Literacy in India", *Indian Journal of Adult Education,* 39, 1, pp. 14-22.

Tirtha, R. (1966), "Areal Patterns of Literacy in India", *Manpower Journal,* 3, pp. 88-118.

Trewatha, G.T. (1953), "A Case for Population Geography", *Annals of the Association of American Geographers,* 43, p. 351.

Truesdell, L.E. (1949), "The Development of the Urban-Rural Classification in the United States: 1874-1949", *Bureau of the Census* Series, Washington, 23, 1, pp. 1-100.

UNESCO (1982), *Population of India,* ESCAPE, Country Monograph, Series-10, Table 220, p. 322.

United Nations (1949), *Population Census Methods* (Population Studies, No. 4), United Nations, New York, p. 3.

United Nations (1950), *Data on Urban and Rural Population in Recent Censuses,* Population Studies, 8, Lake Success, New York.

United Nations (1953), *Determinants and Consequences of Population Trends,* Publication No. 18, New York, p. 135.

United Nations (1953), *The Determinants and Consequences of Population Trends*, New York.

United Nations (1961), *Mysore Population Study Report*, New York.

United Nations (1968), *Demographic Yearbook,* Department of Economic and Social Affairs, New York, pp. 2-5.

United Nations (1972), *Populations Aspects of Social Development,* Economic Commission for Asia and the Far East, Bangkok, p. 67.

United Nations (1980), "Principles and Recommendations for Population and Housing Censuses, Statistical Papers M67, Department of International Economic and Social Affairs, New York.

United Nations (1980), *Principles and Recommendations for Population and Housing Censuses*, Statistical Papers M67, Department of International Economic and Social Affairs, New York.

United Nations (1981), "Estimates and Projections of the Number of the Households by Country 1975-2000", Department of International Economic and Social Affairs, New York.

United Nations (1981), *Estimates and Projections of International Economic and Social Affairs*, New York.

United Nations (1982), *Demographic Yearbook,* Department of Economic and Social Affairs, New York, pp. 132-133.

United Nations (1983), *Rural-Urban Relations and National Centre for Regional Development*, Nagoya, Japan.

United Nations (1983), *Rural-Urban Relations and National Development,* Centre for Regional Development, Nagoya, Japan.

United Nations (1984), *Fertility and Family*, New York.

United Nations (1986), *Determinants of Mortality Change in Developing Countries*, New Delhi.

United Nations (1987), 'Fertility Behaviour in the Context of Development, New York.

United Nations (1989), *World Population Prospects, 1988,* Population Studies No. 106, New York, pp. 49-50.

Usha Rao, N.J. (1982), "Inter-State Disparities in Literacy Rates in Karnataka with Special Reference to Scheduled Castes", in Bhat, L.S. (ed.), *Regional Disparities in India,* Society for the Study of Regional Disparities, New Delhi.

Vaidyanathan, K.E. (1981), "Rural-Urban Redistribution of Population in West Asia", *Population Geography,* 3, 1 & 2, pp. 96-113.

Vallin, J. (1968), "La mortalite dans les pags du ties Monde, *Population,* pp. 845-68.

Vidyarthi, L.P. and Rai, B.K. (1977), *The Tribal Culture in India*, Concept Publishing Co., New Delhi, p. 188.

Visaria, P. (1995), "Demographic Transition and Policy Responses in India", *Demography India,* 24, 1, pp. 1-12.

Visaria, P. and Visaria, L. (1994), "Demographic Transition: Accelerating Fertility Decline During the 1980s", *Economic and Political Weekly,* 29, 51-52, pp. 3281-3292.

Vos, S.D. and Murty K.R. (1985), "Some Reflections on the Demographic Study of the Households in India", *Demography India,* 14, 1, pp. 49-67.

Wirth, L. (1938), "Urbanism as a Way of Life", *American Journal of Sociology,* 44, p. 3.

World Development Report (1992), *Development and Environment*, World Bank Publication, Oxford University Press, Oxford, Delhi, etc., xi-308.

Wyon, J.B. and Gordon, J.E (1971), *The Khanna Study*, Hayward University Press Massachusetts.

Wyon, J.B. and Gordon, J.E. (1971), *The Khanna Study.* Harward University Press, Massachusetts.

Zachariah, K.C. (1962), " Note on Migration" in Glass, R. (ed.), *Urban-Rural Differences in South Asia,* p. 75.

Zachariah, K.C. (1984), *The Anomaly of the Fertility Decline in India's Kerala State: A Field Investigation,* The World Bank, Washington, DC, pp. 1-58.

Zachariah, K.C. (1995), "Transitions in the Determinants of Fertility Decline in India", *Demography India,* 24, 2, pp. 147-161.

Zachariah, K.C. and Ambannavar, J.P. (1967), "Population Redistribution in India: Inter-State and Rural-Urban", in Bose, A. (ed.), *Patterns of Population Change in India, 1951-61,* Allied Publishers, New Delhi.

Zachariah, K.C. *et al.* (1994), *Demographic Transition in Kerala in the 1980s.* Centre for Development Studies Monograph Series.

# INDEX